40° W. 20° W. 0°

IRISH SEA

GREAT BRITAIN

Liverpool

London

Portsmouth

Gosport

Plymouth

Ghent

Paris

FRANCE

BAY OF BISCAY

Marseilles

ITALY

Rome

Naples

SPAIN

MEDITERRANEAN SEA

PORTUGAL

Sicily

Syracuse

AZORES

Fayal

Cape St. Vincent

Cadiz

BARBARY COAST

Malta

Strait of Gibraltar

Algiers

Bougie

Tunis

MOROCCO

Tripoli

MADEIRA ISLANDS

OCEAN

NORTH AFRICA

CANARY ISLANDS

CAPE VERDE ISLANDS

Praia

THE FRIGATES

APPROXIMATE SCALE IN MILES

0   250   500   750   1,000   1,250   1,500

The Seafarers THE FRIGATES

Other Publications:

THE GOOD COOK
THE ENCYCLOPEDIA OF COLLECTIBLES
THE GREAT CITIES
WORLD WAR II
HOME REPAIR AND IMPROVEMENT
THE WORLD'S WILD PLACES
THE TIME-LIFE LIBRARY OF BOATING
HUMAN BEHAVIOR
THE ART OF SEWING
THE OLD WEST
THE EMERGENCE OF MAN
THE AMERICAN WILDERNESS
THE TIME-LIFE ENCYCLOPEDIA OF GARDENING
LIFE LIBRARY OF PHOTOGRAPHY
THIS FABULOUS CENTURY
FOODS OF THE WORLD
TIME-LIFE LIBRARY OF AMERICA
TIME-LIFE LIBRARY OF ART
GREAT AGES OF MAN
LIFE SCIENCE LIBRARY
THE LIFE HISTORY OF THE UNITED STATES
TIME READING PROGRAM
LIFE NATURE LIBRARY
LIFE WORLD LIBRARY
FAMILY LIBRARY:
  HOW THINGS WORK IN YOUR HOME
  THE TIME-LIFE BOOK OF THE FAMILY CAR
  THE TIME-LIFE FAMILY LEGAL GUIDE
  THE TIME-LIFE BOOK OF FAMILY FINANCE

The Cover: With a thundering salvo, the frigate *United States,* under Captain Stephen Decatur, overwhelms her British foe, the *Macedonian,* west of the Canary Islands on October 25, 1812. The damage to the *Macedonian,* as depicted in this contemporary painting by Thomas Birch, was severe but quickly repaired, and the captured ship went into U.S. Navy service.

The Title Page: Stitched onto this woolen banner, the last words of Captain James Lawrence of the doomed frigate *Chesapeake* flew over the flagship of Commodore Oliver Hazard Perry in the fight for Lake Erie on September 10, 1813. When the flag was hoisted to Perry's main-royal masthead, it was the signal to start the action.

THE FRIGATES

by Henry E. Gruppe
AND THE EDITORS OF TIME-LIFE BOOKS

TIME-LIFE BOOKS, ALEXANDRIA, VIRGINIA

Time-Life Books Inc.
is a wholly owned subsidiary of
TIME INCORPORATED

FOUNDER: Henry R. Luce 1898-1967

Editor-in-Chief: Henry Anatole Grunwald
Chairman of the Board: Andrew Heiskell
President: James R. Shepley
Editorial Director: Ralph Graves
Vice Chairman: Arthur Temple

TIME-LIFE BOOKS INC.

MANAGING EDITOR: Jerry Korn
Executive Editor: David Maness
Assistant Managing Editors: Dale M. Brown (planning).
George Constable, Martin Mann, John Paul Porter
Art Director: Tom Suzuki
Chief of Research: David L. Harrison
Director of Photography: Robert G. Mason
Senior Text Editor: Diana Hirsh
Assistant Art Director: Arnold C. Holeywell
Assistant Chief of Research: Carolyn L. Sackett
Assistant Director of Photography: Dolores A. Littles

CHAIRMAN: Joan D. Manley
President: John D. McSweeney
Executive Vice Presidents: Carl G. Jaeger.
John Steven Maxwell, David J. Walsh
Vice Presidents: Nicholas Benton (public relations).
Nicholas J. C. Ingleton (Asia), James L. Mercer
(Europe/South Pacific), Herbert Sorkin (production).
Paul R. Stewart (marketing). Peter G. Barnes.
John L. Canova
Personnel Director: Beatrice T. Dobie
Consumer Affairs Director: Carol Flaumenhaft
Comptroller: George Artandi

The Seafarers

Editorial Staff for The Frigates:
Editor: George G. Daniels
Picture Editor: John Conrad Weiser
Designer: Herbert H. Quarmby
Text Editors: Stuart Gannes, Anne Horan
Staff Writers: Michael Blumenthal. Carol Dana.
Susan Feller, Gus Hedberg, Mark M. Steele
Chief Researcher: Charlotte A. Quinn
Researchers: Feroline Burrage. Patti H. Cass.
Philip Brandt George, W. Mark Hamilton.
Elizabeth L. Parker, Trudy W. Pearson
Art Assistant: Michelle René Clay
Editorial Assistant: Ellen P. Keir

Special Contributors
Champ Clark (Text); Barbara Hicks, Frances G. Youssef
(Research)

Editorial Production
Production Editor: Douglas B. Graham
Operations Manager: Gennaro C. Esposito.
Gordon E. Buck (assistant)
Assistant Production Editor: Feliciano Madrid
Quality Control: Robert L. Young (director), James J. Cox
(assistant). Daniel J. McSweeney. Michael G. Wight
(associates)
Art Coordinator: Anne B. Landry
Copy Staff: Susan B. Galloway (chief).
Elise Ritter Gibson, Sheirazada Hann. Celia Beattie
Picture Department: Marguerite Johnson.
Nancy Cromwell Scott

Correspondents: Elisabeth Kraemer (Bonn);
Margot Hapgood, Dorothy Bacon. Lesley Coleman
(London); Susan Jonas. Lucy T. Voulgaris (New York);
Maria Vincenza Aloisi. Josephine du Brusle (Paris);
Ann Natanson (Rome).
Valuable assistance was also provided by: Enid Farmer
(Boston); Diane Rich (London); Carolyn T. Chubet.
Miriam Hsia (New York); Ian Donaldson (Halifax.
Nova Scotia); Mimi Murphy (Rome); Nancy Friedman
(Washington. D.C.).

The Author:
Henry Gruppe is a graduate of the United States Naval Academy who served on destroyers during the Korean War. He later joined the State Department, rising to Deputy Chief of the special program for African development before retiring to devote full time to his avocations: sailing and the history of the sea. He is the author of The Truxton Cipher, a novel of derring-do in the modern United States Navy.

The Consultants:
John Horace Parry, Professor of Oceanic History at Harvard University, studied at Cambridge University, where he took his Ph.D. He rose to the rank of commander in the Royal Navy in World War II. He has written many books, including The Discovery of the Sea, Europe and a Wider World and Trade and Dominion.

Philip Chadwick Foster Smith is managing editor of The American Neptune, a quarterly journal devoted to nautical history. Formerly curator of maritime history at the Peabody Museum, Salem, Massachusetts, he is the author of several books, including The Frigate Essex Papers: Building the Salem Frigate, 1798-1799.

William Avery Baker, a naval architect and engineer, spent 30 years designing vessels of all sizes for the Shipbuilding Division of Bethlehem Steel Corporation. He is now the curator of the Hart Nautical Museum at the Massachusetts Institute of Technology, where he took his degree. He has done extensive research into sailing vessels, and has reconstructed plans for a number of them, including the frigate Essex.

Commander Tyrone G. Martin concluded a 26-year Naval career as captain of the U.S.S. Constitution during a major restoration from 1974 to 1976. He is the author of A Most Fortunate Ship, a narrative history of "Old Ironsides."

For information about any Time-Life book. please write:
Reader Information. Time-Life Books.
541 North Fairbanks Court. Chicago. Illinois 60611.

TIME-LIFE is a trademark of Time Incorporated U.S.A.

Library of Congress Cataloguing in Publication Data
Gruppe. Henry.
    The frigates.
    (The Seafarers)
    Bibliography: p.
    Includes index.
    1. United States. Navy—History.   2. United States—History. Naval—To 1900.   3. Frigates.
    I. Time-Life Books.   II. Title.   III. Series.
VA56.G7   359'00973   79-10643
ISBN 0-8094-2717-6
ISBN 0-8094-2716-6 lib. bdg.

Contents

Chapter 1 **A navy born to battle pirates** 6

Essay The red-bearded corsairs of the Barbary Coast 34

Chapter 2 **Trial and triumph in the Mediterranean** 40

Essay The strict regimen of life in a seagoing community 68

Chapter 3 **Stunning surprises for His Britannic Majesty** 76

Chapter 4 **The spectacular forays of a dashing captain** 106

Chapter 5 **"Don't give up the ship!"** 132

Essay Saving a gallant ship from the "harpies of the shore" 164

BIBLIOGRAPHY 170

ACKNOWLEDGMENTS 171

PICTURE CREDITS 172

INDEX 173

Chapter 1

A navy born to battle pirates

rom the comfort of an embroidered cushion, Hassan Pasha, favored by Allah as the Dey of Algiers, surveyed the sorry lot of American prisoners who had been seized from the merchant brig *Polly* off Cape St. Vincent on October 25, 1793. He had, he explained in injured tones to the prisoners, been earnestly attempting to negotiate a treaty with the United States. But his peaceful overtures—an offer to call off his marauders in return for tribute to be paid him in both lump sum and annuity—had been ignored by the upstart nation across the Atlantic. For that transgression the Americans would suffer. "Now that I have got you, you Christian dogs," said the Dey, "you shall eat stones."

With that, according to the diary of John Foss, a Newburyport, Massachusetts, youngster who was among the captives, the *Polly*'s men were herded from the Dey's palace to the foul dungeons of the Bilic prison. "When we arrived there," wrote Foss, "we found several other Americans and about 600 Christian slaves of other nationalities with wretched habits, dejected countenances and chains on their legs. Each of us was given a dirty blanket and a small loaf of black sour bread, and on the day after our arrival we were loaded with chains of 25 to 40 pounds in weight fastened to the waist and a ring about the ankle."

Each day, along with the other Christian captives, the Yankees trudged to mountain quarries, where they blasted out giant boulders weighing from 20 to 40 tons each. These were placed on timber sledges and dragged by the prisoners two miles to Algiers harbor, where the rocks were loaded onto scows to be dumped in the construction of an enormous breakwater. Wrote Foss: "The drivers are continually beating the slaves with their stocks & goading them with its end in which is a small spear, not unlike an ox-goad among our farmers." The penalty for even the slightest dereliction, such as showing fatigue, was up to 500 bastinadoes—slashing, blood-bringing blows with a flail, half of them delivered on the buttocks, the other half on the soles of the feet. For more heinous crimes—among them, speaking ill of the Muslim faith—men were either impaled or roasted alive.

The crew of the *Polly* had suffered one of the worst of all possible fates. They had fallen into the hands of the Barbary corsairs, a loose coalition of sea bandits sailing out of Algiers, Tunis, Morocco and Tripoli. The Americans were slaves, and slaves they would remain, living and dying on that Algerian breakwater, unless and until they were ransomed by the U.S. government. Yet, however unknowingly and however unwillingly, the captives of the Barbary Coast by very reason of their pathetic plight evoked a response that would change history's course and the balance of world power: they inspired the birth of the United States Navy.

Decked in a brilliant panoply of flags and pennants, the United States, first-born frigate of the American Navy, rests at her moorings in the Delaware River after being launched and fitted out in 1797. On her bow a spear-carrying goddess of liberty figurehead adds a touch of majesty to the ship's colorful array.

This Navy, begun as a minuscule force amid much doubt and hesitation, would face test after deadly test in the decades to follow, as it defended the young American nation's claims to freedom of the seas. Just a few years after its birth, the infant Navy would be giving and taking devastating broadsides in an undeclared but nonetheless bitter contest with the ships of an erstwhile ally, France. Soon after that it would fight—by itself, without aid from land troops—the first war to be formally declared against the United States, the enemy being the Tripolitans, some of the same corsairs whose arrogant provocations led to the creation of the Navy in the first place.

And by the fateful year of 1812, it would find itself desperately engaged in a struggle with the most fearsome maritime war machine of the age: the British Royal Navy, which numbered nearly 900 ships and had emerged victorious from virtually every one of its actions in recent history. To be sure, Britain was at war with France at the time, and the British Admiralty was preoccupied with keeping Napoleon's powerful fleets penned up in Continental ports. Even so, the British mounted a major naval campaign in the western Atlantic, pitting against the doughty Americans some of the finest vessels and men the Royal Navy had to offer.

As it met these challenges, the United States Navy was to find within its ranks some of the most gallant sea warriors of all time, fighting captains who dueled like knights in ship-to-ship actions that were among the most brilliant in the annals of fighting sail. But it was not only the men who sailed the ships that made the development of America's young Navy the dramatic story that it is. The glory and success—and there would be glory and success aplenty—were shared by the ships themselves, ships that, ton for ton, were the marvel of their day.

These were the long, swift Yankee frigates, a type of warship that was smaller than a great ship of the line but deadly enough for all that, substituting the speed of a greyhound for the power of a mastiff. The United States built frigates because it could afford nothing grander. Yet American shipbuilders and designers would advance the state of the art to the point where their frigates would be the envy of naval architects the world over. There were only a handful of these modest vessels, fashioned of Georgia oak and New England pine, but they would unburden the Royal Navy of the myth of its own invincibility, secure for America a respectable position among seafaring nations and form the nucleus of what would many years later become the mightiest navy on earth. And the first of these remarkable frigates owed their existence, at least in part, to the depredations of the Barbary corsairs.

From their strategic position at the Strait of Gibraltar, the seafarers of the North African littoral had been practicing piracy since the late Seventh Century, when a Tunisian war lord by the name of Musa ibn-Nosseyr recruited shipwrights, built a fleet and settled down to the lucrative business of plundering passing vessels. From time to time the European powers, to protect their commerce in the Mediterranean, attempted to put down the corsairs by attacking the fortified cities out of which the Barbary brigands operated; in 1654, for example, Great Britain's General-at-Sea Robert Blake sailed into the harbor at Tunis and gave the city a proper pounding.

But for the most part the Europeans were too busy fighting among themselves to waste their warships on North Africans, whom they scornfully considered to be sand-pile banditti. It was deemed expedient to buy off the marauders from the Barbary coast by paying tribute—or, in the more dignified term, subsidies—to the deys and the beys and the pashas. None of the involved parties was willing to make known the amounts: "Either shame or jealousy," wrote Thomas Jefferson from his post as American Minister to France, "makes them wish to keep it secret." Yet during the last quarter of the 18th Century the tribute paid by France to Algiers alone was placed by rough estimate at $200,000 a year, and the subsidies extorted from Spain and Great Britain were approximated at even higher amounts.

The American colonies suffered as well. In 1625, only five years after their landing at Plymouth, the Pilgrim Fathers lost two ships to Moroccan pirates who enslaved their crews. And in 1678, after New York merchant Jacob Leiser, his two sons and eight seamen of the ship *Pincke* were captured by Algerian corsairs, New York churches collected contributions to meet the heavy ransom; so much money was subscribed that the surplus was used to begin the construction of Trinity Church on lower Broadway.

Nevertheless, for much of the 18th Century the tribute paid by Britain provided an umbrella of protection for colonial shipping as well, and American trade in the Mediterranean prospered. By 1776 more than 80 Yankee ships were annually calling at Mediterranean ports; the Mediterranean accounted for an estimated one quarter of America's exports of dried and pickled fish and one sixth of its sales of wheat and flour, plus copious shipments of rice, mostly from South Carolina.

The American Revolution naturally ended all British-subsidized immunity from Barbary depredations. The Yankees were now on their own in the Mediterranean. They fared badly, to the extent that Jefferson, writing in 1786 from Paris to his fellow Minister in London, John Adams, baldly expressed the opinion that the best way to deal with the Barbary states was "through the medium of war." This, Jefferson acknowledged, would require "a small marine force."

And there was the rub. The fledgling United States had no navy whatsoever. Of the 35 warships built or purchased during the Revolutionary War, the United States had managed to lose them all. They had been wrecked, captured by the British, or burned or deliberately sunk by the Americans to avoid capture. Now, with trouble looming again, the Americans had to start over if they wanted to build a navy capable of protecting their commerce. In fact, many Americans, especially in the agrarian South and West, did not want such a force, arguing that a navy would inevitably lead to American involvement in European conflicts—the "foreign entanglements" later to be so solemnly decried in George Washington's Farewell Address.

Under the Articles of Confederation the argument was largely academic: with its feeble taxing powers, Congress could scarcely have raised enough money to buy a longboat. But with the adoption of the

Constitution—and with continuing Barbary outrages—the idea of a navy found new life. Returning from Paris to be the nation's first Secretary of State, Jefferson in 1790 submitted to Congress an indictment of the Barbary corsairs and proposals for a small navy. President George Washington added his lament: "Would to heaven we had a navy able to reform these enemies to mankind or crush them into nonexistence!" The Senate approved a measure providing for a navy—only to see it pigeonholed in the House.

Events finally overcame opposition to a navy. In 1793 Portugal, which had long stood as a sort of European sentinel in preventing the marauders from passing through the Strait of Gibraltar into the Atlantic, was persuaded by England to sign a treaty with Algiers. The devious English, content to buy off the corsairs themselves, wanted to encourage attacks on increasingly competitive American shipping. The strait was uncorked, corsairs prowled the great ocean, and by the end of the year 11 American ships had been captured—including the *Polly*, whose men were lectured by the Dey himself on their government's stubborn refusal to pay tribute. The number of American prisoners in Barbary hands rose to 119.

Declaring admiration for John Barry's "patriotism, valor, fidelity and abilities," President George Washington commissions the Revolutionary War hero senior captain of the U.S. Navy in 1797. As commander of the frigate United States (shown in the background scene), Barry cruised the West Indies until 1799, leading U.S. Naval forces against the French.

Still another reason, less urgent to the moment but far more ominous to the long-term American cause, militated in favor of a navy. In February 1793 Revolutionary France had declared war on Great Britain, and as the months passed it became increasingly clear that America was being involved willy-nilly in Europe's brawl. The ships of England and France, manned by conscripts and the unfortunate victims of press gangs, appeared over every horizon and in every harbor, their crews deserting whenever possible to neutral vessels. But these were men that the belligerent navies desperately needed and wanted back—even if it meant taking them at gunpoint from American ships. Nor were the European forces in the least careful about taking only deserters; if men were needed, Americans would do as well as anyone, and many a Yankee found himself hauled protesting from his ship.

The British had a far larger and more aggressive force than the French, and the Royal Navy soon began to halt American merchant vessels and impress members of their crews almost daily. It was an intolerable situation. Even many Americans who had previously opposed building a naval force recognized the compelling need to defend the nation's shipping and its seamen.

On March 27, 1794, the Senate having already approved, the House of Representatives passed an act authorizing the creation of a navy. It was obviously impossible for the new nation to construct a fleet of great ships of the line like those of Great Britain, mounting up to 100 cannon each. The most the United States could hope for was a squadron of smaller frigates, light and nimble, yet perhaps powerful enough for American needs. The act authorized the procurement of six frigates, and appropriated $688,888.82 to start the work.

At best, the measure created a navy in embryo. As a sop to opponents, the act decreed that if a peace was arranged with Algiers, all naval construction should cease forthwith—a condition that would, as it turned out, very nearly kill the new Navy before a single ship was launched. Furthermore, Congress failed to establish a Navy Department to supervise the construction of the frigate force. That task was assigned by President Washington to Secretary of War Henry Knox, a Revolutionary Army general whose main acquaintance with seafaring came from reading Plutarch's *Lives* of such ancient naval commanders as Themistocles and Nicias. But Knox was an excellent judge of men, and he set out to find just the right shipbuilder to serve as chief constructor for America's new Navy.

Fortunately, he did not have to look beyond Philadelphia, then the nation's capital; in that city lived a qualified man who not only wanted the job but had some novel ideas about building frigates. That man was Joshua Humphreys, a partner in the shipbuilding firm of Wharton and Humphreys, and on June 28, 1794, he was appointed "Constructor or Master Builder of a 44-gun ship to be built at the port of Philadelphia." In addition, he was assigned to prepare the designs and molds for the five other frigates authorized by Congress, although they were to be built elsewhere.

Humphreys was a remarkable man. Born in Haverford, Pennsylvania, on June 17, 1751, he had been apprenticed at an early age to William

Penrose, a noted Philadelphia shipbuilder. When Penrose died in 1771 Mrs. Penrose released Humphreys from his indenture and asked him to take over as master shipwright for the completion of a vessel currently in progress. Humphreys then helped design and construct the *Randolph*, a frigate of 32 guns that was larger and faster than ordinary British frigates of her rate; during the Revolution she fought a gallant battle off Barbados against a 64-gun British ship of the line before finally exploding in flames, with the loss of all but four of her crew.

Humphreys' work on the *Randolph* design led him to enter a shipbuilding partnership with his cousin John Wharton, an older man and one of some political influence. Whether Humphreys constructed other warships during the Revolution is not recorded, but the yard apparently prospered, for Humphreys had gained a reputation as one of Philadelphia's leading shipwrights by the time he won his commission to design six new frigates for the nascent United States Navy.

The term frigate was first used to describe a kind of galley that appeared in the Mediterranean in the late 1300s. Over the next few centuries the word was used to characterize any medium-sized, fast sailing ship of moderate armament. But by the early 1800s most navies had standardized the design of their warships. In the Royal Navy, frigates had evolved into long, low ships carrying from 28 to 40 guns capable of firing 12- and 18-pound round shot. Above the main deck, a quarter-deck extended from the mainmast to the stern, and a fo'c's'le deck spanned the distance from foremast to bow. The open space between fo'c's'le and quarter-deck was beamed over but left unplanked. A gangway on each side connected both of the upper-deck sections, and the fo'c's'le and quarter-deck usually carried additional cannon.

Unlike the slow, heavy ships of the line, whose very reason for existence was to engage, like contending herds of elephants, in huge thundering fleet actions, the agile frigates were free-spirited ships with a dozen missions.

Darting here and there on independent duty, the frigate was the cruiser of its day, and its captain was given the widest of latitude so as best to serve king and country. Frigates were nonpareil predators to harass enemy merchant shipping. They were superb and inexpensive weapons with which to confront rebellious despots in faraway colonies; they carried vital messages and important personages; they enforced blockades on the one hand and on the other hand slashed through the lines to relieve beleaguered ports. In any major action swift frigates were the intelligence-gathering scouts, "the eyes of the fleet," as well as marvelous support vessels to tow off big ships of the line damaged in battle. "Frigates!" Admiral Horatio Nelson once cried while campaigning

Laborers haul planks up a gangway for the frigate Philadelphia, paid for by Philadelphia merchants and launched in 1799. Supervising the work is a man in a tricornered hat (center foreground), probably Joshua Humphreys, the principal shipbuilder of the fledgling U.S. Navy.

against the French in the Mediterranean, "were I to die this moment, want of frigates would be found engraved upon my heart."

Hull down, a sleek frigate was often indistinguishable from a great ship of the line. Oversparred and overcanvased by young captains to whom speed and agility were of the essence, frigates often carried proportionately more sail for the hull size than ships of the line. Well and boldly sailed, a proper frigate could thrum through the seas at speeds in excess of 12 knots, thrash up to within six points off the wind and show lively heels to plodding ships of the line.

It was this exact and deadly balance of speed, strength and armament that Joshua Humphreys of Philadelphia had set himself to improve upon. In soliciting his appointment, Humphreys had written to Robert Morris, then a Pennsylvania Senator, urging the need for "such frigates as in blowing weather would be an overmatch for doubledeck ships and in light winds could evade coming to action." In other words, he was proposing a superfrigate, large enough to outsail and outfight other double-deck ships of her class, yet nimble enough to avoid combat in unfavorable circumstances. It was an idea that had already been tried, to a certain extent, by the French and the British.

Both navies had experimented with removing the top deck of a small, three-decker ship of the line, thereby reducing her to frigate class with just two full-length gun decks. These ships were called razees, a name taken from the French *vaisseau rasé*—literally "shaved ship." Against a conventional frigate a razee had one decided advantage; because it had originally been designed and built to be a much bigger vessel, its inner structural timbers and its planking were enormously strong. Therefore a razee could withstand a terrific pounding. Yet razees also suffered from a major disadvantage. Since their underwater hull was unchanged, they possessed the same dull sailing qualities as any normal ship of the line.

Humphreys and some of his contemporaries meant to correct this flaw by constructing Yankee frigates to the same size and with the same inner structural strength as found in a razee—but with graceful tapering lines, from the keel up, for speed and agility. Such frigates would be longer and broader than Royal Navy frigates. Their increased size and stability would make them better gun platforms than His Majesty's frigates, and because of their fine underwater lines they should prove fleet sailers. But like many bold ideas, the brilliance of the concept was matched by difficulties in execution. And not the least of these problems was the animosity that arose between two highly talented men.

In extending to Joshua Humphreys the contract to prepare the designs of the six frigates, General Henry Knox stipulated two important conditions. Perhaps boggling at the image of a frigate with a keel length as long as that of a British ship of the line, Secretary Knox specified a maximum length of 147 feet—several feet less than the smaller British three-deckers. In addition, Secretary Knox specified that Joshua Humphreys was to be furnished with an assistant, one Josiah Fox, to speed the work.

Born in Falmouth, England, in 1763, Fox came from a well-to-do family long connected with the shipping business. It was even said that the

Shipwright Josiah Fox, a stern-faced octogenarian in this 1846 photo, emigrated from England at the age of 30 in 1793 and, as Joshua Humphreys' brilliant associate at the Philadelphia shipyard, played an indispensable role in the design of the new U.S. frigates. His drafting curves are shown at left.

Foxes were distantly related to Sir Francis Drake. Cornishman and Quaker, Josiah Fox was early apprenticed to the master constructor at His Majesty's dockyard at Plymouth, where he learned his lessons well and soon became a qualified shipwright. Because of his family's means, Fox had no real need of a steady job, and for the next seven years he spent his own time inspecting most of the major shipyards in Britain and Europe. Occasionally he went to sea to study how different designs performed under various weather conditions, and he filled notebooks with sketches and comments on the latest in naval architecture and construction methods.

Fox's visit to America in the fall of 1793 was in connection with a study he was making of American shipbuilding timbers—live oak, red cedar, white pine and the like—and how they compared with European woods in weight, strength, flexibility and resistance to rot. Once General Knox learned of the availability of this dedicated young man, Fox was forthwith appointed first as a clerk in the War Office, then as assistant to Humphreys.

It is easy enough to understand why Secretary Knox was so impressed by the brilliant English ship designer, fresh from the yards of Europe and up on all the latest innovations in the design of warships. Knox could hardly be blamed for hedging his bets on Humphreys, a man who, despite his stature as a shipwright, had never before undertaken such a major design job. The quality of Humphreys' work would be of paramount importance, perhaps even to the very survival of the developing nation.

The six frigates represented the first major ships for the official U.S. Navy. Unlike the altered merchantmen and ad hoc new construction of the Revolutionary War, these ships were all to be built along similar lines, constituting a 44-gun frigate class of four ships and a 38-gun frigate class of two ships. The lessons learned from the design, construction and operation of these frigates would be incorporated into the planning of additional ships. It was therefore imperative that the first six frigates represent an advance in the state of the art. Humphreys had already worked long hours without pay, and he was obviously both skilled and honest. But could he deliver? Josiah Fox was there to ensure that he did.

The collaboration began amicably enough. Humphreys rented a large loft for mold making in Philadelphia, and it was now necessary for the two men to agree upon the final design from which work could proceed. The method at the time involved the construction of a scaled-down model of the vessel's hull. Since the two sides of a frigate were mirror images of each other, it was necessary only to model half the ship's hull. These half models were built up of layers, or lifts, of clear white pine pegged together with dowels. Once the lines of the vessel were agreed upon, the half model was taken apart and the lifts were traced on a draft, or line drawing, of the vessel. Then the line drawing was enlarged to the full size of the vessel on the floor of the mold loft. From this full-scale drawing, templates, called molds, of the principal structural parts were constructed out of thin pine boards. Rough molds were also prepared for the use of the woodcutters who would be called upon to select the trees to be felled for each component part.

As work commenced, Joshua Humphreys quickly developed a high regard for Josiah Fox's education and obvious skills. Fox, on the other hand, must have been somewhat bewildered: although titled a clerk, he was clearly expected to play a major role in the design of the new warships. And that was where the trouble started. Fox thought that the new ships, if built to the large dimensions proposed, would prove ponderous. He also quarreled with the slight rake of the Humphreys stem, and thought it should be considerably sharper. He objected to the position of the wales (the thick belts of timber along the sides), to the placement of the widest point in the ship's beam as being too far aft, and most of all to the size of the ships. But Fox was talking to the wrong man; Joshua Humphreys was completely committed to his design for the frigates and would not alter it. Fox, equally adamant, put his ideas into a design of his own. Early in the spring of 1794 both men's designs were submitted to General Knox for adjudication.

Knox was totally unequipped to settle the question. In desperation he turned to William Doughty, a trained shipwright and draftsman who was employed in Humphreys' shipyard. Also consulted were John Wharton, Humphreys' partner and a political friend of Knox's whose influence may have helped Humphreys land the contract in the first place, and other men of prominence. The end result of these decisions by committee was a design, probably drafted by Fox, that incorporated some of his modifications but in general maintained the big-frigate concept advocated by Humphreys.

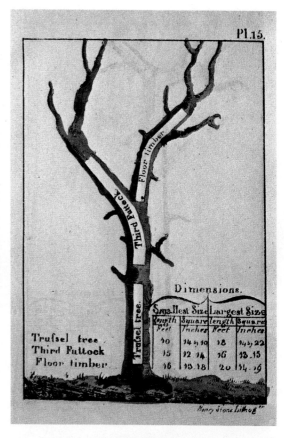

The two men by now were at such loggerheads that Humphreys refused to communicate with Fox except by letter. So bitterly did he resent his young colleague that he dispatched a furious rebuke when he heard that Fox had taken for himself a share of the title naval constructor: "I cannot receive, hereafter or attend to any directions from you, altho directed by the Secretary of War. While you style yourself Naval Constructor You must know that I am at the head of that Department and when you direct a letter to me let it be done in your own style as Clerk of the Marine Department. Whenever the Secretary deems my services no longer necessary, you may then, to other persons, assume such titles as your vanity may suggest."

In later years the descendants of both Humphreys and Fox would claim credit for their respective forebears. They need not have. There were more than enough laurels to be shared in the work, which now proceeded apace despite the open enmity between the two designers.

Once the final designs and templates were in hand, they were turned over to the various shipyards assigned to construct the vessels. Humphreys, of course, had primary responsibility for Philadelphia's 44-gun frigate. In Boston Colonel George Claghorne was to supervise the construction of a 44 to be built at the Hartt Shipyard. In New York the noted shipbuilder Forman Cheeseman was appointed naval constructor of another 44-gun frigate. John Morgan was to build a fourth 44 at Gosport, Virginia. The other two, both 38-gun frigates, were the responsibility of Colonel James Hackett in Portsmouth, New Hampshire, and David Stodder in Baltimore, Maryland.

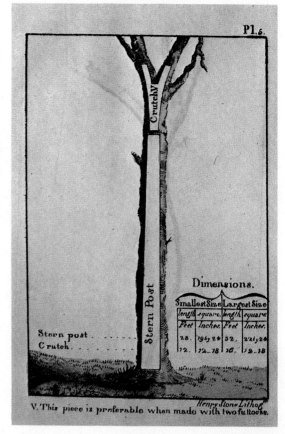

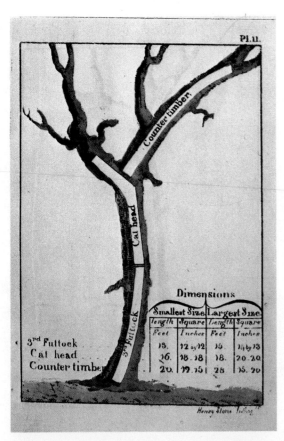

1. Knee in Stock beginning to be hewed.
2. D.o hewed on a straight line, to be shaped on the crook.
3. Timber beginning to be hewed in the Stock.

The next step, and it was one of staggering difficulty, was to procure wood in immense quantities—some 3,000 trees had to be felled for the making of each frigate—and of the required species. For the principal frames of the vessels, the timber of choice was live oak, which was dense, tough and estimated to last five times longer than the white oak then used in European ships. The American builders were correctly convinced that live-oak frames would still be perfectly sound after more than half a century. But specifying the use of live oak was one thing; cutting it to shape and getting it to the yards where the frigates were to be built proved to be quite another matter.

The trees flourished in the low country and on the islands off the coast of South Carolina and Georgia. On October 14, 1794, John Morgan, who had the contract for the frigate to be built in Virginia, traveled southward with 60 axmen to cut the wood for all the frigates and haul it out. He ran into trouble right away.

Because the islands and coastal areas were largely uninhabited and without roads, all the team's equipment and supplies, including the wagons and oxen for hauling the timber, had to be shipped in by sea. The area, moreover, was a quagmire from recent torrential rains, and along with the flooding came yellow fever, then called yellow jack or vomito negro because of the accompanying symptom of black vomit. Some of the axmen took ill and many others quit. Soon there were only three healthy men remaining in Morgan's camp near the present city of Brunswick, Georgia.

Morgan had every reason to be dismayed. His job would have been difficult even in the best of circumstances. Like a sculptor studying a block of Carrara marble, he had to envision the specific knees—the beams or frames—that could be cut from each tree he selected. The trunk of this great oak could be rough-cut into the shape of a sternpost; the curved limb of that one would be ideal for a frame. Morgan was expected to cut out the "crooked timbers" that would be required for each ship. If he did his job properly, the task of the builders would be vastly eased. But the wood was like iron and it was awful work. Often when the live oak was shaped to the molds, pockets of rot, called blackheart, would appear, rendering that particular timber useless for its intended purpose. In a letter to Humphreys, Morgan said, "If you was here, you'd curse live oak."

A fire destroyed some of the patterns and new ones had to be sent for. A vessel carrying precious wood foundered and was lost on the shoals off Cape Hatteras. The dread yellow jack continued to reduce the ranks of the new axmen hired to replace those who had taken ill or had fled. Morgan himself came down with the disease, but fortunately outlived the fears he expressed in a letter to Humphreys. "I have it now,

These plates from an 1823 guide helped woodcutters find oaks of the right shapes and dimensions to provide timbers for the construction of frigates. This practice of building boats from trees chosen for their shapes dated to the ancient Greeks.

everybody is sick here and if I am to stay here until all the timbers is cut, I shall be dead."

The work somehow went forward. Joshua Humphreys sent one of his sons down to help Morgan. More axmen were hired, at outrageous rates, and bent to the work. By the late spring of 1795 there was enough live oak to start the construction of all six frigates.

Though relatively few ships the size of frigates had ever before been built in the United States, many of the American colonists and later immigrants had brought with them skills and rich experience acquired in former jobs in European shipyards. The Yankee frigate builders were as able as any other shipwrights in the world. But they were still inexperienced with the vicissitudes of the American Congress and the salty demands of the first professional American Naval officers. The enterprise would be one of enormous complexity punctuated by the most unexpected of unhappy developments.

The Wharton and Humphreys Shipyard at Philadelphia fronted on the Delaware River, and the shipwrights began by sinking three parallel lines of pilings into the ground descending to the river, each row some 10 feet from its neighbor and about 100 yards long. The individual pilings were lined up according to height, and a track of heavy timbers was spiked to the top of each row so that the three tracks sloped evenly down to the water. The inner track would bear the brunt of the frigate's growing weight during construction, and the outer tracks would guide the cradle when the vessel was launched.

The keel structure consisted of two parts: the keel itself, massive timbers carefully fitted and bolted or spiked together, and a false keel, or shoe, of smaller timbers fixed directly under the keel, which served to protect the keel from damage should the vessel run aground. During the building the keel structure itself was laid upon keelblocks, great square timbers resting upon the middle track.

Meanwhile sawyers were busy at the saw pits, cutting the straight members of the ship's frame. As a man, or men, choking and blinded by sawdust, stood in a pit below the timber, dragging the big frame saw through the wood, the sawyer atop the beam guided the cut along lines true to the nearest eighth of an inch, which was about the thickness of the blade itself. Nearby, adz men hacked and hewed at the rough-cut crooked timbers, smoothing and shaping them to duplicate exactly the patterns from the mold loft. A good adz man could, when the work required it, leave a finish that would impress a cabinetmaker (it was the work of such artists that gave rise to the adage, "Hew to the line, let the chips fall where they may").

The ribs, or frames, of the frigate formed the skeleton of the hull, rising from the keel to the top of the deck railings in one continuous curve. They were fastened into the keel with round copper or iron bolts. Auger men, using enormously long, heavy augers, hand-drilled slightly undersized holes in the wood. The bolts were then hammered through and flattened at the tip, thus crudely riveting the timbers into place. In addition, wooden pegs, called "trunnels," a corruption of treenails, were used to fasten the smaller pieces of timber together.

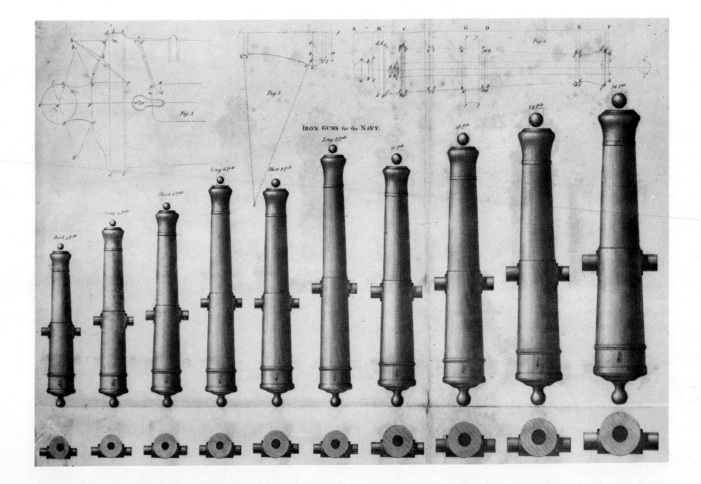

Behind the powerful broadsides of the youthful American Navy were these smoothbore cast-iron cannon, ranging from 4-pounders to 36-pounders (the designation was based on the weight of shot fired). The United States and the Constitution carried 24-pounders on the gun deck; smaller frigates like the Philadelphia carried 18-pounders.

While the installation of the midship frames took place, the sternpost was attached at the end of the keel and the stern built up. Forward, the stem, comprising many pieces of curved wood, was assembled and installed. Since both bow and stern of the frigate became finer and more complex as they tapered at the extremities, the builder no longer used full frames but erected the frames in halves, or cants, one side at a time. The aftercants were installed immediately, but the forward cants were not attached to the keel until the interior work was well along. Thus heavy construction materials could continue to be brought into the vessel through the large cross-sectional opening forward. With keel, stem, stern and midship-frame construction completed, planking could commence while the interior work was also going forward.

The strakes, the horizontal planks that ran the length of the vessel to form its outer shell, were cut from white oak, and each had to be carefully measured so that it would fit snugly to its neighbor. Usually it was sawed, then delicately finished with an adz. The planking varied widely in thickness, depending on its location and the strains that would be put on it. The two planks alongside the keel, called the garboard strakes, were six inches thick, compared with four to five inches for the other bottom planking. The very heaviest planking—the wales, whose precise location Josiah Fox had questioned in Humphreys' model—were

A sturdy platform for seagoing guns

The singular demands of naval warfare made the crafting of a 19th Century gun carriage an art unto itself. The naval gun had to be mobile so that it could be run in and out of gunports. Yet it had to remain stable against the action of the waves. And while the carriage obviously had to be as light as possible, it also had to be enormously strong to withstand the punishment of broadside-to-broadside engagements.

The wood of choice for the carriage was elm, for its strength, durability and resistance to shock. Each carriage was constructed according to formulas based on the diameter of the shot and the weight and dimensions of the gun. The carriage pictured here, destined to hold and control the great bulk of a 24-pounder, was 72 inches long and had side timbers that were five and a half inches thick.

When all went well, the carriage securely supported the cannon, absorbing its recoil through a heavy breeching rope and moving in and out by means of a system of tackles. But ordnance making was an inexact science in those days, and some cannon defied even the best of carriages. It was said that on the *Constitution* one particular cannon had such a fantastic recoil that it was given the nickname "Jumping Billy" because it bounded, carriage and all, several feet into the air every time it was fired.

A 19th Century naval gun carriage, like the one shown here, consisted of two sidepieces, or cheeks, fastened to each other with two massive iron through bolts, and braced by a crosspiece called the transom. A large wooden wedge, or quoin, slid along a slotted stool bed to adjust the elevation of the cannon. To mount the carriage on its wheels, or trucks, the frame was mortised and through-bolted to a pair of thick wooden axletrees.

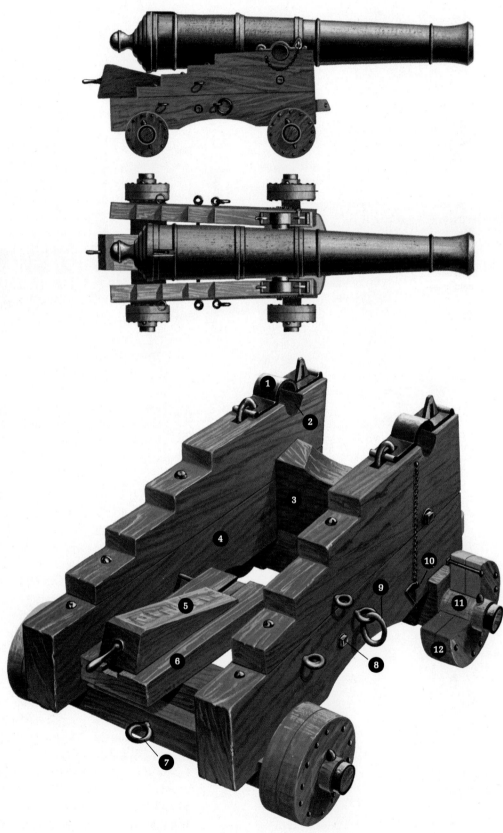

A 24-pound cannon rests evenly on its carriage in the three views seen at left and above. The carriage cheeks angled inward from bottom to top and from back to front to fit the gun barrel's tapering shape. The cannon was cast with two cylindrical support bars, or trunnions, which balanced the gun firmly on the cheeks. The mounted trunnions were then secured by an iron cap square and locked to the cheeks by means of a wedge called a forelock.

1. CAP SQUARE
2. TRUNNION HOLE
3. TRANSOM
4. CHEEK
5. QUOIN
6. STOOL BED
7. TACKLE EYEBOLT
8. THROUGH BOLT
9. BREECHING RINGBOLT
10. FORELOCK
11. AXLETREE
12. TRUCK

seven to 10 inches thick, and were placed on a wide belt beginning at the water line and rising to the gun deck. These wales were the frigate's armor, and her life would depend on their ability to withstand the terrible battering of iron shot.

The frigate's decks were made of yellow pine and white oak, and were constructed from the bottom up. Crosswise beams, secured to the ship's sides and supported in the center by stanchions, were installed first. With this interior scaffolding in place, the deck planks were put down, starting with the orlop deck six or seven feet above the keel (the name derived from "over leap," because this deck spanned the ship directly over the bilge). Then came the berth deck, followed by the gun, or main, deck. After the spar, or upper, deck was laid down, the bow planking was steamed, bent and fastened into place.

It was hard, exacting work at best, and for Joshua Humphreys and his fellow constructors there was an additional complication. The captains of the six frigates had already been appointed and ordered to the appropriate yards to observe the construction of their vessels. These captains were perhaps the most difficult of all the participants in the project; while actually knowing little about naval architecture themselves, they had scant respect for men who built ships but did not take them to sea. Captain Thomas Truxtun of the Baltimore frigate, for example, demanded in a letter to the War Office that "the most experienced sea officers of skill" be consulted before final spar dimensions were agreed upon. He went on to explain: "I mention sea officers because it is almost impossible that any other description of men, who have not had an opportunity of being often at sea, can form a proper judgement on this important subject."

Each captain demanded the right to make major alterations in his ship. Fully expecting that one day they would have to fight these new ships, the captains began to add more and heavier cannon than had been visualized by the designers. Partly because of this great additional weight, the frigates eventually hogged; that is, their bows and sterns sagged downward permanently, thereby somewhat impairing their sailing qualities. As it turned out, the American frigates were generally better sailers than their enemies, but there was no telling how great they might have been had the captains not festooned them with such a weight of armament. Nor were the captains pleased to leave other matters alone. Each captain, as Truxtun had insisted, was granted a major voice in how his ship was sparred and rigged. In addition he, rather than the constructor, determined the quantity of ballast and stores to be put on board.

Despite all such obstacles, construction of the six frigates went well. But then, on March 2, 1796, came stunning news: the United States Senate had ratified a peace treaty with the Dey of Algiers. The Congressional advocates of peace at any price were in the ascendancy, and they were willing to accept utterly humiliating terms: in return for calling off his corsairs and releasing his Yankee captives, Hassan Pasha would receive a lump sum payment of $642,500 and an annual tribute of $21,600 from the United States of America. As one direct and devastating result, a fatal clause of the Naval Act of 1794 took immediate effect: all work was to be stopped on the building of the new Navy.

His Farewell Address just scant months away, George Washington was no longer the potent political force he had once been. Yet through his own agonizing experience he knew as well as any man the cost of military weakness, and he intervened personally on behalf of the Navy. In fact, Congress saw fit to meet him a little less than halfway: it appropriated just enough funds to complete the hulls of the frigates a-building at Boston, Philadelphia and Baltimore; those under construction at New York, Gosport and Portsmouth were to be held up indefinitely. Moreover, Congress reserved for itself the decision as to whether the three hulls to be completed should be fitted out and manned.

Since nothing more could be gained at that point, Washington and others, possibly hoping to breathe life into the three vessels, agreed upon names for them. Thus did Joshua Humphreys' frigate in Philadelphia become the *United States*, the frigate in Boston the *Constitution*, and the frigate in Baltimore the *Constellation*.

The American Navy was unexpectedly—and unintentionally—rescued from its limbo by a onetime ally turned hostile: France. The government of that country had been infuriated with the United States as early as 1793, when President Washington demanded the recall of the French emissary, a certain Citizen Genêt, for attempting to intercede directly with the American people in behalf of the affairs of Revolutionary France. Relations had worsened in that year when Washington, in an effort to maintain U.S. neutrality, refused to let French privateers bring their prizes into American ports. Finally, in 1794 Chief Justice John Jay, acting as a diplomat, had concluded a treaty with England that partially invalidated existing agreements with France.

Over the next several years, relations steadily deteriorated with the Revolutionary government in Paris. French privateers and warships commenced preying not only on British commerce but on Yankee merchantmen as well, and by the summer of 1797 had taken no fewer than 300 American vessels.

In the blaze of popular fury that followed, the Congressional peace doves were put to flight. On July 1, 1797, the House of Representatives, long the sticking point for naval legislation, voted on the question: Should the *United States,* the *Constitution* and the *Constellation* be finished and manned? The ayes won.

Congress did more than that: at long last it established a Navy Department and authorized a Cabinet officer to head it. The new President, John Adams, promptly appointed as the nation's first Secretary of the Navy Benjamin Stoddert, a Revolutionary cavalry major who had become a merchant in Georgetown, overlooking the Potomac at Washington. Stoddert knew nothing whatever about naval affairs. Indeed, he wrote to Adams pleading for the President to help acquaint him with the "knowledge necessary for the Secretary of the Navy to possess to make him useful to his country." As it turned out, Stoddert was not only willing to learn, but able.

No sooner had the Speaker of the House acknowledged the affirmative vote than an 18-year-old messenger set out through Philadelphia in search of Joshua Humphreys, who was restlessly pacing about his little

Benjamin Stoddert, who was appointed the nation's first Secretary of the Navy by President John Adams in 1798, took over an infant fleet that numbered fewer than a dozen vessels of all types. During the hostilities with France known as the Quasi-War, the resolute Stoddert quickly built a fleet of 54 ships that within three years captured 94 armed French ships, including powerful warships.

Signed by President John Adams, this 1797 passport was supposed to guarantee safe passage for a U.S. merchant ship through Mediterranean waters controlled by the Dey of Algiers, with whom the United States had made peace. Scalloped pieces were cut from the tops of such passports and sent to the Dey's captains, who then matched them against the documents to verify their authenticity. But the paper had little effect on other rulers in the area, and their corsairs continued to plunder U.S. shipping.

shipyard. This boy was no ordinary messenger. His father had commanded a privateer during the Revolution, and had conferred his passion for the sea upon his son. The lad's mother had done all she could to quench this yearning. But after a bitter struggle he had been allowed to drop out of the University of Pennsylvania and take a job at a shipping firm near the Wharton and Humphreys Shipyard. He had every intention of entering naval service and had already prepared himself by assiduous practice with pistol and sword.

Something of an athlete and fleet of foot, the boy raced through the streets of Philadelphia on that hot, muggy afternoon. By the time he reached the Wharton and Humphreys yard, he was breathless and hot. He gasped out the welcome news and then sank down upon the stone step of the gatehouse. Although he could scarcely have dreamed it then, by an odd coincidence of history that young messenger, Stephen Decatur, would someday command this very vessel now tied up as an unfinished hull at the shipyard dock.

Joshua Humphreys was ready—more than ready—to get on with the work. Alone among the frigates, the *United States* had already been launched—two months before, on May 10, just as the funds were beginning to run out. The launching had been a moment of high emotion. The vessel herself was covered with all manner of flags and buntings; a huge crowd had gathered in the yard; and several military companies stood by their artillery pieces to thunder out salutes as the big ship began her short slide down the ways.

But then the launch had been marred by an embarrassing—and costly—accident. The ways had been built at slightly too steep an angle. The *United States* crashed heavily into the water, damaging her rudder braces and bending her false keel a few inches out of shape. Humphreys was disconsolate, and all the more so because as May had stretched into June, there was no assurance that the *United States* and her sisters would ever be completed.

Now, with a favorable vote in Congress, Humphreys worked all through July and August to repair the damage and to complete the *United States*. Yet, try as he would, he could never quite undo the effects of the accident at her birth. Because of the slight bend in her false keel, and perhaps also because of the extra weight of a roundhouse on her stern, which increased her displacement aft, the *United States* was to be nicknamed the "Old Waggon" and to be known as the slowest sailer of all the newly constructed vessels.

On September 7 the frigate *Constellation* was launched without incident. But in Boston on September 20, the *Constitution*'s builder was embarrassed by a problem diametrically the opposite of the one that had afflicted the *United States*: the *Constitution*'s launching ways had been set at too shallow an angle, and when the time came to launch her, the big frigate refused to move more than 27 feet, in spite of the fact that the tide was right and jacks and screws were utilized to help her on her way. Nor did she move much more on the second attempt two days later. Finally, on October 21, a month late, Colonel Claghorne succeeded in getting her into the water. Despite the awkwardness of her launch, the *Constitution* quickly captured the seafaring heart of Massachusetts. She

As the gunners of a harbor fort look on, the U.S. Frigate Constellation, with the sloop Hornet at her stern, calls at a French port in this early 19th Century watercolor by noted French marine artist Antoine Roux Sr. The painting once was thought to be of the frigate Boston, but a number of features —particularly the 28-port gun deck, the masting system and the female figurehead —led scholars later to revise their identification.

had been built by New Englanders, who prided themselves on their craftsmanship. Paul Revere himself had supplied the copper bolts and copper sheathing.

In any case, all three frigates were now afloat and in various stages of fitting out. By means of a cranelike device called sheers, the 80- to 105-foot lower masts were lowered, or stepped, into place. White pine was the wood for the masts, and it was preferable that a lower mast be fashioned from a single tree whenever possible. But such trees were very hard to find even in the great timber ranges of North America. Therefore the American builders usually followed the practice of their European counterparts, who built up the lower masts from several timbers of pine, all bound together with iron hoops.

And of course the vessels leaked after launching. It took some time for all the wood to swell and thoroughly close off each seam. Meanwhile the frigates had to be pumped dry regularly. Also, shortly after launching, the frigates had to be careened so as to remove any last underwater vestiges of the launching cradle and to affix the last copper sheathing to hull areas that had been inaccessible during construction.

While all this was going on, ropemakers were hard at work along the

400-yard length of the ropewalks, spinning the tough manila fibers into yarn, winding the yarn into strands and laying the strands into rope. For a frigate the size of the *Constitution*, some four miles of cordage and cable had to be prepared and worked into place. Meantime, in the cavernous expanses of the sail loft, men with dexterous fingers were using heavy needles to fashion great bolts of sturdy linen canvas into sails of various shapes, including extra ones to replace those tattered and lost at sea. A ship the size of the *Constitution* could carry about an acre of sail aloft.

The carpentry shops of the shipyard resounded to the hammer and clank of artisans fashioning gun carriages. And fires blazed in the foundries as ironworkers cast the great cannon and bored them out to the proper dimensions for the shot.

Frigates carried a variety of cannon for different purposes. The main armament consisted of so-called long guns to fire 18- and 24-pound balls for distances of more than a mile. But there were also stubby carronades, which could hurl a far heavier ball, weighing as much as 42 pounds, over shorter distances, and small 3-pound swivel guns for use in boats and in the fighting tops. It was impossible to rate a frigate meaningfully by the total number of cannon that she carried. The standard practice in most navies was to rate their frigates by the number of long guns alone. But that was somewhat misleading, since it omitted the other major guns, the carronades, as well as those long guns added after construction by enterprising frigate captains who were willing to sacrifice sailing qualities for maximum weight of broadside. Thus the *Constellation* was rated a 38-gun frigate but actually carried 48 long guns when she fought her first battle; the *United States* was rated a 44, but in reality had 50 long guns; the *Constitution,* while also rated a 44, actually mounted 60 long guns when she put to sea.

There were differences as well in the true weight of the shot fired by a cannon of a given rating. A British 18-pounder, for example, fired a ball weighing just about that amount. But French cannon, because of different casting techniques, generally fired a ball weighing one or two pounds more than the cannon's rating. And American cannon, because of various casting deficiencies, usually fired a ball weighing a pound or so less than the cannon's rating. American cannon balls also were known to break in two upon hitting the target, and occasionally even to fly into pieces in midflight. Poorly cast cannon also burst on occasion. Finally, American powder was somewhat inferior to that of the European navies, slightly reducing range and hitting power.

To make up for these deficiencies, the Yankee gunners drilled endlessly, forming strong attachments to their weapons and giving them names such as Raging Eagle, Spitfire, Mad Anthony and Defiance. The entire crew of a Yankee frigate, in fact, was made up of proud and highly motivated men, perhaps even more so than the crack crews of the Royal Navy frigates. For one thing, their pay was superior to that of other seamen—and indeed to that of many working men ashore. President Adams had seen to that personally. In organizing the Navy, Adams had studied the employment opportunities of the day, and after learning that a skilled artisan ashore earned $12 to $14 per month and a merchant

FRIGATE CONSTITUTION.

TO all *able-bodied* and *patriotic Sea-men*, who are willing to serve their Country, and Support its Cause :

The President of the United States, having ordered the Captain and Commander of the good Frigate CONSTITUTION, of 44 guns, now riding in the harbor of *Boston*, to employ the moſt *vigorous exertions* to put ſaid ſhip, as ſpeedily as poſſible, in a ſituation to ſail at the ſhorteſt command.

Notice is hereby given, That a HOUSE OF RENDEZVOUS is opened at the ſign of the *Federal Eagle*, kept by Mrs. BROADERS, in Fore-ſtreet ;—where ONE HUNDRED and FIFTY able Seamen, and NINETY-FIVE ordinary Seamen, will have an opportunity of entering into the ſervice of their country for One Year, unleſs ſooner diſcharged by the Preſident of the United States.—To all able bodied Seamen, the ſum of SEVENTEEN DOLLARS ; and to all ORDINARY SEAMEN the ſum of TEN DOLLARS per month, will be given ; and two months advance will be paid by the Recruiting Officer, if neceſſary.

None will be allowed to enter this honorable ſervice, but ſuch as are well organized, healthy and robuſt ; and free from ſcorbutic and conſumptive affections.

A glorious opportunity now preſents to the brave and hardy Seamen of New-England, to enter the ſervice of their country—to avenge its wrongs—and to protect its rights on the ocean. Thoſe brave Lads, are now invited to repair to the FLAGG of the CONSTITUTION now flying at the above rendezvous ; where they ſhall be kindly received, handſomely entertained, and may enter into immediate pay.

SAMUEL NICHOLSON,
Commander, United States Frigate Conſtitution.

At the above rendezvous Lt. CLARK of the Marines, will enliſt three Sargeants, three Corporals, one Armourer, one Drummer, one Fifer, and fifty privates to compoſe a company for the Ship CONSTITUTION. None can be inliſted who are not five feet, ſix inches high.

Boſton, Maſſachuſetts, May 12.

Captain Samuel Nicholson's urgent 1798 appeal for sailors for his Constitution emphasizes patriotism and short enlistments, inducements U.S. recruiters relied on in lieu of the impressment favored by the British. But the one-year term proved troublesome, since ships were often forced back to port for new crews.

seaman $8 to $10 per month, he had fixed the pay of American enlisted men at $10 to $17 per month.

Candidates enlisted for a one-year hitch (compared with indefinite terms in the Royal Navy) and were allowed to look over their ships before signing on. They could see the relatively roomy decks in which they would sling their hammocks, and inspect the ration list, which guaranteed at least a pound of meat per man each day, with satisfying quantities of rice, cheese, molasses and other foods. In addition, each sailor was entitled to half a pint of spirits or a quart of beer daily. Compared with the diet of most workingmen, it was excellent fare, and a considerable inducement.

To all of this could be added a genuine patriotic anger directed at both the Barbary corsairs and the French privateers who were preying on American merchant shipping. And if a man, by helping to put a halt to such depredations, could line his pockets with a share of prize money from a captured enemy vessel, then so much the better. Thus the frigate captains easily filled the complements of their ships with elite crews, content with their lot and eager for combat.

The *United States*, under Captain John Barry, sailed down Delaware Bay and put to sea toward the end of June 1798. Once out, she cleared away for Cape Cod and later ran down to the West Indies on her shakedown cruise. At about the same time, Captain Thomas Truxtun sailed the *Constellation* past the Virginia capes and out into the Atlantic, convoying a dozen merchantmen beyond the capes to protect them from French privateers.

On July 22, 1798, the *Constitution*, Captain Samuel Nicholson commanding, cleared Boston Roads and stood to sea. She dropped down to Newport, Rhode Island, and then took up cruising station between Cape Henry, at the mouth of Chesapeake Bay, and Florida, in search of French armed ships.

So the first three of the new Yankee frigates all appeared at sea in little more than a month. And because these ships were so big and so strikingly different from other frigates, officers of foreign navies were quick to take notice.

Somewhat smugly, the Royal Navy concluded that Humphreys, Fox, Doughty and all the others had succeeded only in bringing forth an ungainly hybrid, part frigate, part ship of the line, possessing few of the best qualities of either. With their extended length, their strange flush decks overweighted with cannon, their several feet of extra beam and the distinct inward curve of their upper sides above the wales (called "tumble home" by marine designers), the new Yankee frigates seemed freakish in the eyes of the British. Their very tall masts, just scant feet shorter than those of a British ship of the line, supported enormous quantities of canvas, sometimes even a skysail above the royals. Most Royal Navy officers speculated that the American frigates would make lubberly sailers.

But one British captain was soon to be disabused of this notion. In 1799 the *Constitution* appeared in the West Indies to serve as flagship of the small American force stationed there to fight what had become known as the Quasi-War with France. Since the days of Sir Francis

Drake, the West Indies had been lush cruising grounds for the British, and the Royal Navy maintained several bases in the islands. The normal courtesies were exchanged between Captain Samuel Nicholson of the American squadron and his British counterparts. One English master, a Captain Parker, after inspecting the *Constitution*, politely expressed the opinion that his own frigate, the *Santa Margaretta*, could beat her hands down in a sailing match. And since Parker had called at Madeira on his way to the Caribbean, he offered to wager a cask of splendid Madeira wine to prove his point. Nicholson accepted the challenge. At the appointed time, both frigates rendezvoused, a signal gun was fired to start the race and the two ships were off.

The *Constitution*'s sailing master was a brilliant young lieutenant by the name of Isaac Hull, who at 25 had already logged considerable experience as a merchantman officer and captain. In the brisk breeze Hull piled on every piece of canvas the big ship could hold, until it seemed as

Breaking the law—but in a "handsome manner"

Swarming out of a commandeered sloop, raiders from the Constitution capture the French-owned Sandwich in the West Indies in 1800.

if her masts would surely snap. But the masts held, and as the *Constitution* flew through the Caribbean it quickly became apparent that the race was no contest. By sunset the British frigate was hull down astern and the *Constitution* was hove to so that the Royal Navy could catch up. That night an English boat crew delivered one cask of very fine Madeira to the Yankee crew, whose grins proved that Joshua Humphreys and his associates had known very well what they were about.

But even though the Yankee frigates had shown that they could sail, there was still a reason why the Royal Navy looked upon them with some disdain. The robust Yankee frigates were designed to mount long 24-pound cannon. The British had experimented with 24-pounders but had discarded them as too cumbersome. In British eyes, what might be lost in weight of metal between a 24- and an 18-pounder was more than made up for by the rapidity with which the lighter gun, to which the Royal Navy had committed itself, could be reloaded and fired again.

So eager were the men of the U.S. Navy to prove their prowess that they would stretch the law to the breaking point in order to discomfit the enemy. Such was the case on the *Constitution* in May of 1800, during the so-called Quasi-War with France.

While patrolling in the West Indies, the *Constitution*'s Commodore Silas Talbot learned that a French-owned ship, the former British packet *Sandwich*, was loading coffee in the harbor at Puerto Plata, Hispaniola. Under a 1795 treaty, Spain had ceded its territory on Hispaniola to France, but because no formal surrender of Puerto Plata had taken place, the harbor was still under Spanish protection. And Spain was neutral in the hostilities between the U.S. and France. Weighing the diplomatic complications against the glory of taking a prize, Talbot decided to chance it.

To execute the operation, Talbot selected his 27-year-old first lieutenant, Isaac Hull. Because it would be too risky to take the *Constitution* into the shallow harbor, the Americans chose what Talbot termed "a suitable vessel for disguise." She was a privately owned American sloop named the *Sally*, which had been running contraband between the area and the U.S. and was well known at Puerto Plata.

Before dawn on May 9, Hull and a group of volunteers boarded and commandeered the *Sally* as she lay at rest in a bay. The next day, taking the *Sally*'s master along to lull any suspicions, they set out for Puerto Plata, about 15 miles away. There were some 90 Americans in the party—half a dozen on deck and the rest below.

Entering the harbor at noon on Sunday, May 11, the Americans found that their intended prize, as Talbot later reported, was "a beautiful copper-bottomed ship" that mounted four 6-pound cannon and two 9-pounders. Not a soul could be seen on deck; her crew was apparently below eating dinner. Beyond her, the town and the fort overlooking the harbor dozed in the noonday heat of the tropics.

The capture was ridiculously easy. While a party of Marines went ashore to spike the fort's guns, the *Sally* coasted silently up to the *Sandwich*. Hull and his men surged over her sides, brandishing cutlasses and pistols. Utterly surprised, the *Sandwich*'s crew surrendered forthwith.

The next morning, Hull delivered both ships to the *Constitution*. The Americans, from Talbot and Hull on down, considered both the *Sandwich* and the *Sally* legitimate prizes. But they were in for a disappointment.

In the diplomatic uproar that followed, the U.S. government decided that it was more important to soothe injured Spanish feelings than to hold the French trader. The seizure of the *Sandwich* was declared illegal on the ground that the ship had been under the protection of a neutral power. The vessel was handed over to Spain, and no prize money was paid. The *Sally* was condemned for trafficking with the enemy, and was sold soon after; the money went to Spain as indemnity.

Despite the official displeasure, the men of the *Constitution* were regarded as heroes. Commodore Talbot commended Hull and his crew for "the handsome manner and great address with which they performed this daring adventure." And in a personal letter to Talbot, Secretary of the Navy Benjamin Stoddert extolled "the spirit which dictated and the gallantry which achieved an enterprise which reflects honor on the American Navy."

The ships of both navies also mounted heavy carronades. But these were short-range, bludgeoning weapons—for use in the final stages of battle. The weapon of choice was the lancelike long gun, loved by fighting captains who relied on superior tactics, seamanship and rapidity of fire. The Americans did not disagree about the merits of the long gun as such. They simply believed that the edge went to the bigger, stronger frigates with additional crewmen to handle the heavier and longer-ranged 24-pounders. What is more, given the slight deficiencies in American munition making, it was only prudent to compensate for those imperfections by mounting a heavier gun and learning to fire it as rapidly as possible.

The first test of the American cannon came soon enough. A little after midday on February 9, 1799, the *Constellation*, under Truxtun, was cruising near Saint Kitts in the Caribbean to protect American shipping from French privateers. If the French were looking for trouble, Truxtun was just the sort to accommodate them. A successful Revolutionary War captain, he was vain, jealous of rank, as touchy toward his numerous friends as toward his many enemies—and a man who loved nothing better than a fight.

At 12:30 p.m. in the Caribbean the *Constellation*'s lookout sighted a sail near the island of Nevis. The *Constellation* was put before the brisk wind and settled on a course to intercept the stranger. As the two ships drew together, an angry squall struck the area, causing the *Constellation* to lose a studding-sail boom and the other ship to lose her main-topmast. On both vessels the wreckage was quickly cleared away. By then the stranger had hung out the tricolor and had been identified as the *Insurgente*, reputed to be a crack frigate, the fastest ship in the French Navy. Like the *Constellation*, she was rated at 38 guns. But the French, following the British lead, had opted for lighter cannon than the Americans, and so her main armament consisted of 18-pounders, compared with the *Constellation*'s hefty 24s.

Shortly after 3 p.m. the two ships closed to within 100 yards, and both crews were at battle stations and staring out at each other over loaded cannon. It was not a moment for faint hearts. Nor was it a moment when the Americans of the *Constellation* would be found wanting. Convincing himself that the Frenchman meant to shoot, the bellicose Thomas Truxtun made quick to get off the first broadside, his 14 long 24-pounders roaring at once from the starboard battery. While the *Constellation* was still feeling the recoil of the enormous synchronized explosion, the *Insurgente* returned the compliment with her own full broadside of 18-pounders.

As both frigates blazed away, the French followed national custom by aiming high, hoping to dismast the enemy before outmaneuvering and closing for the *coup de grâce*. The *Insurgente* came up into the wind in an effort to cross the American's bow and deliver a broadside directly down the length of the *Constellation*. But the loss of the French ship's topmast had reduced her speed and maneuverability. Unable to get in front of the American, she found herself head on to the *Constellation*'s gun-studded starboard side. Crossing in front of the French vessel's bow, Captain Truxtun seized his advantage and raked the *Insurgente* with the

Private Signals by day for the ships of War of the United States.

Private Signals by night for the ships of War of the United States.

Private Signals for the American Fleet

Pages from Commodore John Barry's signal book, used during the naval war with France, detail a system of flag recognition signals for use by day (left), as well as a more involved combination of gunpowder flashes and verbal exchanges for sending messages at night (right).

kind of broadside fusillade the enemy had intended to deal the *Constellation*. Splinters flew, French cannon were dismounted, and French sailors fell everywhere.

The *Constellation* continued on across the *Insurgente*'s bow, and both ships turned onto parallel courses, presenting their hitherto unengaged sides to each other, port for the *Constellation*, starboard for the *Insurgente*. Truxtun's men swiftly shifted to their already loaded port-side cannon and continued to pour on broadside after broadside. But the *Insurgente*'s gun crews were still dazed from the ferocious raking they had just endured, and they had trouble manning their new batteries. Some men began to panic and run below; others gamely went to their new stations. But by now the *Insurgente*'s rigging was hanging in shreds, her mizzen-topmast had been shot away, and the remains of her fore-topsail dangled in streamers.

As for the *Constellation*, a French 18-pound ball had struck her fore-topmast, just above the cap. Amid the smoke and confusion David Porter, the midshipman in command of the foretop, could not catch Captain Truxtun's attention to point out to him that the mast was likely to topple over. Just past his 19th birthday, the youngster climbed up into the rigging hand over hand, cut the lines while the enemy's shot whistled about him, and lowered the fore-topsail yard, thereby saving the damaged mast. It was good that he did, because Captain Truxtun chose that moment to come up into the wind, cross the *Insurgente's* bow and rake the Frenchman again.

By now the Frenchman's plight was pitiable. No quartermasters remained to handle the frigate's wheel. Repeated calls to her fighting tops brought no response. Every gun on her main deck was dismounted. Dead and dying French sailors lay everywhere; 70 of her 409-man crew were casualties. Once more the *Constellation* turned, prepared this time to deliver a full raking broadside into the weak and unprotected Frenchman's stern. Captain Barreaut of the *Insurgente* had no recourse but to haul down his flag.

Later, Barreaut stepped aboard the *Constellation* and complained, "Why have you fired upon the national flag? Our two nations are not at war." In a report to the Secretary of the Navy, Truxtun wrote, "The French Captain tells me, I have caused a War with France, if so I am glad of it, for I detest Things being done by Halves." The *Insurgente* was taken as a prize, and three days after the contest the two ships came to anchor at Saint Kitts.

The *Constellation* had just proved that an American frigate could sail and fight with the best. And if there was any lingering doubt about it, almost a year later she was to prove it again, this time by routing the 52-gun French frigate *Vengeance* in a five-hour night battle off Guadeloupe. By aiming high the *Vengeance* so damaged the *Constellation's* rigging that Truxtun was unable to close and board. But the punishment he handed out in return was more than enough to persuade the Frenchman to depart the scene with great haste, finding refuge at the Dutch island of Curaçao. During the battle the *Constellation* suffered 39 casualties, the *Vengeance* four times that many.

The engagement between the *Constellation* and the *Vengeance* was the last major confrontation of the Quasi-War. Napoleon Bonaparte had seized power in France, and his grandiose plans for conquest did not include settling trifling disputes with the remote and relatively impotent United States.

But America was no longer as weak as Bonaparte might have supposed. Congress had had second thoughts because of the hostilities with France, and provided more funds. Within 14 months after the *Constellation's* victory over the *Insurgente*, the other three of the group that American sailors and naval historians came to refer to fondly as the "six original frigates" had been launched, doubling the big ship strength of the United States Navy.

Construction of the frigates originally assigned to the yards at Gosport, Virginia, Portsmouth, New Hampshire, and New York, which was halted by Congress in 1796, had started up again in 1798. Design of the Gosport ship had by then been turned over to Josiah Fox, who reduced her size, with the result that instead of carrying the planned 44 guns she was rated a 38. Yet when she slid into the water on June 20, 1799, as the *Chesapeake* under Captain Richard Dale, she was as trim and handsome

In the most famous encounter of the brief undeclared war between the United States and France, the Constellation and the Insurgente exchange broadsides in the Caribbean on February 9, 1799. Although one of the best French frigates on American station, the Insurgente was no match for the Yankee, and struck her colors in scarcely 75 minutes.

a vessel as any master could desire. She was also destined for a career plagued by bad luck.

The New Hampshire ship, christened the *Congress*, 38 guns, was launched on August 15, 1799, and the New York frigate, christened the *President*, 44 guns, slid down the ways on April 1, 1800. For reasons never entirely clear, the *Congress* was to prove the least distinguished of America's first six frigates; she spent much of her time laid up at dockside and was finally broken up at Norfolk in 1836. The *President* was entirely another matter. Her final design had been delegated to Joshua Humphreys' old helper, William Doughty, who altered her lines so as to make her lighter and lower, with less freeboard. Of the three 44s, she was the fleetest—a quality that would stand her in good stead in the conflicts to come. And they would come soon.

Scarcely a year after the last of the frigates was launched, the U.S. Navy was called upon to go into action against the Barbary corsairs. The Dey of Algiers was not the problem this time; he had remained quiet, apparently content with his annual pay-off. But extortion breeds extortion, and there were other sea rovers along the North African coast lusting after American gold.

The red-bearded corsairs of the Barbary Coast

When the U.S. Navy sailed into the Mediterranean in 1801 to engage the Barbary corsairs, it was going to war with a pirate tradition that dated back many centuries. Marauders from North Africa had been prowling Mediterranean waters, plundering and taking slaves, since the end of the Roman Empire. And they had risen to become a major force around 1500 with the arrival of two daring sea rovers. These were the brothers Barbarossa, or Red Beard—so called because of their flaming auburn whiskers.

Very little is known of the brothers' early lives, save that they were born in Greece, became seafaring brigands and turned up as Muslims in North Africa at the dawn of the 16th Century. The elder of the pair, Aruj, was apparently the dominant brother, for contemporary accounts say next to nothing initially about the younger Barbarossa, Khair-ed-Din. Aruj soon found an ally in the King of Tunis, who offered him a safe harbor in exchange for one fifth of his pirate plunder. The bargain struck, Aruj immediately embarked on an exploit that was to elevate him overnight to status as the premier pirate of the Mediterranean.

Lying off the Italian littoral in 1504, Aruj spotted a great treasure galley flying the colors of Pope Julius II and rowing leisurely toward Civitavecchia, the principal port of Rome. Never dreaming that a Moorish pirate would be so far north, the Christians panicked at the first sight of turbans. A storm of arrows and shot concluded the issue, and the pirates had their prize.

Shortly after, a second large treasure galley belonging to the Pope hove into view. Manning the captured galley, Aruj and his men forced their prisoners to strip and herded them belowdecks. The corsairs then donned the Christians' clothes, tied their own small ship astern of the galley to make it appear to be a prize, and waited for the enemy to sail into the trap. Once again surprise was complete and Aruj quickly took his second papal treasure ship.

It was the first time in history that two papal galleys had been captured by a pirate in a single day. But that was just the beginning. Aruj next defeated and captured a Spanish warship defended by a force of 500 soldiers. By 1512 he had assembled a force of 12 galliots with cannon, gathered 1,000 armed men and fortified an island off Tunis as his base. Not content with plundering forays, Aruj launched two unsuccessful attacks on the Spanish-held North African city of Bougie, during which he suffered the loss of his left arm. Undaunted by these setbacks, in 1516 the daring corsair marched 5,000 of his men into Algiers, overthrew the local rulers and brutally seized power.

So grave were the Barbarossa depredations that in 1518 Charles, the new King of Spain, dispatched a force of 10,000 soldiers to put an end to the Moorish pirates. According to legend, the Spanish managed to surprise Aruj and 1,500 of his men outside of Algiers. Vastly outnumbered, Aruj strewed gold and jewels behind his force in hopes of distracting his pursuers as he fled toward the safety of the city. But the Spaniards caught Aruj at the River Salado and slaughtered the corsair king and all of his men.

The Spanish then withdrew from most of the area, believing that they had dealt the pirates a crippling blow. But they reckoned without Aruj's brother, Khair-ed-Din. This young man had all Aruj's cunning and courage. But he was a statesman too, shrewd in ways that Aruj was not.

Khair-ed-Din's first goal was to consolidate and legitimize his power. Where Aruj had contented himself with making alliances with local princes, his brother in 1519 enlisted the support of the entire Ottoman Empire, offering his services and seeking the favor of Sultan Selim I. The Sultan, in return for Khair-ed-Din's loyalty, sent 2,000 janissaries to bolster the corsair's forces and appointed the Barbarossa brother Governor-General of Algiers.

Khair-ed-Din was now no longer a renegade, but a legitimate servant of a great emperor. He soon retook several towns still held by Spain near Algiers and extended his conquests to the rest of the Barbary States. Between 1533 and 1544, as admiral of the Sultan's fleet, he ravaged the coasts of Greece, Spain and Italy, and caused the Sultan's flag to be feared throughout the Mediterranean. In 1543 he plundered the Italian province of Reggio di Calabria, seized as his bride the Governor's 18-year-old daughter and, for their honeymoon, carried her along with him while he continued to raid Italy.

By the time Khair-ed-Din died peacefully in 1546, he and his brother, Aruj, had established a corsair tradition on the Barbary Coast that would continue to plague Christian mariners for some 300 years.

A 16th Century Dutch engraving reflects the European fear of the piratical Barbarossa brothers, whose names lived on for centuries among the North African brigands, known as the Barbary corsairs. The legend gives the Dutch spelling of the brothers' names, Aruj (left) and Khair-ed-Din, and declares that the pair are "Kings of Algiers."

ARUCH En CHERIDYN BARBAROSSA
Koningen van Algiers.

Slaves who made the pirates rich

While rare prizes of silk and gold glad-
dened every Barbary captain's heart,
the most valuable and common booty
by far was a captured ship's passengers and crew. These hapless souls
were sold into slavery, one of the oldest institutions in the Muslim Mediterranean. So important were slaves to
the Barbary economy that at times they
made up 25 per cent of the total population of some cities.

The slaves were generally hustled to
shore soon after capture, since their
extended care and feeding aboard ship
was impractical. At the slave marts,
such as the one at right, they were seg-
regated by sex, inspected for fitness
and then sold either singly or in lots.

Wealthy men whose families could
ransom them quickly were commonly
treated well. And for those men who
were skilled—such as carpenters, surgeons and shipwrights—slavery was
sometimes little different from life at
home; they were often allowed to set
up a business and keep part of their
earnings toward their ransom. But for
the unskilled men chained in quarry
gangs or to a galley rowing bench, life
was a purgatory of awful food, bloody
whippings and, soon enough, death.

For women life was perhaps even
worse. The fairest were traditionally
sent to Constantinople as concubines
for the Sultan. Comely women who
were not among the most beautiful
were fated for similar service to a local
prince or in the city's brothels. For the
rest it was a wretched, brutish life of
foul scullery work, house cleaning or
selling water in the streets.

*Manacled Christians are displayed
singly and in lots in the slave market at
Algiers. Interested buyers examined a
prospect's hands and teeth, forced him to
run to check his fitness and then beat
him with a stick to see how he reacted.
Women slaves, according to one
writer, could be viewed more intimately
in a "concealed latticed shop."*

Ministering to a captive see

There were various altruists on the fringes of the Barbary slave trade who provided food, medicine and spiritual succor to the captives. The best-known of these were the Trinitarian Fathers, a staunch band of priests who took on the job of ministering to Christians in the hands of infidels.

Founded at the close of the 12th Century, the order was headquartered in Europe; its members journeyed to the Barbary States, where the rulers welcomed them because the priests were active in arranging for ransoms.

To raise the ransom money demanded by the slaveowners—and enough extra to meet the expenses of their far-flung ministry—the priests commonly painted pictures of Barbary brutality even more hellish than reality "in order," as one observer put it, "to excite the charity of the faithful."

Though over the years the fathers ransomed many victims of the slave trade, the commerce itself continued until the early 19th Century.

A priest bargains over ransom with a Barbary slaveowner in this engraving from Father Pierre Dan's Histoire de Barbarie et de Ses Corsaires. The volume was widely circulated throughout Europe to strengthen the efforts of Christians to succor the slaves.

Fire, hot wax and crucifixion are tortures depicted by Father Dan, who claimed that Muslim slaveowners thus attempted to convert Christians. But Spanish author Miguel Cervantes, himself a slave for two years, asserted that cruelty was an end in itself. Writing of an Algerian slaveowner in Don Quixote, he noted: "Every day he hanged a slave, and cut the ears off another. He did it merely for the sake of doing it."

These piously entreating statuettes, carved in the 17th Century to resemble Hamburg sailors held in bondage in North Africa, were placed over collection boxes in German churches to elicit the donation of ransom money. Unlike richer captives, whose families could raise ransom easily, poor sailors had to depend on charity — though a special tax was sometimes levied in their behalf.

Chapter 2

Trial and triumph in the Mediterranean

n May 14, 1801, a gang of ax-toting Tripolitans appeared before the U.S. consulate in Tripoli and began hacking away at the flagpole, which soon toppled onto the terrace, leaving only a stump. By that deed, seemingly an act of mindless vandalism, Yusef Karamanli, the Pasha of Tripoli, declared war on the United States of America. In the desert wasteland of the Barbary Coast, wood was a precious commodity. Trees tall and sturdy enough to make a flagpole were virtually nonexistent (most diplomats solved the problem by cadging a spare spar from one of their nation's ships). Because of the short supply, flagpoles carried a special significance, and chopping them down was the traditional way for the Barbary States to announce that they were opening hostilities.

The Americans had had fair warning. One of the Pasha's sons earlier had darkly informed the U.S. consul, William Leander Cathcart, that "when the American flag staff comes down it will take a great deal of grease to get it up again." To be precise, $20,000 a year worth of grease. That was the annual tribute that the Pasha of Tripoli, least of the Barbary States in both population and wealth, was demanding as his price for letting American merchant ships pass through what he deemed to be his waters. After all, the U.S. was paying the Dey of Algiers $21,600 yearly, and Yusef Karamanli saw no reason why he should not get the same.

The young American republic was not ready for a war. The Revolution had ended only 18 years before; for the last three years there had been hostilities at sea with France. Most Americans earnestly desired a period of calm. But news of the Pasha's demands sent a wave of public indignation surging through the country. The meager U.S. Treasury was already being stretched to pay off the Dey of Algiers; to accede to a second extortionate demand was insupportable. Angry speeches were made in Congress, and President Thomas Jefferson declared: "It is money thrown away. There is no end to the demands of these powers, nor any security in their promises. The real alternative before us is whether to abandon the Mediterranean or to keep up a cruise on it."

News of the Pasha's declaration of war had not yet reached the United States. Jefferson could not wage war on the Tripolitans without legislative sanction, and Congress, for all the rumblings, was not yet ready to go that far. But Jefferson did dispatch a naval squadron to show the flag and signal U.S. determination not to be denied the Mediterranean. It was a delicate matter, and he put the squadron under such restrictions as might make a fighting captain weep: "We enjoin on you the most rigorous moderation, conformity to right & reason, & suppression of all passions, which might lead to the commitment of our Peace or our honor."

And so on June 2, 1801, a small U.S. Navy force made sail from the Virginia capes, bound for the Barbary Coast. It comprised the frigates *President*, 44 guns, *Philadelphia*, 36, and *Essex*, 32, and the schooner *Enterprise*, 12 guns. Two of those ships were of unusual genesis: in the outburst of patriotic passion that had accompanied the undeclared Quasi-War with France, the people of Philadelphia had themselves collected the funds to build the frigate named after their city, and the citizens of Salem, Massachusetts, had subscribed to the construction of the beautiful little *Essex*. (Similarly, the frigates *John Adams* and *New York*

His back to a window framing warships at anchor, Commodore Edward Preble clasps a chart diagraming his intrepid attacks against the Tripolitan corsairs in this 1805 oil by the famed Rembrandt Peale. Preble was greeted as a national hero upon his return home. "I cannot," he remarked, "but be a little flattered with the reception I have met with here."

had been financed by public contributions in Charleston, South Carolina, and New York, respectively.) Aboard the *President* and acting as commodore of the little fleet was Captain Richard Dale, whose moment of greatest glory had come during the Revolutionary War, when he had served as a young first lieutenant under John Paul Jones. On the moonlit night of September 23, 1779, Dale had swung from a rope on the *Bonhomme Richard* to lead a victorious boarding party onto H.M.S. *Serapis*.

Now, delayed by foul weather, Dale arrived off Tripoli on July 24. He learned of the Pasha's declaration of war and was setting up a blockade when he found that he was running short of fresh water. To fetch some from Malta, he dispatched the *Enterprise* under Lieutenant Andrew Sterrett—a very tough young man. While serving as a lieutenant on the *Constellation* during her 1799 battle with the French *Insurgente*, Sterrett had killed an American seaman who attempted to desert his station. As he later explained it to a friend: "One fellow I was obliged to run through the body with my sword, and so put an end to a coward. You must not think this strange, for we would put a man to death for even looking pale aboard this ship." In the latter assertion he was speaking in hyperbole, of course; life in the U.S. Navy was not nearly so barbaric. But the act—and Sterrett's defense of it—told much about his fierce character.

On August 1, while on his water run, Sterrett sighted and approached the Pasha's ship of war *Tripoli*, with 14 guns and a crew of 80. Since Great Britain was at peace with Tripoli, the *Enterprise* was flying the Union Jack, a common deceptive practice of the day. Hailing the *Tripoli*, Sterrett asked what business had brought her to sea. The enemy commander replied that he was hunting Americans but had not, alas, been able to find any. Down went the *Enterprise*'s British flag, up went the American colors, and Sterrett's men fired their muskets across the Tripolitan deck; the *Tripoli* answered with a ragged broadside.

For three hours the two ships flailed away at each other. Time after time the Tripolitans struck their colors; time after time, as the Americans approached to board the supposedly surrendered ship, the corsairs again hoisted their flag and renewed the battle. Finally the Tripolitan admiral, Rais Mahomet Rous, was wounded; this time, as a guarantee that his ruse would not be repeated, he threw his flag into the sea. Of the 80 men with whom he had begun the fight, 30 were killed and 30 injured. Astonishingly—and in testimony to the poor quality of Tripolitan marksmanship—not a single American suffered so much as a scratch.

Dale's news of the Tripolitans' declaration of war and of Lieutenant Sterrett's smashing response to it had a galvanizing effect on Congress. The heretofore reluctant legislators passed a resolution commending Sterrett and his men, awarded an extra month's pay to everyone on the ship and voted Sterrett a commemorative sword. Then the Senate and House adopted a resolution that amounted to a declaration of war against Tripoli. It authorized President Jefferson to use the Navy however he pleased to protect American shipping from the Barbary brigands.

Despite this lifting of restrictions on action, a long lull followed in the Mediterranean. Dale's blockade effectively prevented Tripolitan corsairs from venturing out of port, and on April 14, 1802, because the enlistments of the *President*'s men were running out, Dale took the ship back to Norfolk and shortly resigned from the service in a dispute over rank; he wished to be elevated to admiral, but that rank did not yet exist in the U.S. Navy and Congress refused to create it for him.

A new commodore was named to command the Mediterranean squadron. All he would have to do was maintain the blockade. But Dale's successor proved a disaster.

The new squadron commander should have been Captain Thomas Truxtun, hero of the *Constellation's* fight with the *Insurgente*. But since he would be acting as a commodore, the status-conscious Truxtun demanded that the Navy follow European practice and place a captain under him to sail his flagship, the 38-gun *Chesapeake*. When the Navy Department refused, Truxtun resigned from the service—and the U.S. lost one of its stoutest fighters.

Truxtun's replacement in command was Richard Valentine Morris, an inexperienced man who had been promoted to captain less than a year before. Although events were to prove Morris hopelessly inept as a naval commander, it would have been difficult to improve on his political connections. His father, Lewis Morris, had been a member of the Continental Congress and had signed the Declaration of Independence. His uncle, Gouverneur Morris, was a leading light of the Constitutional Convention. His brother, Lewis Robert Morris, as a member of the House of Representatives, had played a key role in Jefferson's Presidential election over Aaron Burr.

On April 27, 1802, the new commodore sailed forth in the *Chesapeake* from Hampton Roads to wage war with the Pasha of Tripoli. Morris was accompanied, incredibly, by his wife and small son, and he took his time before joining his fleet. He arrived at Gibraltar on May 31, 1802, and tarried there, socializing with British officers, until August 17. He then set out to pay calls on various Spanish, French and Italian ports, winding up at Malta. By year's end he had yet to lay eyes on the shores of Tripoli. At last, on January 30, 1803, he made sail for his squadron, but a gale blew the *Chesapeake* back to Malta. On February 10 he departed again, not for Tripoli but for Tunis, to confer with the American consul, William Eaton. While there, unbelievably, the commander of the U.S. Mediterranean squadron managed to get taken hostage by the Bey of Tunis.

This mortifying event occurred after Morris had completed his business with Eaton and was preparing to return to the *Chesapeake*. Somehow he forgot to bid a proper diplomatic farewell to his host, the Bey, and that affronted monarch had him seized until restitution was made— in money. The figure the Bey had in mind was $34,000. Morris was released only after Eaton had paid $12,000 from his personal funds and the Danish consul had stood bond for the remaining $22,000—which Morris sent ashore after arriving back on the *Chesapeake*.

And from there at last he sailed to Tripoli. Commodore Richard Valentine Morris arrived on station in late May, 1803, more than a year after departing from the United States. All the while, the U.S. squadron, under an interim commander, had held a loose blockade of the Tripolitan coast, and the Americans now greeted their new commodore with a minor victory. Early in June the patrolling squadron came on a dozen grain boats hidden in a small bay 35 miles west of Tripoli. The Americans swept into the bay and sank them all, sending to the bottom 25 tons of wheat badly needed by the Pasha. Now Morris made his last and most egregious error. Elated at the success of the raid, he decided to play the diplomat by treating with the Pasha for peace.

Under a flag of truce, he went ashore and proposed to the Pasha that the United States henceforth pay Tripoli $5,000 each time it sent a new consul to that country, with an additional $10,000 to be turned over if the Pasha behaved himself for five years. The Tripolitans, up to now so thoroughly blockaded, could scarcely believe their ears. Thinking the Americans daft, the Pasha upped the ante to an immediate payment of $200,000—plus reimbursement for the sunken wheat-carrying feluccas. When word of these negotiations reached the United States, the reaction was sulfurous. On September 11, 1803, Commodore Morris received instructions ordering him home, and once he got there Thomas Jefferson stripped him of his commission without benefit of court-martial.

The same orders that recalled Morris named his replacement. Again, Jefferson had reached down his list of captains, bypassing five senior officers. But this time he had come up with a fighter, in the gaunt person and vinegary personality of Captain Edward Preble.

Edward Preble was born in Portland (then called Falmouth), Maine, on August 15, 1761. His father was Brigadier General Jedediah Preble, renowned in New England both for having fought beside General James Wolfe when the British and the American colonists won Quebec from the French in 1759 and for having been the first man to ascend to the top of New Hampshire's Mount Washington. ("Brigadier Preble," it was said, "went up and washed his hands in the clouds.") The son Edward was a hot-tempered child who became a terrible-tempered man. But he was also one in whom loyalty loomed large, whose every thought and indeed every passion was directed toward the betterment of those who served with him.

Like many Americans of his day, Edward Preble had excellent cause to detest the Royal Navy. He had scarcely turned 14 when the town of Falmouth, including the Preble family home, was burned to the ground in a British effort to "chastise" the people of New England during the Revolutionary War. Old Jedediah by then had turned from soldiering and mountain climbing to potato farming, a vocation that held no attraction whatever for young Edward.

One day in his 16th year he flung down his hoe, traveled to Newburyport, Massachusetts, and signed articles on a privateer setting out on an Atlantic expedition. When he returned, his father arranged an appointment for him as an acting midshipman aboard the frigate *Protector*, 26 guns. Edward Preble saw action in the sinking of the British *Admiral Duff*, 32 guns, and again in an inconclusive fight against the *Thames*, also a 32. Eventually the *Protector* was captured by the Royal Navy, and Preble was consigned to the prison hulk *Jersey*, moored amid the mud flats off Brooklyn. Edward Preble was one of the lucky few who survived that hellhole. He had hardly spent a month among the men dying of filth, starvation and louse-borne typhus aboard the *Jersey* when he was unexpectedly exchanged for a captured British officer. Once

Berthed in New York Harbor, the disease-ridden British hulk Jersey became prison for Midshipman Edward Preble after he was captured from the American frigate Protector during the Revolution. Thousands of American seamen died of fever aboard the Jersey, but Preble's exchange was arranged by a Loyalist who had known his father in happier times.

repatriated, he served out the War as a lieutenant aboard the *Winthrop,* 12 guns, cruising off the coast of Maine and capturing several good-sized British privateers.

During the next two decades he spent most of his time in the merchant trade, eventually becoming master and owner of his own ship. A dour, irascible New Englander, Preble earned a reputation as a severe disciplinarian, but a fair-minded man and an excellent mariner withal. He entered the new U.S. Navy soon after it was established but in 1802, as a relatively junior captain, he attempted to resign. He cited ill health as his reason, perhaps in reference to the stomach ulcers from which he suffered chronically. Robert Smith, who had succeeded Benjamin Stoddert as Secretary of the Navy, refused Preble's request. Instead, after reviewing Preble's service record, he placed this strange, complex man on sick leave until a suitable berth could be found for him. The opportunity came with the recall of Commodore Morris. And Preble soon showed his mettle.

On September 10, 1803, the new Mediterranean flagship *Constitution,* 44 guns, under Commodore Edward Preble, lay off Cadiz before passing through the Strait of Gibraltar. Low-hanging clouds and thick haze made for a starless, moonless night watch. Suddenly the dim shape of a vessel loomed out of the darkness. Preble came on deck and the *Constitution* cleared for action. The stranger refused to identify herself, so Preble mounted the mizzen shrouds and bellowed through his speaking trumpet: "I now hail for the last time. If you do not answer, I'll fire a shot."

The reply came in a cool, clipped upper-class English accent: "If you do, I'll return a broadside."

Preble's choler, never far from the surface, now rose. "I should like to catch you at that! I now hail for an answer. What ship is that?"

"This is His Britannic Majesty's eighty-four gun ship of the line, *Donegal*, Sir Richard Strachen commanding. Heave to and send a boat."

The young officers aboard the *Constitution* nudged one another. An 84 would crush the *Constitution* in the first broadside. Surely the old man would have to back down.

Not Preble. "This is the *Constitution*, 44 guns, Captain Edward Preble commanding," he replied. "I'll be damned if I'll send a boat to any ship." Flinty eyed, he stared down the *Constitution*'s long spar deck at the row of sputtering fuses held aloft by the gunners. "Blow up your matches, boys!" he called.

It was the crestfallen British who sent the boat. With embarrassment they confessed that their ship was not the 84-gun *Donegal*, but the 32-gun frigate *Maidstone*. Still, the point had been made. The old man was ready to fight an enemy twice his size, and the word spread swiftly throughout the Mediterranean.

Upon his arrival in that ancient cradle of commerce and arena for war, Preble took command of a squadron of six warships in addition to his *Constitution*. There were the 36-gun *Philadelphia*, two 16-gun brigs, the *Argus* and *Siren*, and three 12-gun schooners, the *Enterprise*, *Nautilus* and *Vixen*. Preble immediately set about whipping their crews to a peak of efficiency unknown before. Taking one look around, he pronounced the young officers commanding these vessels as nothing but "a pack of boys." It was an exaggeration; most were in their early 20s and the oldest among them was 30. But in the navies of the day, these were very young ages for command. In any case, the words would stick. One day these men would bear the designation "Preble's Boys" as a title of high honor. Some, to be sure, would quietly slip from history's notice. Others would die bathed in their own blood on oaken decks. But many of them would graduate from Edward Preble's "nursery of the Navy," as it came to be called, to enter the pantheon of American Naval heroes (*pages 47-49*).

But before then they had much to learn. They were full of strut, as proud and touchy as bantam fighting cocks. Most of them saw the Navy as an opportunity for excitement and individual glory, not as a service in which tedious chores and brave deeds alike were performed silently and diligently for a common purpose. Though willing to inflict discipline on others, they were themselves unruly and imprudent. And those who had already served in the Mediterranean, enduring either Dale's efficient but static blockade or Morris' buffoonery, smoldered with frustration. Denied the opportunity to close with an enemy who taunted them from Tripoli's shores, they were all too eager to fight with casual strangers or even with one another at the cock of an eye or the curl of a lip.

Stephen Decatur, the same lad who had carried to Joshua Humphreys the good news that the *United States* could be launched, was typical of these young roosters in both their virtues and their vices. When Preble arrived, Decatur was in command of the little brig *Argus*, 16 guns. He was 24 years old and a lieutenant. With his curly chestnut hair and

The heroes known as "Preble's Boys"

In every great fighting force there is a core of gifted officers whose leadership and bravery inspire their men to extraordinary heights. In the Royal Navy at the turn of the 19th Century, that core was Horatio Nelson's magnificent "Band of Brothers," victorious at the Nile, Copenhagen and Trafalgar. In the nascent U.S. Navy of the day, there was a similar group, and it was known as "Preble's Boys."

Trained under the stern eye of Commodore Edward Preble, these young officers numbered perhaps a dozen—among whom Stephen Decatur, Isaac Hull, Charles Stewart, William Bainbridge, James Lawrence, Thomas Macdonough and David Porter would attain the greatest fame.

The sons of doctors, lawyers, whalemen and merchant captains, these officers had little in common in family circumstances, education or temperament. Yet each of them manifested such courage and enterprise fighting the French in the Quasi-War in the West Indies and the Barbary corsairs in the Mediterranean that they were soon marked for success. Indeed, in 1803 Navy Secretary Robert Smith wrote that with "further improvement" the young officers assigned to Commodore Preble might one day lead the nation "when she shall, as she no doubt must, be engaged in a more serious warfare than the present."

When that test came a decade later in the War of 1812, the boys were now men, and they performed brilliantly. For though they commanded only a handful of the Navy's vessels, they were responsible for virtually all of the major American naval victories.

Stephen Decatur, who became a national hero at 25 when he destroyed the seized frigate Philadelphia in Tripoli, was so impatient for fame that early in the mission he chose not to wait for a brig bringing extra men. "The fewer the number," he said, "the greater the glory."

CHARLES STEWART, who would later captain the Constitution in the War of 1812, was an instant success in his first command in 1800. Given an armed schooner in the West Indies during hostilities with France, he seized two small enemy warships and retook several captured American merchant vessels.

JAMES LAWRENCE, who perished on the Chesapeake in 1813, was a daredevil as a lieutenant. In the early 1800s he crossed the Atlantic in a small gunboat — though it had only a foot of freeboard.

THOMAS MACDONOUGH, who led U.S. forces on Lake Champlain in 1814, showed such a gift for command in 1803 as prize officer of a captured Moroccan vessel that he earned the respect even of the enemy. When the ship was later returned, the Moroccans vainly tried to tempt Macdonough into their service.

ISAAC HULL, who in 1812 won the War's first great victory when his Constitution defeated the Guerriere, had already proved himself a superb fighter. In 1803 he bombarded a Tripolitan warship three times the size of his schooner Enterprise, killing the captain and forcing many of the 220 crewmen to leap overboard.

DAVID PORTER, who was captain of the Essex in 1812, sealed his reputation for leadership in 1803 when he pressed an attack on Tripolitan grain boats, although he was wounded in both thighs.

WILLIAM BAINBRIDGE, later another victorious commander of the Constitution, suffered the embarrassment of letting the Philadelphia fall into Tripolitan hands in 1803. But he made amends during his captivity by devising a plot to burn the vessel and smuggling the message in invisible ink out to Commodore Preble.

brilliant dark-brown eyes, he was as handsome as Lucifer and as proud. A fellow officer described him as having a "peculiarity of manner and appearance calculated to engross the attention—the form and look of a hero." Another said flatly: "Decatur is an officer of uncommon character, of rare promise, a man of an age, one perhaps not equalled in a million." Stephen Decatur would prove to be all of that, but he had so far established himself mainly as an enthusiastic participant or helpmate in duels to the death.

On his first ship, the *United States*, Decatur had challenged the mate of a merchantman who had refused his demand for the return of some Navy deserters. In the duel that followed, Decatur crippled the mate with a shot in the hip but remained unscathed himself. Later, as the first lieutenant serving on the *Essex*, Decatur sent indignant word that he would call the very next morning on the commander of a Spanish guard ship that had fired over the American frigate's shore boat. The Spaniard was astute enough to absent himself from his ship by the time Decatur stepped on board, but the young Yankee left him the message that "Lieutenant Decatur pronounces him a cowardly scoundrel and that, when they meet on shore, he will cut his ears off." Happily, the two never met, but the Spanish stopped harassing the Americans.

Just a few months before Preble took command of the squadron, Decatur had been a prime mover if not a principal in a much more serious affair. It involved Midshipman Joseph Bainbridge, then barely 16 years old, of the *New York*. Bainbridge and several of his messmates quietly took their seats one night at the opera in Malta, only to be subjected to loud, pointed observations about Yankee courage from officers of the Royal Navy sitting nearby. As Midshipman Bainbridge left the opera house, he was followed and further insulted by the British Governor's young private secretary, an excellent marksman notorious for having killed several men in duels. Bainbridge knocked him flat. Cards were quickly exchanged. But the next morning the English officer representing the Governor's secretary was in for a surprise, devised by Stephen Decatur, who had volunteered to act as Bainbridge's second.

"The usual terms, pistols at ten paces?" inquired the Englishman.

"Yes, it will be pistols," replied Decatur. "But pistols at *four* paces."

The Englishman's eyes widened. "Good Lord, sir," he exclaimed, "that looks like murder."

"Not murder," Decatur corrected, "but surely death." He went on to explain: "Your man is a professional duelist while mine is not."

The duel was held according to Decatur's specifications. The young Englishman, unaccustomed to staring into the muzzle of an opponent's pistol at such close range, wavered, and his shot missed the American midshipman altogether. Bainbridge, instructed by Decatur to hold low against the recoil if he valued his life, shot his antagonist dead.

Obviously, Commodore Preble's main challenge was to curb the tempers of his young men without breaking their spirits. One possible approach was to break up the cliques and factions that had formed, but wholesale personnel changes could severely damage morale. Preble ordered some shifts in the men's assignments but he moved cautiously and with a light hand.

The dirk, such as this one carried by Stephen Decatur, was standard equipment for midshipmen and for many junior officers in the early 19th Century. Descended from the short sword worn by Scottish Highlanders, it was frequently used during boarding engagements.

In Preble's rearrangement the *Argus* was taken away from Decatur and given to Lieutenant Isaac Hull, a 30-year-old New Englander with a reputation for brilliant seamanship and steadfast service. Apple cheeked and somewhat portly, the workman-like Hull was modest and reliable, given to deeds instead of words. The *Argus* was a good command for him, something of a reward because she was a sweet sailer, and Commodore Preble himself had supervised her construction. Because Hull was clearly his senior, Decatur could have no complaint, especially when Preble assigned him to command of the handy little schooner *Enterprise*. For second-in-command of the *Enterprise*, Decatur retained his lieutenant from the *Argus*, James Lawrence, a handsome lad whose easygoing ways had made him the most popular officer in the squadron.

Not surprisingly, Preble decided to leave the frigate *Philadelphia* under the command of Captain William Bainbridge, the young duelist's older brother. Six feet tall, powerfully built and self-educated, William Bainbridge preferred his hard sailor's fists to more sophisticated weapons as a means of settling arguments. He had been an 18-year-old first mate on a merchantman whose crew mutinied and was about to throw the captain overboard when Bainbridge came on deck. Bainbridge instantly piled in, fists flying, scattered the mutineers and clapped the ringleader in irons. For that exploit he became, at 19, a merchant master and, during the Quasi-War with France, a Navy captain.

But his career was shadowed by misfortune. During the Quasi-War, when his schooner *Retaliation* was hopelessly outgunned by the French frigates *Insurgente* and *Volontaire*, Bainbridge had become the first U.S. Navy captain to strike his colors; to his great chagrin, he would soon become the second as well. It would be another decade before he fully redeemed himself and took his rightful place in U.S. Naval history. Assigned to the *Philadelphia* as Bainbridge's second-in-command was Lieutenant David Porter, the former midshipman who had so distinguished himself in the battle against the *Insurgente*.

The brig *Siren*, 16 guns, soon joined Preble's force, commanded by Lieutenant Charles Stewart, a thin-faced youngster with ginger-colored hair and all the charm and psychic insights of his Celtic inheritance. Stewart had a reputation as an officer who stayed out of his commanding officer's path whenever possible but who obeyed orders to the letter. Barely literate when he first joined the Navy, he had educated himself and he later became a writer of considerable talent.

The little schooner *Nautilus*, 12 guns, was placed under the command of Lieutenant Richard Somers. Dicky Somers, Charles Stewart and Stephen Decatur had grown up together in Philadelphia, and a sort of three-musketeers relationship had evolved among them. Somers was gentle in deportment but fearsome when aroused. One evening he had been walking unarmed with two fellow officers in the Sicilian port city of Syracuse when the group was set upon by five *banditti*, brandishing swords and bent on unburdening the Americans of their pay. At the cost of a severe wound, Somers parried a thrust with his bare hand, took the sword away from his assailant, killed him and put the other brigands to flight.

Rounding out Preble's squadron was the schooner *Vixen*, 12 guns,

commanded by Lieutenant John Smith. With this squadron of two frigates—one his own flagship, the *Constitution*—and five smaller vessels
thus organized, Preble rightly assumed that his high-spirited youngsters
would soon produce a superb fighting force if he could only pull them
together and teach them that individual heroics should be subordinated
to iron discipline, with first consideration given to the squadron rather
than to personal pride. Accordingly, he detached the *Philadelphia* and
the *Vixen* to maintain the blockade off Tripoli, while he took the rest of
the squadron offshore to continue gunnery and sailing drills.

Preble went by the rules—his own. There were no fewer than 106
articles and regulations in a document entitled "Internal Rules and Regulations for U.S. Frigate *Constitution*, 1803-1804, by Captain Edward
Preble." There is some question whether Preble devised them all himself
or adapted the general orders already in force for another frigate, possibly those for the *Philadelphia*. In any case they were a masterpiece of
particularity, and Preble enthusiastically enforced each and every one of
them throughout the squadron.

Preble's hotspurs were to maintain a "polite address, and decent deportment from one officer to another" at all times, since "the character of
a gentleman and an Officer can never be Separated." Special attention

With sail crowded on, the 36-gun
Philadelphia runs with the wind shortly
before being captured by Tripolitan
corsairs. Captain William Bainbridge, who
was criticized for not blowing up his ship,
responded tartly to his detractors: "I
never presumed to think I had the liberty
of putting to death 306 souls because
they were placed under my command."

was "to be paid to the regulations relating to the cutting up of fresh beef, that choice pieces be never purposely selected for the Officers." Neither were officers allowed to "select casks of the best wine or spirits for their own use from those intended for the Ships Company." Discipline was strict: "The officers of the ship will not suffer the most trifling thing under them to be executed with indifference." But punishment in the form of the rattan cane was to be used only "with discretion." Moreover, officers were ordered to keep a sharp eye out for "those persons who are particularly cleanly, alert and obedient in order that the deserving may see that their merits are not disregarded." Even those most wretched of creatures, the ships' boys, came in for Preble's attentions: "The Master-At-Arms is to keep a list of the boys and their cloaths and to their conduct, cleanliness and behavior."

But in all this, Edward Preble never for a moment lost sight of the reason for his squadron's presence in the Mediterranean. And it was by no means unintentional that the longest—precisely 500 words—and most thoroughly detailed of his rules related to gunnery and the boarding of enemy vessels.

Regulation No. 102 began by requiring that "the strictest silence is to be observed by the men at their guns"; it continued: "Particular orders will be given in sufficient time for the manner of shotting the guns; It is most likely that 2 round shot will be ordered for the two first rounds on the Gundeck, one round shot and one load grape for the two first rounds on the upper-deck. The captains of the guns are ordered not to attempt to put any other charge into their guns, than that which is expressly ordered, as the fatal consequence of loading the gun improperly has been too often experienced with the loss of their lives. The greatest attention is ordered to be paid in pointing and elevating the guns, as it is most necessary and essential to fire a well directed shot and to fire often."

He concluded: "The officers commanding at their different quarters, are directed to see the Decks wetted and sand or ashes strewed upon them whenever the ship is going into action, also that water in the proper casks is supplied for the people in action, and it is my directions that they make known immediately at all times any articles deficient at their quarters. The boarders who may be called upon either to board the enemy or to repel the enemy are to be attentive to the drum and upon the call of the long roll they are immediately to assemble on both gangways according to their Stations, from which place their Officers will lead them on."

Under the spur of this demanding commodore from Maine, who firmly believed that "loyalty down begets loyalty up," Preble's boys became men in a very short while. Scarcely eight weeks after their confrontation with the British in Malta, the Americans were called into fierce action in the aftermath of an unmitigated disaster—the taking by the Tripolitans of the *Philadelphia*.

On October 31, 1803, the *Philadelphia* was standing off Tripoli harbor when a lookout sighted two Tripolitan ships making for the safety of shore. Bainbridge set off to intercept them—and almost immediately ran the *Philadelphia* hard aground on an uncharted reef. It was a disas-

trous situation: the big frigate was wedged up and careened over at a crazy angle, so that her guns were useless against the Tripolitans who soon came swarming to the scene of the wreck. The unfortunate Bainbridge had no choice but to surrender.

Yusef Karamanli, the sinister Pasha, now had more than 300 Americans to hold for ransom. Moreover, at high tide the Tripolitans managed to haul the *Philadelphia* off the reef; they moored her just inside the harbor of Tripoli so that her broadside of 18 guns, now double shotted, enormously added to the Pasha's defenses.

On board the *Constitution*, now the only frigate the Americans had left, Preble reacted angrily. "Would to God," he wrote in a letter to the Secretary of the Navy, "that the Officers and crew of the *Philadelphia*, had one and all determined to prefer death to slavery; it is possible such a determination might save them from either." In any case the *Philadelphia* must somehow be destroyed before the Tripolitans could fit her out for sea. Bainbridge had drawn the same conclusion and communicated it from his prison in a ciphered correspondence conducted

Enraged Tripolitans gesticulate wildly from the shore at the fleeing Intrepid (left), whose crew, commanded by Stephen Decatur, has just torched the captured U.S. Frigate Philadelphia. Some of the Intrepid's crewmen felt there was more danger in the blaze than from the enemy's tardy and inaccurate cannon fire.

Ornately engraved along its 29-inch blade and scabbard, this sword was given to Stephen Decatur by Congress in 1804 "as testimony of gallantry, good conduct and services" exhibited in destroying the frigate Philadelphia while the ship was held by the enemy.

through the good offices of the Danish consul. It seemed well nigh impossible. But it was intolerable to leave the *Philadelphia* in the hands of the Tripolitans. Preble searched among his officers and carefully selected his man: Stephen Decatur.

Preble's written orders to Decatur went directly to the point:

"Sir: You are hereby ordered to take command of the prize ketch *Intrepid*. It is my order that you proceed to Tripoli, enter the harbor in the night, board the *Philadelphia*, burn her and make good your retreat. The destruction of the *Philadelphia* is an object of great importance and I rely with confidence on your intrepidity and enterprise to effect it. Lieutenant Stewart will support you with the boats of the *Siren* and will cover your retreat with that vessel. On boarding the frigate, it is possible you may meet with resistance. It will be well, in order to prevent alarm, to carry all by sword.

"May God prosper you in this enterprise.

"Edward Preble"

The moonless night of February 16, 1804, was chosen for the attempt. With 75 men, all volunteers, Lieutenant Decatur in the *Intrepid* glided through the dark, moving within reach of the chains that supported the *Philadelphia*'s bowsprit against the pull of her canvas. He intended to swing in under the chains and use them to climb aboard. Then an errant puff of wind arose. The little ketch was taken aback to the breeze, placing the *Intrepid* full under the *Philadelphia*'s entire port battery and within the gaze of the Tripolitan night watch. The Yankees had shipped an Arab-speaking Maltese on board for just this eventuality, and he now went into his act; cursing and yelling, he indicated that the ketch was without anchors and requested a line. A hawser was obligingly passed, and a moment later, with the ketch fastened to the frigate, the Americans clambered aboard, crying *"Philadelphia!"*

It was not much of a fight. The sleepy Tripolitans never expected a gang of howling Americans to appear in the midst of a harbor protected by a massive fortress. Many of the Tripolitans simply leaped overboard; others fled below to the orlop deck; the rest were quickly cut down. Shortly after, a rocket soared over the *Philadelphia*, informing the *Siren* that the American frigate was once more in American hands.

After the event considerable controversy arose over what happened next. It was claimed that Decatur and his men could easily have sailed the *Philadelphia* out of the harbor, thereby restoring her to Preble's squadron. But Preble's instructions had been specific—"burn her and make good your retreat." And Stephen Decatur had, with difficulty, learned to obey orders.

Fires were started in every corner of the ship, and the flames began to lick up into the tarred rigging. Decatur was the last man off—in a flying leap into the rigging of the *Intrepid*. The *Philadelphia*'s guns began to let go in the intense heat; her cables burned through, and she began to drift, an aimless funeral pyre, crazily circling about while erratically discharging her cannon. When she was just under the Pasha's castle, the fire finally reached her magazine and she exploded with an immense thunderclap that reverberated over the town and showered its inhabitants with blazing remnants. By that time the *Siren*'s boats had hooked onto

the *Intrepid* and were towing her out. Surgeon's Mate Lewis Heerman quickly dressed the wounds of the one injured American.

Stephen Decatur finally had the fame he had so anxiously sought. When the tale was told at home, the nation rejoiced in the derring-do of this *enfant terrible*. Congress voted him a sword and promoted him over seven other officers to captain; at 25 he was by far the youngest officer to hold that rank. But even before he learned of his promotion, he was involved in another fierce engagement.

On August 3, 1804, after months of successful but wearying blockade, Commodore Preble moved to attack the harbor of Tripoli itself and thus force the Pasha to release his American captives. For this assault he borrowed six gunboats and two bomb vessels from the friendly King of the Two Sicilies. The gunboats were small, nimble craft mounting one or two long guns and were used mainly for coastal and harbor patrol; the bomb ketches were armed with heavy mortars and were designed exclusively for shore bombardment. Preble manned them mostly with Americans, though a number of Sicilians volunteered to join the attack and were welcomed.

To defend the harbor, the Tripolitans had massed 11 gunboats, and as the assault got under way, the odds against the Americans suddenly lengthened ever further. Just as the Americans were making their approach, the wind shifted and only three of the gunboats succeeded in gaining the harbor: Gunboat No. 4, commanded by Stephen Decatur; Gunboat No. 2, commanded by his younger brother, Lieutenant James Decatur, and Gunboat No. 6 under Sailing Master John Trippe. These three gunboats closed to attack their Tripolitan counterparts.

It was close, hot work under the August sun. The American tactics were brutally simple: to pull within point-blank range, then sweep the enemy's deck with deadly canister—musket balls loaded in a canvas bag that burst as the cannon was fired, spraying out the grape-sized pellets as if from an enormous shotgun. Before the enemy could recover from this murderous weapon, the Americans were to close and board. These tactics worked perfectly for Gunboat No. 4, and Stephen Decatur quickly captured the first prize. However, Gunboat No. 2 happened upon misfortune.

James Decatur had managed to work his little vessel into an advantageous position against her opponent. The Tripolitan captain surrendered his boat—but as Decatur leaped aboard to take possession, the captain, with gun in hand, shot him in the head. James Decatur collapsed and fell back into the American gunboat. In the resulting confusion the enemy escaped. Gunboat No. 2 dropped behind and carried the dismay-

In mortal combat with the captain of a Tripolitan gunboat, Stephen Decatur (center foreground) is about to slay his enemy with a pistol as seaman Daniel Frazier (standing, center) prevents a second Moor from cleaving Decatur's skull with a scimitar. Though outnumbered, 11 Americans had boarded the enemy vessel to avenge the death of Decatur's brother James, killed while capturing another gunboat. Decatur and his men killed 17 Tripolitans; the remaining seven surrendered.

ing news to Stephen Decatur. Roaring with rage, he set his gunboat in pursuit of his brother's killer.

Which of the Tripolitan boats he caught is moot. Perhaps he caught the one commanded by his brother's killer, perhaps not. In any case, he reached a Tripolitan vessel, and 11 Americans went over the rails against a score or more of armed and desperate corsairs.

The giant Tripolitan captain came at Decatur with a boarding pike. In parrying the thrust, Decatur snapped his sword off at the hilt. The captain thrust again, this time slashing through Decatur's arm and piercing his chest. Decatur grappled with his opponent, and as the two rolled about on the deck another Tripolitan took a swipe at Decatur with his blade. A wounded American sailor, some say Reuben James, others say Daniel Frazier, body-blocked the Tripolitan officer out of the way, taking the slash himself. Decatur managed to extricate a small pistol from his pocket, pushed it against the Tripolitan captain and pulled the trigger. The gunboat action was over. With the death of their captain, the remaining Tripolitans on board immediately surrendered. And the other gun-

The frigate Constitution, with her supporting squadron, pours a deadly barrage into the Barbary corsairs' lair. Although the Pasha of Tripoli had lowered his ransom demand for 307 American prisoners from three million dollars to half a million dollars, the commander of the American fleet, Edward Preble, hotly declared, "I had rather spend the rest of my life in the Mediterranean than consent to either."

boat crews, seeing that two of their vessels had been captured, fled deep into the harbor.

But the squadron's battle continued. While Decatur was fighting for his life, Commodore Preble sailed the *Constitution* close to the entrance of Tripoli harbor and pounded the shore batteries. Preble narrowly escaped death when a 32-pound cannon ball passed through an open gunport and headed directly for him, but at the last moment it ricocheted off a quarter-deck gun and burst into fragments, wounding an American Marine. With the shore batteries silenced, the *Constitution* sank several Tripolitan merchantmen and fired about 50 rounds into the Pasha's castle and the town of Tripoli.

The American prisoners in Tripoli were greatly heartened by the sight of the Yankee frigate so near the Pasha's harbor, coolly sailing to and fro and lashing out thundering broadsides. The captured Captain Bainbridge had been brought before the Pasha when the *Constitution* first appeared—presumably to witness her defeat.

Bainbridge later reported: "At the commencement of the bombard-

ment, the Pasha surveyed the squadron from his palace windows, and affected to ridicule any attempt which might be made to injure either the batteries or the city. He promised the spectators on the terraces that rare sport would presently be enjoyed by observing the triumph of his boats over the Americans. In a few minutes, however, he became convinced of his error, and precipitately retreated with an humble and aching heart to his bomb-proof chamber.''

Nevertheless, the Pasha refused to release his captives. Preble had to break off the engagement because of poor weather, but later resumed his campaign of harassment, seeking not to capture Tripoli but to force the Pasha to capitulate. On August 7 and 25, and again on September 3, Preble bombarded Tripoli, inflicting heavy damage.

On September 4, the ketch *Intrepid*, which Decatur had used to burn the *Philadelphia*, was fitted up as a floating mine, her hold filled with 100 barrels of gunpowder and the deck above heaped with explosive shells. Volunteers were solicited to sail the *Intrepid* into Tripoli harbor and blow her up in the midst of enemy shipping while the raiders escaped in the *Constitution*'s gig.

Sheets of flame, splintered planking and bursting shell erupt into the night sky over Tripoli as the American fire ship Intrepid explodes while attempting to set ablaze the enemy's anchored fleet. The ill-fated ketch, loaded with 100 barrels of gunpowder and 150 shells, had a crew of 13 volunteers, none of whom survived to reach the American ship at right, awaiting them just outside the harbor.

Under Preble's leadership, Yankee *élan* by now was so high that most of the squadron volunteered. Preble selected Master Commandant Richard Somers, Lieutenant Joseph Israel and Midshipman Henry Wadsworth to lead the perilous expedition. Four seamen from the *Nautilus* and six from the *Constitution* completed the party. Before leaving, Dicky Somers gave his volunteers one last chance to back out of the hazardous mission, but the men answered with three cheers. Somers took a ring from his finger and snapped it into three pieces, keeping one and giving the others to his boyhood friends, Stephen Decatur and Charles Stewart.

As the *Intrepid* set out, carried toward the harbor by a faint breeze, a thin veil of low-lying sea fog rose to obscure what happened next from the view of the Americans in the squadron offshore. The watching Americans saw the flash of an alarm gun and heard its report shortly after the *Intrepid* faded from view. Then the Pasha's shore batteries opened a tremendous bombardment. An instant later the Americans saw a great blossom of flame in the direction of the *Intrepid*, and heard a monstrous explosion. By the light of the flash, they could see masts and other debris blown above the fog and rain down amid a fireworks display of exploding shells.

To this day no one knows precisely what happened to the *Intrepid*. There have been suggestions that the members of the ketch's crew suddenly found themselves trapped between the fort's fire and Tripolitan guard boats, and blew themselves up to avoid capture. A likelier possibility is that the *Intrepid* suffered a direct hit from a red-hot cannon ball in her cargo of munitions.

The Pasha never explained what had happened—if, indeed, he knew. But he did force his prisoner, Captain William Bainbridge, to view the mutilated remains of 12 brave Americans whose bodies had washed ashore. The 13th was never found.

The *Intrepid* incident provided a bitter end to Edward Preble's superb Mediterranean career. Five days after Dicky Somers and his *Intrepid* shipmates died, reinforcements arrived off Tripoli—the frigates *President*, *Congress*, *Constellation* and *Essex*. Aboard the *President* was Commodore Samuel Barron, who because he was senior to Preble superseded him as the squadron commander.

The Secretary of the Navy had expected that Preble would be willing to remain in the Mediterranean as a subordinate commander in Barron's squadron. This Preble had no intention of doing under any circumstances, and he decided to return to the U.S. The commodore's leave-taking was emotional. "This supersedure lacerates my heart," he said. Stephen Decatur presented the peppery old fighter with a scroll, signed by every one of his young tigers, in which they recorded their admiration. Preble's trip home was a triumphal procession in which he called at Malta, Syracuse and Naples. At each port, cannons boomed salutes and the sailors of other nations manned their yards and cheered his ship to its anchorage. In Rome the Pope observed that Preble's small force "has done more for the cause of Christianity than the most powerful nations in ages." And when Preble finally reached Washington on March 4, 1805, the United States Congress voted him a sword

"Valiant leader, defender of American commerce at Tripoli, 1804," reads the laudatory Latin inscription on this gold medal presented to Commodore Edward Preble by President Thomas Jefferson in 1805. Preble's fierce attack on the city is depicted on one side and a portrait of the hero is imprinted on the other.

and a gold medal, and in speech after speech showered on him the gratitude of his people.

The Tripolitan war dragged on for another three months, with no further major actions. Commodore Barron, a considerably less aggressive type than Preble, was content to keep the Tripolitans tightly bottled up in their harbor, and watch them slowly starve for want of wheat and other foodstuffs. Eventually, as unrest mounted among his people, Pasha Karamanli decided to strike the best bargain he could with the Americans. He agreed to a peace in which he would cease harassing American vessels in the Mediterranean, and in return for a payment of $60,000 he would release the *Philadelphia*'s Captain Bainbridge and his more than 300 crewmen. Considering that the ransom came to approximately $200 per man, and that there was scant hope otherwise of securing the release of the captives, it was not too bad a deal for the Americans.

From his retirement in Portland, Maine, Commodore Edward Preble viewed all this with a fighting man's eternally suspicious eye for diplomatic maneuver. He had been retired for less than two years when he died on August 25, 1807, after a painful bout with tuberculosis and ulcers. Had he lived, he would have been prouder than ever of his boys. For they now formed the heart of a United States Navy, bloodied off Tripoli, that would come into its own as a world institution in another war, soon to be waged.

The finest fighting sailor of them all, Horatio Nelson, may well have sensed what was coming. Watching the *Constitution* clear Gibraltar one day, Admiral Nelson was impressed by the way the big frigate came up into the wind, shook out royals and topgallants, and cleared away on a new heading. With prophetic insight, the victor of the Battles of the Nile and Copenhagen observed: "In the handling of those transatlantic ships lies a nucleus of trouble for the navy of Britain."

Horatio Nelson always was far ahead of his time, and in the years immediately following the Tripolitan war there was little to suggest to the British Admiralty that the Americans were to be taken seriously. As always in a democracy, and particularly in the American model, peace meant demobilization. During the remainder of the decade after the corsairs were brought to heel, the Navy suffered from lack of appropriations: a number of ships were forced out of commission or restricted to limited duty, officers resigned or were relegated to shoreside posts, and morale sank to the lowest level since the organization of the Navy.

Yet it was precisely during these years that a new and infinitely serious threat to American freedom of the seas arose. This time it came not from the Moors of the Mediterranean but from the British, and it extended everywhere American ships dared to sail. At the heart of the conflict was the growing British practice of impressment—of halting American ships at sea and seizing men to serve on board British vessels.

In the Royal Navy's view, impressment was vital to Britain's national defense. Ever since 1793 Britain had been engaged in an increasingly desperate struggle with France, and the nation's survival depended upon its Navy. By 1806 the Royal Navy comprised well over 800 ships, most built in England but many captured from its enemies. Manning this vast fleet, a matter of desperate importance, required no fewer than 150,000 men. Press gangs roamed the British countryside, searching for able-bodied men to impress into the Royal Navy. Anyone would do. Not even the rector of St. Paul's Church in Halifax, Nova Scotia, the Reverend Dr. Robert Stanser, was safe. In the early 1800s that unfortunate clergyman found himself dragged aboard one of His Majesty's vessels, much to the embarrassment of the station's commander in chief, who lost no time in releasing him.

For most of the impressed seamen, America offered a hope. Royal Navy deserters as well as British merchant seamen, afraid of being impressed from British ships or British ports, flocked to American coastal craft, where they found much better pay and more humane working conditions. The English were determined to get them back—but it was difficult if not impossible to distinguish them from real Americans. Confronted by this dilemma, the British government struck upon a sweeping policy: once an Englishman, said the British, always an Englishman. This meant that in English eyes all so-called Americans born before 1783—the year the British acceded to American independence—were British subjects and could be impressed, even if they had to be taken at gunpoint from American ships.

Understandably, the United States violently disagreed. Given this impasse, it was small wonder that tempers flared and occasionally British and American cannon roared. Ugly scenes became commonplace. There was, for example, the shocking incident that occurred after a British deserter managed to gain the U.S. Frigate *Essex*, lying in English waters and awaiting the arrival of dispatches. Hardly had he hidden himself when a British boat crew arrived in pursuit, the deserter's lieutenant aboard and obviously able to single out his man. No case could be made in the man's defense, and the Yankees could only stand by unhappily as the deserter was dragged forth.

At the gangway the unfortunate sailor, probably realizing that he was soon to be flogged into imbecility, requested permission to go below and fetch his belongings. But once released, he rushed instead to the carpenter's bench, seized an ax and lopped off his own left hand. As onlookers gaped in horror, the sailor flung his ghastly, bloody sacrifice at the British officer's feet—and swore that he would cut off a foot before serving again in the Royal Navy. After 10 years of war with the French, England had more than enough maimed and crippled men, and the one-handed sailor was left behind.

The situation kept growing worse. Early in 1807, as the *Chesapeake* was being readied for a Mediterranean cruise, the British consul at Norfolk officially protested to Captain Stephen Decatur, now commander of the Navy yard there, that the American frigate was shipping four Royal Navy deserters—William Ware, Daniel Martin, John Strachen and Jenkin Ratford. This was true—so far as it went. What the British neglected to mention was that they had themselves impressed three of the four from an American merchantman in the Bay of Biscay. The fourth man, Jenkin Ratford, swore vehemently that he too was an American. Reas-

sured that the four men had as good a claim as any to American citizen-
ship, Decatur, later backed by Secretary of State James Madison, refused
the British demand that the men be returned.

On June 22 the *Chesapeake* put to sea. Her men were still engaged in
stowing away cables, while the decks were encumbered with cabin fur-
niture, personal effects, chicken coops and provisions for the long voyage. At 3 p.m. the *Chesapeake* was hailed by H.M.S. *Leopard*, 50 guns,
and courteously requested to heave to so that dispatches destined for
Europe could be placed aboard. But instead of dispatches, the British
boarding officer delivered a demand for the release of the four men.

The commander of the *Chesapeake*, Commodore James Barron—
younger brother of the officer who had relieved Preble—refused the
British request. When the British boat crew returned to the *Leopard* with
that message, the British frigate forthwith delivered several broadsides
into the *Chesapeake*. Totally unprepared to return the fire, Commodore
Barron decreed that before the flag was hauled down one gun should be
fired—and so it was, but only after young Lieutenant William H. Allen
had succeeded in juggling a live coal from the galley fire in his bare
hands to ignite the cannon's fuse. Then Barron surrendered.

*Spectators at Plymouth lift rousing
cheers as the flag-bedecked Royal Navy
warship Hibernia slips down the ways
in 1804. The ship was one of the mightiest
vessels built or acquired by the British
in the years before the War of 1812.*

The *Chesapeake*'s sails were riddled with grape and canister shot, she had been hulled 21 times, and her blood-soaked decks carried three dead and 18 wounded.

Of the four "deserters" taken by the British, only two survived. On Monday, August 31, 1807, Jenkin Ratford was hanged from the fore-yardarm of H.M.S. *Halifax*, then buried somewhere above the high water line in an unmarked grave along the foreshore of McNab's Cove, Halifax Harbor. William Ware, Daniel Martin and John Strachen were each sentenced to receive 500 lashes upon their bare backs with a cat-o'-nine-tails, a punishment hardly more merciful than Ratford's. But before the sentence could be carried out, William Ware suddenly died, and upon President Jefferson's strongest appeal, Daniel Martin and John Strachen were returned to the *Chesapeake*.

When the *Chesapeake* returned to Norfolk after this humiliating encounter with H.M.S. *Leopard*, Stephen Decatur was ordered to relieve Commodore Barron of his command. Responding to a storm of public indignation, the Navy convened a court-martial, and Decatur, appointed to the board, made known his views: a wiser man than Barron would not have sailed in a warship unprepared to fight; a more courageous man would not have hauled down his colors.

In his happier days Barron had served as president of a court-martial that had exonerated Captain William Bainbridge on charges of running the *Philadelphia* aground and losing her to the Tripolitans. Perhaps Barron expected the same understanding and clemency from the court that tried him. As a commodore, he based his case upon the responsibility of the ship's commanding officer, Captain Charles Gordon, to have properly cleared his ship for action. Whatever his expectations, Barron was found guilty of taking an unready ship to sea and was dismissed from the Naval service for five years.

In fact, James Barron was a proud and able officer, and he had reason to see himself as a scapegoat. The focus of his resentment soon centered on Commodore Stephen Decatur's broad pennant, floating over Barron's former command, the unlucky *Chesapeake*. In years to come Barron would have his revenge.

Americans never forgot the *Chesapeake*'s humiliation. Once again the Royal Navy had trampled on the pride of the young republic and the public temper flared hot. "Never since the Battle of Lexington," said President Thomas Jefferson, "have I seen this country in such a state of exasperation." If Jefferson had summoned Congress to a special session, he could have had war. He did not, and the passions gradually cooled, but the deep resentment continued to fester for years. The whole nation cheered when the U.S. learned that it too could play the *Chesapeake-Leopard* game. On May 1, 1811, the British frigate *Guerriere*, 38 guns, stopped the American brig *Spitfire* off Sandy Hook, New Jersey, and her boarding party impressed a passenger named John Deguyo, a native citizen of the United States. This, finally, was too much for the American government, which had hitherto been exceedingly forbearing.

The frigate *President*, Captain John Rodgers commanding, was ordered to search out the *Guerriere* and return Deguyo. During the dark

Smirking in triumph after attacking and boarding the U.S. Frigate Chesapeake on June 22, 1807, British officers from the frigate Leopard order four crewmen, three of them American, impressed into the Royal Navy. "Never since the Revolution has public indignation been so aroused," observed one American.

night of May 16, Rodgers caught up with a vessel presumed to be the *Guerriere*. It was never established which ship fired first in the confusion that followed, but both sides soon opened in earnest. After several minutes of this, the British ship was rendered unmanageable and ceased firing. The *President* stood off a little way from her victim until daybreak. And then Rodgers discovered that the battered vessel was not the *Guerriere* but a 22-gun British sloop named the *Little Belt*. She had suffered severely in the engagement, with 11 killed and 21 wounded. It is not known whether Rodgers offered apologies. But he did offer assistance—which the British captain furiously declined before limping off over the horizon.

The action only exacerbated what was already an explosive situation. The British public was outraged, and loud were the demands for revenge. In the U.S., Rodgers was cleared of any wrongdoing, and in fact was regarded as something of a public hero—particularly since the Royal Navy showed no signs of slackening its campaign of impressment. By the fall of 1811 more than 6,000 cases of impressed Americans were registered in Washington; even the British admitted to 3,300.

In the United States Congress national pride and ambition came to a

Clashing in the twilight of a North Atlantic evening, the Yankee frigate President and British sloop of war Little Belt trade thundering broadsides on May 16, 1811. No match for the 44-gun President, the 18-gun Little Belt suffered 32 casualties in the first few minutes, before escaping in the gathering darkness and limping back to Halifax Harbor.

boil with the slogan, Free Trade and Sailors' Rights. Aside from the impressments, there were angry issues of commerce on the high seas. Britain, in its continuing struggle with France, was halting the ships of neutral nations and confiscating all cargoes that might find their way to the French; in consequence, the swiftly expanding American trade with Europe was suffering greatly.

The House of Representatives that convened on November 5, 1811, was extraordinary in its brilliant array of fierce and fiery newcomers, soon to be known as the "young war hawks." Their number included John Caldwell Calhoun, as cadaverous as Cassius and as eloquent as Cicero; his fellow South Carolinian, Langdon Cheves, known as one of the South's shrewdest lawyers; Tennessee's Felix Grundy, who had resigned as chief justice of his state's supreme court so that he might vote in Congress for war against England; Peter B. Porter, a fat, hard-minded New York trader whose business had been hurt by the troubles with Britain; and, by far the most important of all, Henry Clay of Kentucky, dazzling in his flowered waistcoat, spellbinding in his golden oratory, who was elected Speaker of the House on his very first day in that body. All were burning at the indignities suffered by American ships at British hands. And all, moreover, dreamed of a greater America.

Against them, and leading the antiwar forces, was one of the most peculiar men ever to enter Congress: John Randolph of Roanoke, Virginia. He claimed descent from Pocahontas, always wore silver spurs and carried a riding crop, which he used to brandish at his opponents in debate. Entering the House chamber with his favorite hound at his side, he spent his days quaffing mugs of porter provided by an assistant doorkeeper. Randolph also had a poisonous tongue, and he reserved his special venom for Calhoun and Clay, whom he loathed. Years later, when Calhoun was presiding over the Senate as Vice President and Randolph had moved from the House to the upper chamber, Randolph addressed the chair: "Mr. Speaker! I mean Mr. President of the Senate and would-be President of the United States, which God in His infinite mercy avert...." And he abusively described Clay, with whom he would one day fight a bloodless duel, as "this being, so brilliant and yet so corrupt, which, like a rotten mackerel by moonlight, shines and stinks and stinks and shines."

Now, in his losing antiwar effort, Randolph of Roanoke began to filibuster, droning on and on throughout day and night sessions and yielding the floor only to colleagues of like mind.

By the night of June 18, 1812, the war hawks had had enough. As an elderly New Englander rambled through a long and tedious antiwar speech to a handful of snoozing Representatives, the hawks, who had gathered in the lobby, burst into the chamber, seized spittoons from the floor and banged them about amid wild cries. The startled speaker sat down, thus giving up the floor. Speaker Henry Clay instantly put the question: Shall the United States of America declare war on Great Britain? By 79 to 49 the House voted in the affirmative. After some debate the Senate later concurred.

And so, amid the clanging of Congressional cuspidors, the United States entered the War of 1812.

The strict regimen of life in a seagoing community

In the 1800s, any town with a population of 400 or 500 would have sprawled over many acres. Yet that same number of men lived for months at a time—crowded in with cannon, ammunition, provisions and penned animals—on board a U.S. Navy frigate scarcely bigger than a good-sized country barn. In such conditions, a crowd of men, as one captain remarked, were "ripe for any mischief or villainy." And only through the most careful regimentation of life in this wooden-walled community were captains able to keep crews in order and ready for war.

It was not uncommon for an American frigate captain to issue 100 different regulations at the start of a voyage. A seaman was assigned to one of two watches, which alternated duty every four hours around the clock. During the day, while one watch attended to working the ship, members of the other watch were expected to scour the decks, scrub clothes and hammocks, repair tackle and sails, clean the cannon and practice all the techniques of combat at sea.

Though life in the U.S. Navy was more humane than in the Royal Navy, rules were nonetheless strictly enforced. Officers were quick to punish laggards with a sharp rap of a rattan cane or by withholding the daily grog ration. For the more serious charge of "neglect of duty"—most often sleeping on watch—a man could be confined in irons or flogged with cat-o'-nine-tails until his back was bloody.

Breaks in the round of drudgery came at eight in the morning, noon and 4 p.m., when men had an hour to eat their rations and have a smoke. If no special activity was scheduled, men were also allowed a few hours in the evening to play fiddles, swap yarns, play checkers or whittle tough chunks of salt meat into a bizarre brand of scrimshaw.

Men off watch were expected to be in their hammocks and asleep by 8 or 9 p.m. But sailors habitually griped that sleep on board ship, as one man sourly put it, was "but a mockery and a name." Because of the watch schedules, a seaman could never count on more than four hours of uninterrupted sleep a night. And frigate crews never knew at what hour they might be jolted awake by "the cannonading drum beating to quarters." For some captains were such sticklers for drill that they roused their men to sail down an imaginary enemy in the dead of night.

A boatswain pipes reveille at dawn.

As men tumble from their hammocks at reveille, a boatswain's mate runs through the berth deck, applying a knotted rope—known as a "starter"—to laggards who have failed to heed the pipe. The men had exactly 12 minutes to take down their hammocks, bundle them up and stow them in the railed "nettings" on the spar deck before they reported for duty. Then, according to the orders of one captain, "decks, gun carriages, port sills, and chains are to be washed"—all of this to be done in time "to admit of piping to breakfast precisely at 8 o'clock."

As some seamen raise the jib and weigh anchor preparatory to getting under way, officers, attendant crewmen and a Marine honor guard snap to attention at the gangway to receive the squadron commodore on board. Led by the captain (center), the officers and midshipmen salute by doffing their hats, while the seamen and the piping boatswain show their respect by tugging at their forelocks. Meanwhile, the first lieutenant barks orders to other crewmen through his speaking trumpet.

At morning sick call, the surgeon
examines a patient in a cot as his mate
tends to men lined up to report their
complaints. While the crowded conditions
produced illness aplenty, every crew had
malingerers who sought excuses to snuggle
into cots in a sick bay warmed by
suspended buckets of hot coals—causing
captains to refuse grog to any man
whose name appeared on the sick list.

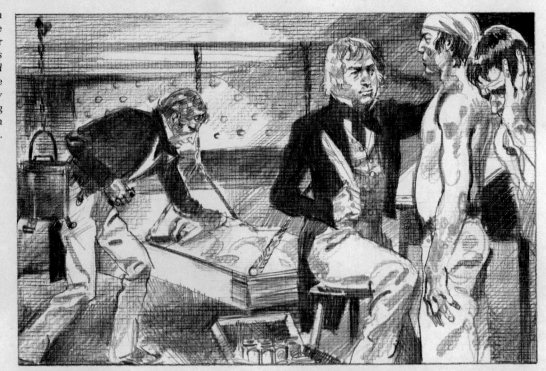

While one cook bastes a roast for the
officers' dinner, another samples the
crew's fare in giant "coppers" sunk
into the galley stove on the gun deck. The
seamen ate a stew made from salt beef
or pork. Each eight-man "mess" was
entitled to a 10-pound chunk of meat
a day, and sent representatives, seen here
selecting cuts from a cask, to choose
and tag the best pieces they could find.

A shot from the frigate, half a mile away, splashes into the sea near the empty barrels used as a target for gunnery drill. Practice with live ammunition was rare aboard British vessels, but the U.S. Navy encouraged the use of powder and shot in the belief that only by actual firing would crews learn speed and accuracy.

Sailmakers tend to their canvas, the cooper mends casks, the cordwainer sews a leather powder bucket and the barber wields his razor on the gun deck, where shipboard craftsmen went about their daily tasks. The barber was the busiest of all; many captains did not allow individual razors on board for fear they would be used as weapons, and to shave hundreds of sailors twice a week, the barber worked all day every day.

As a seaman extends his cup for the daily half pint of the whiskey-water mix called grog, another sailor barters a twist of tobacco for an extra tot of the brew. Most captains disapproved of grog trading, and limited their men to one ration, to be gulped down at the tub.

As their mates eat supper sitting around mess cloths, four seamen cheer their favorites in a weevil race, to be won by the first insect crossing the circle charcoaled on the canvas. Ship's biscuits were so weevil riddled that no sailor would bite into one without rapping it on the deck.

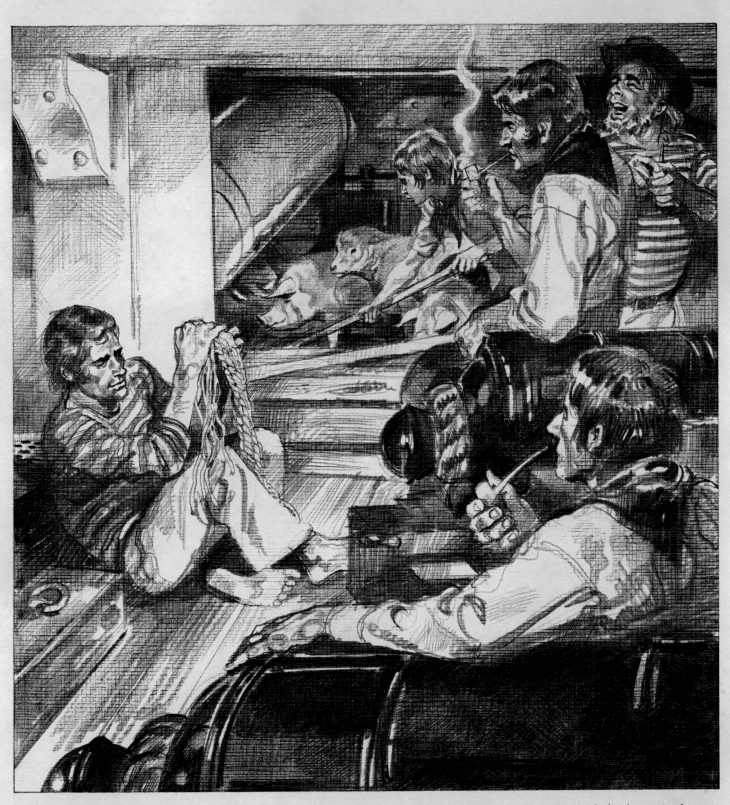

Lounging near the manger on the gun deck, where animals
were kept to provide fresh meat, three seamen pass the time after
dinner with a smoke and gossip while a fourth laces cords to
make a piece of decorative macramé. Smoking was one of the few
pleasures allowed men aboard a frigate, but because of the fire
hazard, it was restricted to the area forward of the galley.

Chapter 3

Stunning surprises for His Britannic Majesty

hen war finally came, it opened timidly for the Americans. Both President James Madison and Secretary of the Navy Paul Hamilton were of the opinion that the small number of American warships should be held in port to serve as coastal defense vessels rather than be risked at sea against the mighty British Navy.

This decision was not as pusillanimous as it might have first appeared. In the years since the menace of the Barbary corsairs had faded, the U.S. Navy had been allowed to deteriorate from the strong young fleet that had numbered 54 vessels in 1801. By 1812, the entire Yankee Navy consisted of but 17 seagoing vessels: the 44-gun frigates *President, United States* and *Constitution*; the 36-gun frigates *Chesapeake, Constellation* and *Congress*; the light frigate *Essex*, 32 guns; and the corvettes *Adams*, 28 guns, and *John Adams*, 24 guns. Of seagoing sloops, brigs and schooners, the Americans had but eight: the *Hornet* and *Wasp*, 18 guns; the *Argus* and *Siren*, 16 guns; the *Nautilus*, 14 guns; the *Enterprise* and *Vixen*, 12; and the *Viper*, 10. The rest of the Navy consisted of either Great Lakes craft or coastal gunboats.

Against this minuscule force the British counted some 900 warships ranging from awesome 100-gun ships of the line down to sloops and brigs. The Royal Navy boasted a total of 860,990 naval tons against only 15,300 for the Americans, 27,800 cannon against 442, and 151,572 men against 5,025. Most of the British ships had to be kept in European waters to counter French thrusts in the continuing Napoleonic Wars. But even at the outset of the hostilities with America the Royal Navy had almost 100 warships deployed in the western Atlantic from Halifax to the Indies, and these vessels mounted nearly seven times the entire armament of the Yankee Navy. No wonder that on June 10, 1812, *The Statesman* of London trumpeted: "America certainly can not pretend to wage war with us; she has no navy to do it with!" Given these long odds against the U.S., President Madison and Secretary Hamilton appeared to be using simple common sense.

But the line officers of the Navy were in open and violent disagreement, and two of their members, William Bainbridge and Charles Stewart, rushed to Washington to present the Navy's case. Against the Cabinet's plaint that the Royal Navy had been supreme to date in naval warfare, the two American officers marshaled their arguments. For one thing, the fact that the British Navy was heavily engaged against the French and Spaniards would limit its response to the new American war. The British would undoubtedly attempt a blockade before long, but

With a murderous broadside of 24-pound shot, Stephen Decatur's United States crushes the Macedonian, one of the Royal Navy's most powerful frigates, off the Canary Islands on October 25, 1812. As the Macedonian's masts toppled, Decatur urged his men to lower their aim for more lethal effect: "Her rigging and spars are going fast enough; she must have a little more hulling."

unless they assembled the entire British Navy off the American coast-line, it would be impossible to prevent single ships, cloaked by darkness or bad weather, from escaping to the open sea. The British, moreover, with their long history of triumph, would be likely to underrate any American opponent. And if an American frigate could catch one of these cocksure Britishers in a fair, ship-to-ship fight, the Americans might well deal haughty old John Bull a bloody nose he would long remember.

The Yankee frigates were bigger, stronger and faster than their opposite numbers in the Royal Navy, Bainbridge and Stewart pointed out. American Naval cannon had gun sights to improve firing accuracy, while British guns had none, perhaps because Horatio Nelson himself had discouraged sights on British cannon on the ground that Royal Navy ships should always be so close to the enemy that they could not miss. The innovative American use of thin, sheet-lead powder cartridges had eliminated the need to meticulously sponge out the cannon between rounds; there was no danger that scraps of smoldering flannel left behind by cloth powder bags would ignite the next charge prematurely. The British, who used flannel bags and therefore had to sponge between shots, could get off only two rounds to the Americans' three. And American Marines had a superior method of directing small-arms fire down upon opposing quarter-decks: only the best backwoods marksman did the sniping, while six other Marines loaded rifles for him.

These and other innovations, coupled with higher morale and greater will to fight, would ensure Yankee success eight out of 10 times, Bainbridge and Stewart argued. How they arrived at this stunning figure is unknown. Most likely they plucked it out of thin air. And they went boldly on. The two officers reminded Madison and his Cabinet that the vaunted British record was achieved against the French Navy, which had been demoralized by inactivity and by the politics of revolution against the monarchy. It was a navy in which the authority of the officers, many of whom were of noble birth, had been thoroughly undermined. And the French Navy had proved ineffective in battle when gunners who had spent the greater part of their service at anchor tried for the first time to hit one moving vessel from another.

President Madison and Secretary Hamilton listened to the bold arguments of Bainbridge and Stewart with interest. Finally a compromise was reached. Madison overruled his Cabinet and agreed to permit each of the Navy's ships to make one cruise apiece before being converted into harbor defense craft. And this was all the Yankee Navy needed.

By a curious coincidence, the War began almost identically for each side as the two fleets groped for each other. On the 21st of June Commodore John Rodgers, who had taken the British *Little Belt* in 1811, shaped a course southeast out of Sandy Hook, New Jersey. Rodgers' small squadron consisted of the frigates *United States*, with Stephen Decatur commanding, the *Congress*, with John Smith as captain, and the *President*, in which Rodgers still flew his flag. In addition, he had the sloop of war *Hornet* and the brig *Argus*. Rodgers' purpose was to intercept a fleet of about 100 British merchantmen that had been reported to be sailing from Jamaica to England. Because the orders he received suggested timorous-

OFFICE OF
THE FREEMAN'S JOURNAL,
AND
PHILADELPHIA
Mercantile Advertiser.
SATURDAY, June 20, 1812.
ONE O'CLOCK.
Official Declaration of War.
[*From the National Intelligencer Extra,*
June 19]

AN ACT
Declaring War between the United Kingdom of Great Britain and Ireland and the dependencies thereof and the United States of America and their Territories.

BE it enacted by the Senate and House of Representatives of the United States of America in Congress assembled, That WAR be and the same is hereby declared to exist between the United Kingdom of Great Britain and Ireland and the dependencies thereof, and the United States of America and their territories; and that the President of the United States be and he is hereby authorised to use the whole land and naval force of the United States to carry the same into effect; and to issue to private armed vessels of the United States commissions or letters of marque and general reprisal, in such form as he shall think proper, and under the seal of the United States, against as vessels, goods, and effects of the government of the same United Kingdom of Great Britain and Ireland, and of the subjects thereof.
June 28, 1812.
APPROVED.   JAMES MADISON.
[*Subscribers are requested to call at the Office for this Supplement.*]

Conveying the text of the United States declaration of war, this broadsheet was distributed by a Philadelphia newspaper on June 20, 1812. At the outset, President Madison issued an invitation for privateers to prey on British shipping.

ly that he remain in the vicinity of New York, Rodgers' sortie was the American equivalent of Nelson clapping the telescope to his blind eye during the Battle of Copenhagen so as not to see a general recall order.

The squadron crowded on all sail and headed east. At dawn on June 23, when the little fleet was 35 miles due east of New York, Rodgers saw a sail on the northeast horizon. But the stranger was no merchantman. She proved to be the British 36-gun frigate *Belvidera*, Captain Richard Byron commanding. Rodgers and his squadron immediately set out in chase as the *Belvidera* fled to the northeast.

By late afternoon the *President* had outdistanced the other American ships and was in range of the *Belvidera*. Commodore Rodgers went to the fo'c's'le and, with a fine sense of history, fired the opening shot himself from one of the *President*'s bow chasers. He thus became the first American to fire a cannon at the enemy in the War of 1812.

On the main deck directly beneath Rodgers, the foremost gun on the starboard side was trained fully around so that it, too, could be brought to bear. Three shots were fired in quick succession by these two guns; all struck the *Belvidera*, killing and wounding nine men. But then came disaster. When the gun on the main deck was fired again, it burst and ignited the nearby "passing box," which contained powder for the next shot. In the resulting explosion 16 Americans were killed or wounded. The commodore, standing on the fo'c's'le deck directly above the exploding gun, was catapulted into the air and came crashing down with a broken leg. Though in terrible pain, he waved aside medical attention, ordered his officers to hold him on his feet and courageously continued to direct the fight. But it was a frustrating business.

With the *President*'s fo'c's'le in a shambles and with the British frigate beginning to hit home with her stern chasers, Rodgers yawed the *President* to port and delivered an entire broadside. However, the American shot did little except to punch a few holes in the *Belvidera*'s sails, and this became the pattern of the battle—the *Belvidera* shooting frantically out of her stern ports, hoping to dismast her opponent, and the American frigate trying to stay within range while yawing from side to side to deliver broadsides. By early evening the British had cut away the *Belvidera*'s anchors, and thrown many of her boats and most of her food and water over the side. Thus lightened, she pulled away from the *President* and three days later gained Halifax Harbor.

Mortified by his failure to capture the *Belvidera*, Rodgers rejoined his squadron and pressed ahead in his search for the Jamaica convoy. On July 1, fogbound and far eastward of the Grand Banks, he saw large amounts of orange rind, coconut shells and lemon peels floating in the water ahead. Believing his quarry was within reach, he urged his ships onward. But the sea ahead was empty of vessels and he never found the source of the garbage. Rodgers was within 200 miles of the British Isles on July 13, when he reluctantly decided to turn back, reaching Boston on August 29 after 69 days at sea. Though he had not caught the *Belvidera* and had missed the Jamaica convoy, he had had the consolation of taking eight small prizes, all British merchantmen, on the way home.

More important, this initial sortie by the Yankee Navy in squadron strength had taken the British by surprise. The Royal Navy had planned

only to station single ships off American ports. But now that was obviously impossible, and these lone patrols were withdrawn until reinforcements could be mustered. Thus, in the first months of the War, the American ports were wide open and dozens of American merchantmen came and went almost as they pleased. What is more, although the British could congratulate themselves on the escape of the *Belvidera*, they had little to cheer about a few weeks after that event when the roles were exactly reversed.

During the prewar years, Captain Isaac Hull's chief concern had been the speed of his ship, the U.S. Frigate *Constitution*. Hull was an officer of wide experience, including that of commanding the *Argus* off Tripoli under Preble, and from the moment he took command of the *Constitution* in mid-June, 1810, he found the big frigate to be the dullest of sailers. And no wonder. In a calm sea off Hampton Roads, divers examined the ship's copper-sheathed bottom and found it to be covered with what Hull estimated to be 10 wagonloads of oysters, mussels, barnacles and weeds, all hanging on "like bunches of grapes," as he disgustedly put it.

Hull sailed up to the head of Chesapeake Bay to let fresh water kill some of the ship's marine growth, and managed to scrape off the rest by dragging an iron contraption of his own devising back and forth along

Silhouetted against a luminous sky, the President rides at anchor off the southern coast of France in this watercolor painted in 1802. The first frigate to engage the enemy in the War of 1812, the President was commanded by Commodore John Rodgers, who lamented bitterly the escape of the British frigate Belvidera after a running battle. He watched the departing frigate, he said, "with more mortification than words can express."

the ship's bottom. Next, he replaced a number of heavy 42-pound carronades on the *Constitution*'s spar deck with lighter, but longer-range, 32-pound cannon, and this too helped the big frigate's sailing qualities. Still Hull continued to fret over her speed, and finally, in April 1812, he arranged at the Washington Navy Yard to have her bottom completely recoppered and her ballast increased. The effect of all these changes was to make the *Constitution* as fleet as any frigate afloat, and to cost the British an easy capture when the War began.

In the early afternoon of Thursday, July 16, while Rodgers and his squadron were still at sea, the *Constitution* was cruising north along the New Jersey coast when her lookouts sighted four sets of sails toward the land and a fifth out to sea. Since five ships was the exact size of Rodgers' small command, Isaac Hull rejoiced in the thought that he had come upon the American squadron, and would now join forces. But he was cautious as he stood out to sea toward the solitary stranger, coming within six to eight miles of her by 10:30 p.m. Hull had lights raised aloft in the prearranged recognition signal and when no reply came he suspected that he had come across enemy ships.

He turned south to avoid the vessels, and they turned with him. The dawn revealed, to Hull's horror, that he was surrounded by a British squadron. Captain Philip Bowes Vere Broke had fortuitously trapped the *Constitution* within his squadron, consisting of the 64-gun ship of the line *Africa*, the 38-gun frigates *Shannon* and *Guerriere*, the 32-gun *Aeolus*, and the *Belvidera*, which after escaping to Halifax had joined Broke.

The Britishers were already flushed with success, having chased and captured the American 14-gun brig *Nautilus* the day before. And now they had one of the big American 44s within their grasp. But suddenly the wind, which had been faint through the night, fell off entirely.

As the six vessels drifted in the calm, Hull desperately launched the *Constitution*'s boats and started towing the big frigate out of her trap. He next had two 24-pounders run out the stern cabin windows on the gun deck and another 24-pounder and an 18-pounder run out the stern holes cut on the quarter-deck.

The toil on the oars was backbreaking under the hot sun in the airless morning, the little boats barely able to stir the vast bulk behind them. The British immediately saw what was happening, and soon set their own small boats to towing, to work their squadron up into range of the *Constitution*. For almost three hours the agonizing tortoise race continued. And then, just as the *Shannon* closed into gun range, a faint breeze arose. Hull was the beneficiary. Having had the wit to wet his sails to make them less porous, he gathered way, and while his boat crews rowed frantically to keep up, began to move away from the *Shannon*.

Within 30 minutes Hull had gained half a mile on his pursuers. But then the breeze died. Soon the *Shannon* was back into gun range and experimenting with a few salvos from her bow chasers. It looked hopeless for the Americans. At that point Lieutenant Charles Morris, another Tripoli veteran, proposed an extreme measure; Isaac Hull agreed to try it.

The sounding line showed 22 fathoms, or 132 feet, of water beneath them. Those of the *Constitution*'s crew not employed in the towing operation were set to work getting up all the rope in the ship and splicing it into a line half a mile in length. One end of this enormously long hempen hawser was fastened to a kedge anchor, a particularly sharp-fluked device. The kedge anchor was carried far ahead by the *Constitution*'s cutter while the other end of the line was held by the ship's crew standing in the bow of the ship. At its farthest extremity, the anchor was dropped and all hands hauled on the line as they walked aft. Upon reaching the stern, each man released his grip, ran to the bow and began again. There were no jolly chanteys now, just the grunting of shirtless, sweating men as they pulled for their lives. Meanwhile, what was left of the ship's rope was spliced into a second line so that as the *Constitution* was being pulled forward to one anchor, another anchor was being hauled out. The distance between the *Constitution* and the *Shannon* quickly opened. But once the British understood why the American frigate was gliding out of their reach, they set about the same task.

On and on it went. Occasionally small puffs of wind ruffled the surface and gave Hull a chance to pick up his boats and rest his weary men. These pickups on the run called for superb seamanship; any error in judgment would result in the certain capture of a boatload of Americans. And after each respite in the fluky airs, the British were right behind him. To lighten ship, Hull had the *Constitution*'s drinking water pumped out—2,335 gallons of it. In the July heat he kept the sails wet continuously by having men haul buckets of sea water up to the great height of the *Constitution*'s masts to douse the canvas. Late in the afternoon the small breeze returned and this time stayed for four hours, enough to rest the men weary from kedging.

But by sunset, the breeze had died, and the work was resumed until midnight. The *Shannon*'s crew was apparently even wearier than the *Constitution*'s, for the British failed to regain gun range during this interval. A faint breeze stirred again at midnight, the boats were taken in, and the heavy ships lumbered through the darkness, their sails carefully trimmed as each captain tried to make the most out of the weather. Very, very slowly the *Constitution* began to win this game, to draw ahead of her pursuers. Before nightfall Hull had observed a summer squall bearing down upon the ships. Since the British had followed his every tactic faithfully, he now endeavored to deceive them with a feigned move.

Just before the squall struck, Hull had the *Constitution*'s heavy canvas reefed and his light canvas taken in—exactly as though he were expecting a heavy blow. The British quickly followed suit, for to lose a yard or topmast would mean loss of the race. However, the squall was light, as Hull had perceived, and as soon as it was upon the *Constitution*, he had as many sails set as the big frigate could carry. With the squall now hiding the *Constitution* from her pursuers, the frigate thundered along at 11 knots, opening more distance between her and Broke's squadron.

When the squall cleared, it was all over. The British could still see the *Constitution*, but she was close to the horizon and thumping along mightily. The pursuers held on doggedly all through the night, but by next morning, the *Constitution*'s sails were barely in sight. Since there was no way for Broke to close the gap, he had to give up the chase. Isaac Hull had made good his escape.

The entire affair reflected great credit upon Isaac Hull. He had some-

Members of the crew of the becalmed Constitution, trying to work the frigate away from pursuing British warships, row out ahead of their vessel to drop kedge anchors. The Constitution was then moved forward as men hauled in on the anchor lines. By such means Captain Isaac Hull managed to conduct the Constitution to safety during a three-day battle of wits against the British.

how managed to extricate his ship from a British squadron that seemingly had him in its clutches for three days and three nights. One slip, one miscalculation on his part would have delivered the *Constitution* and almost 500 Americans into British hands. Yet there was no glory in escaping from the Royal Navy, only a sort of tit for tat satisfaction after the *Belvidera*'s escape from Commodore Rodgers' squadron. But Isaac Hull—a rotund, steadfast, undemonstrative former cabin boy from Derby, Connecticut—was to have another chance for glory; fate was about to bestow on him the first real battle opportunity of the War.

A few days after Hull had sailed the *Constitution* away from Broke's squadron, the British commander was faced with a vexing problem. Somewhere out in the Atlantic, he knew, Commodore Rodgers was on the prowl with his five-ship squadron, perhaps shooting up the Jamaica convoy. The British squadron would have to set out in pursuit. However, Broke's frigates could not remain at sea much longer without reprovisioning. Therefore Broke decided to detach one vessel at a time to take on fresh water and stores at Halifax. As the first vessel to go, Broke chose the *Guerriere*, a 38-gun French frigate captured off the Faroes in July 1806. So, while the *Constitution* shaped a course for Boston on July 19, she was followed a week later by the *Guerriere*, making for Halifax but initially following the same route.

The *Constitution* did not remain long in Boston. For one thing, her master had a problem paying for provisions the ship needed. Since the Navy's agent in Boston had no funds, Isaac Hull had to borrow, without authority, from one William Gray, a wealthy shipowner. To linger in port, using up the new supplies, would be an imposition on Gray's patriotic largess. Secondly, there were no orders from Washington awaiting Hull in Boston. The captain rightly suspected that when those orders did arrive he would be told to lay up his ship and attempt no more sorties. Isaac Hull did not wait for orders; he took the *Constitution* to sea on August 2. The stage was now set for an event whose impact was to explode across the young American nation.

Just before 2 p.m. on Wednesday, August 19, 1812, the *Constitution* was bowling along south-southeast through choppy, oyster-colored seas. The wind gusted from the northwest. The skies were cloudy. The Yankee was some 200 miles east of Halifax. When at four bells a lookout called down that there were sails on the horizon, the crew became tense with excitement; the men's blood was up. It was a Royal Navy frigate.

On board His Britannic Majesty's *Guerriere*, en route to Halifax, there were 38 murderously efficient cannon, iron discipline and supreme confidence. Her tall, able captain, James Richard Dacres, was mindful of the *President*'s prewar action against the *Little Belt* and he was determined sooner or later to avenge that small, ill-fated British ship. The *Guerriere*'s topsails were painted with his message: THIS IS NOT THE LITTLE BELT. Twenty-eight years old, the son of an admiral, James Dacres had commanded Royal Navy ships for the past six years. He knew his business and now he was anxious to get on with it.

As the next hour passed, the gap between the two light heavyweights narrowed. At 3:30 Dacres backed the *Guerriere*'s topsails and spun her around so that she now waited, rolling easily in the choppy seas. Captain William B. Orne, master of a recently captured American merchantman named the *Betsey*, was called to join Dacres on the *Guerriere*'s quarterdeck. Captain Dacres turned to him and observed tartly that the *Constitution* bore down "rather too boldly to be an American." Still, he noted, "the better he behaves, the more honor we shall gain by taking him."

In a few more minutes the men of both ships began to take in light sail and clear for action. As the drums rolled, sand and ashes were scattered about spar and gun decks to ensure firm footing on bloody planking. The surgeons hurried below with their crude and dreadful instruments. Ports were opened, and gun carriages creaked and rumbled as the 18- and 24-pounders, cannon capable of hurling balls of those weights a distance of more than a mile, were rolled out.

A little before 5 p.m. Hull turned the *Constitution* away for a moment to pick up speed and to make a last check that all was in readiness. When the *Constitution* turned back toward the *Guerriere*, absolute silence prevailed, in accordance with the decade-old, standing ship's order of irascible old Commodore Preble. There was only the creaking of the top-hamper, the hiss and slap of the waves against the frigate's cutwater, the cold, rough feel of the black-iron brutes to comfort the gunners. A long moment later the *Guerriere*'s battle flags broke out at every mast, and flicks of orange flame with billowing clouds of acrid smoke erupted from her starboard side.

As the approaching ship, the *Constitution* was at a disadvantage in the initial stage of the battle. Forced to keep her bow toward the *Guerriere*, she could bring only her forward guns to bear, while the British frigate could—and did—fire, fall off, come up again, and fire another broadside. Under these circumstances, Hull preferred not to fire at all until the time was exactly right.

At about 6 p.m. he was within 50 yards of his enemy. The *Guerriere* was firing relentlessly. The British officers could now be clearly seen moving about the *Guerriere*'s deck and encouraging their gunners. On board the *Constitution*, ropes twanged as they parted and sails collapsed as great holes appeared in them. The vessel reeled as shot struck her hull, and the spar deck seemed enveloped in a great thrumming sound as round shot and grape flew overhead. Two men were killed and several were wounded. First Lieutenant Charles Morris asked Captain Hull for permission to open fire. Hull responded coolly: "Not yet, sir." The anxious gunners faced aft, looking at their captain, as three times Lieutenant Morris made the same request. And three times Isaac Hull uttered the same response. At last, at half pistol shot—a distance of scarcely 25 yards—the *Constitution* turned broadside to the enemy, and Hull cried: "Now, boys, pour it into them!" The portly captain gave this command so forcibly, it was said, that his trousers split, exposing his backside as the *Constitution* let go with everything she could bring to bear.

The effect of this broadside, delivered at such close range that not a gun could miss, was catastrophic to the *Guerriere*. Her entire side was virtually crushed in. Splinters flew in every direction, some as high as the mizzen top. The ship visibly staggered under the blow.

Firing now as fast as her guns could be reloaded, the *Constitution*

The "Constitution": a wooden ship with "iron walls"

In the spring of 1813 a stunning order went out from the Admiralty to all Royal Navy frigates patrolling the Atlantic. Under no circumstances were they to engage an American heavy frigate unless they had the Yankee outnumbered at least 2 to 1.

Embarrassing though it was, the order made very good sense. The U.S. Frigate *Constitution* had just defeated two British frigates, the *Guerriere* and the *Java*, in deadly single-ship actions, and her sister ship, the *United States*, had bested yet a third. Clearly, prudence must be placed before pride until the Admiralty learned to deal with these superships.

Constructed between 1794 and 1797 at Hartt's shipyard in Boston, the *Constitution* was designed from the start to overmatch any Royal Navy frigate. Her length from taffrail to billethead was 204 feet, 50 feet longer than the standard British frigate; her beam, at 43.5 feet, was three feet wider; and her 2,200-ton displacement was greater by nearly a quarter. Her masts, pieced together from the heartwood of New England white pines, towered a maximum of 189 feet above the water and could carry 42,000 square feet of sail.

But these specifications were only part of the explanation for the *Constitution*'s superiority. Her frames were as heavy as those used to construct a ship half again her size. They were secured to her keel at intervals averaging only one and a half inches—making her sides virtually solid walls of oak 15 to 20 inches thick. Her nickname is attributed to a sailor who, watching cannon balls bounce off her hull, remarked, "Her sides are made of iron!"

Yet for all her massiveness, "Old Ironsides" was so fine lined that she could sail at 14 knots and work as close as six points off the wind, qualities that enabled her to elude most pursuers and fight only whom she chose. Overall, as one of the ship's foretopmen fondly declared, "She was an object which the criticising eye of a sailor would wish to gaze ardently upon at any time, a superb looking frigate."

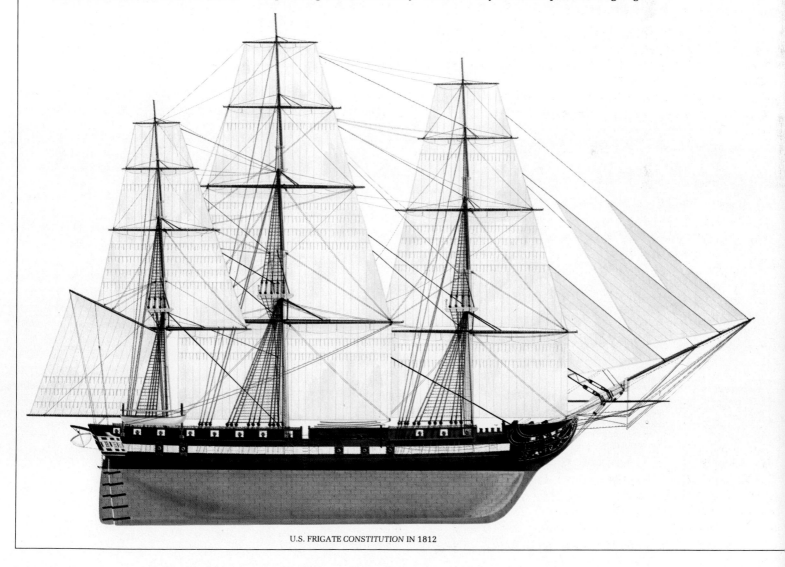

U.S. FRIGATE CONSTITUTION IN 1812

To berth and provide working space for her crew of 400 officers and men, 100 to 150 more than on the premier British frigates, the Constitution's hull was divided into a hold and four deck levels—the two uppermost of which bore her wartime armament of 24 carronades, thirty 24-pounders and an 18-pound bow chaser.

Her topside, known as the spar deck, was remarkably clear of clutter to facilitate the handling of her 37 sails, whose lines and halyards ran to fife rails and pinrails at deck level.

Just forward of the mizzenmast was the ship's wheel, where the helmsman—standing to windward on the high side of the deck—steered the ship, eyeing a compass in one of the binnacles on either side of the wheel.

The Constitution had two capstans —enormous spools of oak that turned independently on the same axis—one on the spar deck for working the rigging, and the other on the gun deck below for weighing anchor. They were turned by sailors straining on spokes that fitted into the capstan crowns.

Built as a flagship, the Constitution could accommodate both her captain and a squadron commander in identical sleeping cabins at either side of her stern. These officers shared a day cabin and aftercabin, but each had a private head located in the quarter galleries—glassed-in balconies protruding from both sides of the stern.

Most of the crew slung their hammocks on the berthing deck, while aft on the same deck officers inhabited tiny locker-like cabins. Below lay the orlop deck. Except for berthing the surgeon's mates in the cockpit, it was given over to storage space for rope, sails, food and the thousands of feet of hempen anchor cable—22 inches in circumference—passed down dripping wet from above. Gunpowder was kept in two magazines located well below the water line, where enemy fire would be least likely to penetrate.

1. DAVIT
2. CAPTAIN'S GIG
3. TAFFRAIL
4. AFTERCABIN
5. QUARTER GALLERY
6. RUDDER
7. PINTLE
8. GUDGEON
9. BREAD ROOM
10. CAPTAIN'S DAY CABIN
11. QUARTER-DECK
12. QUARTER BOAT
13. MAST FOR SPANKER SAIL
14. MIZZENMAST
15. STEERING WHEEL
16. BINNACLE
17. WARDROOM

18. ORLOP DECK
19. AFTER POWDER MAGAZINE
20. LIEUTENANT'S CABIN
21. DECK BEAM
22. AFTERCOMPANIONWAY
23. 32-POUND CARRONADE
24. HAMMOCK NETTING
25. SPAR-DECK CAPSTAN
26. GUN-DECK CAPSTAN
27. DEADEYE TO SECURE SHROUDS
28. SIDE PLANKING
29. COPPER SHEATHING
30. ANCHOR CABLE
31. HAMMOCKS
32. GROG TUB AND SCUTTLEBUTT
33. BOARDING PIKES
34. FIFE RAIL

35. MAINMAST
36. ENTRY PORT
37. HANGING SHOT RACK
38. 24-POUND LONG GUN
39. MAIN HATCHWAY
40. CABLE SCUTTLE
41. FRAMES
42. GUN PORT
43. SHEET ANCHOR
44. CANVAS OVER HAMMOCK RACKS
45. PINRAIL
46. GALLEY SMOKE PIPE
47. GALLEY STOVE
48. MOORING BITTS
49. BERTHING DECK
50. ARMORY
51. STORES IN HOLD

52. SAIL LOCKER
53. FOREMAST
54. BULKHEAD
55. SICK BAY
56. BOWSPRIT BITTS
57. FORECASTLE
58. ANCHOR BITTS
59. 18-POUND BOW CHASER
60. GAMMON LASHING
61. BOWSPRIT
62. BILLETHEAD
63. BOOMKIN FOR BOW RIGGING
64. TRAIL BOARD
65. CATHEAD TO SUPPORT ANCHOR
66. HAWSEPIPE
67. STEM
68. KEEL

maintained a murderous bombardment. The maimed and dying quickly began to pour into the surgeon's cockpit on the *Guerriere*. The English frigate's main yard crashed into the slings. A few moments later her mizzenmast plunged overboard. When the mast struck the water, it acted like a huge rudder, forcing the *Guerriere*'s bow up into the wind.

"By heaven, that ship is ours," Hull cried. He tried to sail the *Constitution* across the *Guerriere*'s bows so that the Yankee frigate's shot could rake the length of the *Guerriere*. But in the excitement and confusion, the *Constitution*'s bow was driven too far into the wind and hung there, her topsails taken aback, her torn rigging dragging in the water. The frigates were now so close together that the white and gold figurehead of the *Guerriere* could be touched with American hands. The English bowsprit hovered over Captain Hull's head.

Lieutenant William S. Bush of the *Constitution*'s Marine detachment leaped to the railing and called to Hull: "Shall I board her?" Bush was shot in the head, reeled back and died instantly. The ships rocked so close together that an American seaman, having fired his pistol at a British sailor and missed, flung the empty weapon at his adversary and struck him in the chest. Captain Dacres leaped to the hammock nettings on the *Guerriere*'s starboard fo'c's'le and, facing aft, waved his sword

While a powder boy hurries up with a charge and a gunner opens the cannon's port, the crew of a 24-pounder on the Constitution cheers lustily at word from Captain Isaac Hull that they are about to take on the British frigate Guerriere.

forward. An American musket ball took him in the back and he collapsed onto the deck. Then, before further boarding attempts could be organized, the ships wrenched apart, the *Constitution* meanwhile continuing her ferocious, raking fire. As the *Constitution* drew away, the *Guerriere*'s foremast came crashing down, pulling her mainmast with it.

The first frigate action of the War of 1812 was almost over. It had taken the *Constitution* less than 30 minutes to do what only a handful of Britain's enemies had been able to accomplish during the past 100 years.

The *Constitution* ran off out of cannon range and Hull swiftly repaired his cut-up rigging. When the Yankee frigate returned, the *Guerriere*'s flag was still flying. Captain Hull immediately dispatched Lieutenant George Read to demand the *Guerriere*'s surrender. Seeing the Union Jack that had been hung from the stump of the mizzenmast as an act of bravado on the part of one British tar, Read asked Dacres if he had struck his flag or not. The valiant Dacres, in great pain from his wound, replied thoughtfully: "Well, I don't know. Our mizzenmast is gone, our fore and main masts are gone. I think on the whole you might say we have struck our flag." At this point, the impatient Lieutenant Read offered to return to the *Constitution* so that the battle could be resumed. Dacres bowed to the inevitable; the *Guerriere*'s battle ensign came down immediately from the stump of the mizzenmast.

The captured American captain, William Orne, described the sight aboard the *Guerriere:* "At about half past six o'clock in the evening, after the firing had ceased, I went on deck, and there beheld a scene which it would be difficult to describe; all the *Guerriere*'s masts were shot away, and she lay rolling like a log in the trough of the sea. Many of her men were employed in throwing the dead overboard. The decks were covered with blood, and had the appearance of a butcher's slaughterhouse; the gun tackles were not made fast and several of the guns got loose, and were surging to and fro from one side to the other. Some of the petty officers and seamen, after the action, got liquor, and were intoxicated; and what with the groans of the wounded, the noise and confusion of the enraged survivors of the ill-fated ship rendered the whole scene a perfect hell."

Under the circumstances, Read suggested that the British surgeon might like some assistance from the *Constitution*'s surgeon. Captain Dacres agreed, but noted that aboard the *Constitution* the surgeon must be busy enough. "Oh, no," Read replied. "We have only seven wounded, and they were tended to long ago."

Lieutenant Read was only telling the truth, galling though it was to Captain Dacres. A more one-sided battle would be hard to find in British Naval history. Aboard the *Guerriere* there had been 101 casualties out of a crew of 302. Aboard the *Constitution*, there had been only seven killed and seven wounded out of 456 men. Physical damage to the *Constitution*, other than some cut-up rigging, was very slight. The *Guerriere* was a wreck, dismasted and with no fewer than 30 holes deep in her hull.

James Richard Dacres and Isaac Hull had already met on several occasions. As Captain Dacres, his wounded back paining him terribly, slowly mounted the *Constitution*'s rail to tender his sword, Isaac Hull stepped forward. "Dacres, give me your hand," Hull said. "I know you are hurt."

Captain James Dacres of the Guerriere tempted fate when he boldly challenged any U.S. frigate equal to his to "a few minutes tête-à-tête." Although he confidently predicted the Guerriere's victory over the Constitution "in 45 minutes," he was forced to strike his own colors in less than half an hour.

When Captain Dacres proffered his sword, Hull gently pushed it away. "No, no, I will not take the sword from one who knows so well how to use it," he said.

Hull then busied himself with rendering every assistance he could to the *Guerriere*'s wounded. In his subsequent official battle report, Dacres noted: "The conduct of Captain Hull and his officers to our men has been that of a brave enemy; the greatest care being taken to prevent our men losing the smallest trifle, and the greatest attention being paid to the wounded." The aristocratic Dacres had behaved equally well. Even though he was short handed, before the battle he had permitted 10 impressed Americans aboard the *Guerriere* to take shelter below rather than be forced to fire upon their own flag.

As the work of assisting the wounded went on, it soon became apparent that the *Guerriere* was finished. Hull decided not to try to save her, but to blow her up and transfer her men to the *Constitution*. He asked Dacres if there was anything left on board that the English captain particularly wanted. "Yes, there is," Dacres replied, "my mother's Bible." The Bible was immediately sent for, and then the *Guerriere* was destroyed.

Her sails hauled up for battle at close quarters, the Constitution (right) ranges in on the British frigate Guerriere in the first of four paintings (shown here and on the following two pages) by Michele Felice Cornè. The works were commissioned by the American Captain Isaac Hull to commemorate his stunning victory.

At 6:15 p.m., after 10 minutes of furious fire from the Constitution, the Guerriere's mizzenmast has toppled and the American frigate has shaken out more sail for greater maneuverability. As the mast fell, an American gunner whooped, "By God, we've made a brig of her! Next time we'll make her a sloop!"

On August 30, 1812, the *Constitution* reached Boston, where the news of the *Guerriere's* sinking swept over the town. The harbor seethed with pleasure boats as the big frigate was worked up to her moorings. Church bells pealed as the news quickly spread across the land. Isaac Hull, aghast at being made a celebrity, shrank from his new role—though he did not deny that he deserved it. To the Secretary of the Navy, he wrote: "It's my opinion that the less there is to be said about a brilliant act, the better." Of his crew, he said: "From the smallest boy in the Ship to the oldest Seaman, not a look of fear was seen. They all went into action, giving three cheers and requesting to be laid alongside the enemy."

While New England erupted with unrestrained enthusiasm for this victory peculiarly its own, Isaac Hull quietly turned to his back correspondence. One letter that probably caught his eye was from the Secretary of the Navy. Too late to reach the *Constitution* before she sailed to meet the *Guerriere*, it had directed Hull "to remain at Boston until further orders." Hull discovered that in the few weeks he had been at sea, his brother had died and family affairs were in some disarray. Among other events that rocked the Hull family was the fact that Isaac's uncle, General William Hull, had surrendered Detroit to the British without

firing a shot and was now about to be court-martialed. Reluctantly, Hull concluded that his primary responsibility at this time was to his family, particularly to his widowed sister-in-law and fatherless nieces and nephews. It would not do for him to be away at sea for an extended period. Therefore, at Isaac Hull's own request, on September 15, 1812, he was replaced by Captain William Bainbridge as commanding officer of the *Constitution*.

As for the British, they were stunned by the *Constitution*'s victory over the *Guerriere*. The London *Times* observed: "It is not merely that an English frigate has been taken, after what we are free to express, may be called a brave resistance, but that it has been taken by a new enemy, an enemy unaccustomed to such triumphs, likely to be rendered insolent and confident by them. Never before, in the history of the world did an English frigate strike to an American." The *Times* historian must have overlooked the capture of the *Serapis* by the *Bonhomme Richard* during the Revolutionary War. But perhaps the Duke of Wellington was recalling that earlier defeat as well as the *Guerriere*'s when he remarked, "I have been very uneasy about the American naval successes. I think we should have peace with America."

At 6:25 p.m., 20 minutes after the Constitution fired her first broadside, the Guerriere is losing her foremast and mainmast; the enemy, according to the U.S. ship's log, managed only to get "one of his guns to bear on us, which he discharged with little or no effect."

By 6:30 p.m. the Guerriere, dragging her spars and rigging, drifts helplessly, while the Constitution draws off to eastward. preparing to deliver one last broadside. But the British frigate could fight no longer and—said the Constitution's log— "fired a gun in token of submission."

But while all Britain was astounded by the unexpected American victory, that unhappy event could at least be ascribed to chance. In the next encounter, all were agreed, the Royal Navy would surely demonstrate the valor and experience that had made it supreme. That opportunity was, in fact, to come quickly.

As the war clouds had gathered, the officers of both the American and the Royal Navies had gone out of their way to be hospitable to each other. Stephen Decatur, the hero of Tripoli, was no exception. In February 1812, while at Norfolk, Decatur was pleased to act as host to one Captain John Surman Carden, commander of His Majesty's 49-gun frigate *Macedonian*.

There were the usual professional comparisons of each other's command. At 41, Carden was Decatur's senior by eight years and a captain of great experience. He was certain that the *United States*'s 24-pounders were decidedly inferior to the 18-pounders on the *Macedonian*. Carden reasoned that the American 24-pounders were too heavy to be handled as rapidly and efficiently as the British 18-pounders. The *Macedonian*, moreover, was only two years old while the *United States* was 14. "Besides, Decatur," he told the American, "though your ships may be good enough, and you are a clever set of fellows, what practice have you had in war? There is the rub. We now meet as friends, and God grant we may never meet as enemies; but we are subject to the orders of our governments, and must obey them. Should we meet as enemies, what do you suppose will be the result?" It was clear that Carden thought he knew the answer. The question would come back to haunt him before the year was out.

Shortly after Commodore Rodgers' unsuccessful attempt to find the Jamaica convoy at the start of the War, the American commander had taken his squadron on a second sortie. Leaving Boston on October 8, 1812, Rodgers sailed due east for four days with his three big frigates and two smaller warships. Once again they failed to find a major British convoy—or any Royal Navy ships to fight. In the *United States*, Decatur chafed at the frustrating lack of action, and all the more so when on the return leg to Boston he learned from a passing American ship of Isaac Hull's triumph in the *Constitution* over the *Guerriere*.

But then at last came the chance for individual initiative. Still three days out of Boston, Commodore Rodgers detached the *United States* and the *Argus* for a further sweep of the Atlantic. The remainder of Rodgers' squadron had hardly dropped over the horizon when Decatur in turn detached the *Argus* for independent duty. Perhaps he thought the little 16-gun brig would be more effective on her own. Then, too, perhaps he wanted the stage to himself for a solo performance, a virtuoso presentation that would dazzle his countrymen.

For two weeks Decatur cruised the *United States* in mid-Atlantic, his impatience mounting with each passing day. In the meantime, his old acquaintance of Norfolk days, Captain John Carden, had sailed from Portsmouth with orders to take station in the West Indies. Carden felt no particular sense of urgency; he had not heard of the *Constitution's* victory over the *Guerriere*. The *Macedonian* called at Madeira, where her officers invested in some excellent wine. At Madeira too, Captain Carden was informed that the U.S. frigate *Essex* was loose, and that he should keep a weather eye out for her.

While the information was incorrect, it shaped in Carden's mind a strategy that subsequently proved disastrous. Hoping to find the *Essex*, Carden sailed south. On Sunday, October 25, 1812, the *Macedonian* was on the extreme western edge of the Sargasso Sea, 500 miles west of the Canary Islands. It was a splendid, sunny morning, the semitropical sea faintly yellowed by the algae brought up in the ocean currents. Just after breakfast, with the crew dressed in their Sunday best and making preparations for the Sabbath service, a sail was sighted to the northwest and called down to the deck.

The stranger was soon identified as a large frigate bearing down on the *Macedonian* under easy canvas, the spray flashing over her fo'c's'le, the foam cresting under her bow. Carden had his frigate cleared for action. Soon, through his glass, Carden could glimpse the officers grouped on the stranger's quarter-deck, could see her gunports opened, her guns run out with gunners standing by, and her fighting tops packed with armed men. Carden had his British colors hoisted and sent aloft the Royal Navy's recognition signal. For answer, small lashed bundles soared up to the stranger's three mastheads and to the spanker gaff. A moment later, the lashings were tugged open and the Stars and Stripes floated over the frigate.

Aboard the *United States*, Stephen Decatur was wearing an old straw hat and his seediest uniform, the style he favored at sea. His final preparations for combat were interrupted by the approach of a grizzled old quartermaster with a ship's boy named Jack Creamer in tow. The little powder boy had requested permission to speak to the captain, and under the ship's rules the quartermaster had brought him aft to do so. What the boy wished was to be formally entered on the *United States*'s muster roll. He was only 10, the son of a crewman who had died on board, and he had been allowed to ship out as a sort of mascot. He now wanted Decatur to waive the legal 12-year age limit for enlistment.

"What for, my lad?" Decatur asked.

"So that I can share in the prize money when we take the Britisher, sir," Jack Creamer responded.

Decatur chuckled and granted the boy's request. Then there were other matters to attend to.

The *Macedonian* fired the first shots—three guns from her port battery to test the range, the balls splashing into the sea short of the Yankee frigate. Then, to get just within range of his 18-pounders, the confident Carden wore ship; that is, he put the *Macedonian*'s stern through the wind, so that the entire starboard broadside was presented to his enemy. The two ships were now barely a mile apart and sailing easily on slightly converging courses toward the morning sun. Both ships had backed their mizzen-topsails—steering rap-full, it was called—to steady their decks and afford their gunners every opportunity to demonstrate their marksmanship. A little after nine the ships exchanged a few salvos, the shot passing through their rigging, the smoke from the Yankees' guns billowing out to form a large white halo between the two ships.

The frigates were now fully in range of each other. The preliminaries were over. Years later a man who had been a British powder boy aboard the *Macedonian* recalled what happened next: "A strange noise, such as I had never heard before, arrested my attention—it sounded like the tearing of sails just over our heads. This I soon ascertained to be the roar of the enemy's shot. By and by I heard the shot strike the sides of our ship; the whole scene grew indescribably confused and horrible; it was like some awfully tremendous thunderstorm whose deafening roar is attended by incessant streaks of lightning, carrying death in every flash, and strewing the ground with victims of its wrath—only in our case, the scene was rendered more horrible than that by the presence of torrents of blood which dyed our decks. Our men kept cheering with all their might. I cheered with them, although I confess I scarcely knew for what.

"So terrible had been the work of destruction around us, it was termed the slaughter house. Not only had we several boys and men killed or wounded, but several of the guns were disabled. The one I belonged to had a piece of the muzzle knocked out of it and when the ship rolled, it struck a beam in the upper deck and became fixed in that position. A fellow named John was carried past me, wounded. I distinctly heard the large blood drops fall pat, pat, pat on the deck. His wounds were mortal. Even a poor goat, kept by the officers for her milk, did not escape the general carnage. Her hind legs were shot off and poor Nan was thrown overboard."

By now Captain Carden realized his mistake in taking on the *United States* and young Stephen Decatur. For all his brags about British guns and gunnery, he could not match the Americans. The big 24-pounders opposite him were being fired with magnificent discipline and awful effect, fired by divisions, and not simply aimed at the bulk of the *Macedonian*, but at specific targets aboard her. Further, they were firing twice as fast as his 18-pounders, so rapidly that the *United States* sometimes appeared to be on fire. Indeed, men aboard the *Macedonian* thought the *United States* was in flames and began to cheer. But then the smoke parted and the Yankee officers could be seen coolly walking about and directing fire, the American gunners stripped to the waist and wearing bandannas on their heads.

In a last desperate effort, Carden ordered the *Macedonian*'s helm put to port and called for boarders. It was hopeless. Yankee shot parted the braces leading to the foreyard, and the sail slatted over, throwing the *Macedonian* up into the wind. While the British frigate hung there, the *United States* pulled across her bow and fired into the crippled ship with heavy 42-pound carronades. The fight by now was 90 minutes old. Both the *Macedonian*'s fore- and main-topmasts had been shot away at the caps. She had received over 100 cannon shot in her hull. All of her boats except the jolly boat towed astern had been smashed to splinters and most of her guns had been silenced. Then, although the *Macedonian*'s battle flag still flew from the stump of the mizzenmast, the Yankee suddenly stopped firing.

In this sudden lull in the battle, all that could be heard on the *Macedonian* were the cries and groans of the wounded, the slosh of water through the main-deck gunports as the British frigate wallowed in the sea, the creaking of the badly strained hull each time she rolled. Then the smoke parted and the Yankee frigate, still apparently not suffering any major damage, could be seen sailing away. Was there another British frigate looming over the horizon? Were the Yankees on the run? A few men began to cheer insanely. It was a forlorn hope. Within an hour the *United States* returned, her rigging repaired, her crew still at their guns. There was hurried council of war on the quarter-deck of the *Macedonian*. Sometime about noon Captain Carden gave the order and the *Macedonian* struck her colors.

The *United States* lowered a boat and Lieutenant John B. Nicholson was rowed over to take possession of the British frigate. Boarding the *Macedonian*, the Americans were appalled at what they had wrought. The British frigate had more than 100 casualties. "There were fragments of the dead scattered in every direction, the decks slippery with blood, one continuous agonizing yell of the unhappy wounded," recalled an American. As on the *Guerriere*, the remainder of the *Macedonian*'s 301-man crew had broken into the spirit room and many were now roaring drunk. With difficulty the Americans made their way through the bloody gun deck to the steerage, which was packed with the dead and the dying. Lieutenant Nicholson greeted the *Macedonian*'s

The gentlemen of the King's Navy

Although a seaman's life in the King's fleet was a hell of execrable food, stinking water and frequent applications of the lash, for officers life was as gentlemanly as the Navy could make it.

Just as egalitarian democracy in America influenced—to a point—the U.S. Navy, so the rigid class system of the island nation pervaded British ships. Officers ate their own hearty and carefully preserved provisions, sipped wine and (as these contemporary paintings by English artist Augustus Earle suggest) were comfortably berthed in relatively spacious quarters in which they could pursue a variety of recreational, cultural and religious activities. Young midshipmen, as apprentice officers, benefited from the schoolmasters employed to instruct them at sea. During their off-duty hours they relaxed companionably on the berth deck to read, write letters and play the games their landbound peers would play in any boarding-school common room ashore. While on duty, they enjoyed absolute authority over the ordinary seamen on board, and in their dress uniforms they strutted the decks in garb only slightly less splendiferous than that of full-fledged officers.

The senior officers enjoyed private living quarters, servants and, on some voyages, the companionship of their wives or children, who were allowed to share their accommodations. They ate in the genteel comfort of the captain's mess or the wardroom and used private toilets protected from the weather and heaving seas. In port they were free to invite friends and local notables on board for Sabbath services, social calls and meals. Not surprisingly, it was virtually unheard of for an officer of any rank to jump ship.

In the painting entitled Midshipmen's Berth (top), an apprentice officer, lounging on deck, studies his book and slate while his shipmates shave, frolic with a pet gibbon, paint, play the pipe and gossip. In Bible Reading on Board (bottom), Navy and Marine officers, a few seamen and some well-dressed civilians, including a lady, listen and follow along with varying degrees of attentiveness as the captain, in his flag-draped chair, reads from the Scriptures.

surgeon, who shook his head sadly, and said: "You fellows have made wretched work with us."

Captain Carden's trip to the *United States* was mortifying. Boarding the Yankee frigate, he could see that she was only slightly damaged (she had also suffered only minor casualties: seven dead and five wounded). He noted bitterly that some of the *United States*'s crew obviously had been British deserters. "Nelson" was painted over one of the American frigate's gunports, "The *Victory*" over another. Captain Decatur's appearance startled him. It was bad enough to have lost his ship, but now he was offended at having to surrender to an officer dressed like a farmer. In a scene almost identical with the meeting between Dacres and Hull two months before, Carden offered his sword to Decatur, who, as was customary with a stout enemy, refused to accept it. "I cannot receive the sword of a man who has so bravely defended his ship," said Decatur. Carden observed that he was ruined. "I am an undone man," he said, "the first British naval officer that has struck his flag to an American."

Not so, Decatur responded, "your *Guerriere* has been taken. The flag of a frigate was struck before yours." This news, later reported Decatur, seemed to cheer Carden somewhat.

Finding that the battered *Macedonian* could be jury-rigged for an attempt to bring her back to America, the *United States* lay to for the next several days while her crew attended to the wounded, buried the dead, rigged new topmasts and sponged out the bloody decks of their prize with vinegar. Every courtesy was extended to the British prisoners, the American officers even repaying the *Macedonian*'s officers when they helped themselves to the Madeira wine. During this brief interlude Decatur one day spotted the 10-year-old powder boy, Jack Creamer.

"Well, Jack," Decatur asked, "we have taken her and your share of the prize money if we get her safe in may be $200. What will you do with it?"

"I will send half to my mother, sir," he replied, "and the other half shall pay for my schooling."

Decatur was so impressed with the boy's response that he arranged a midshipman's commission for the youngster when they returned to America. Creamer subsequently went on to become a senior officer in the American Navy.

Among his other prisoners from the *Macedonian*, Decatur found that he had captured a complete eight-man French band. Under the terms of their contract they were to be protected from combat, and had been hidden in the cable tier when the battle was joined. When the bandsmen at last emerged they discovered that they were now expected to play "Yankee Doodle." The French band elected to remain with the *United States*, and more than 30 years later, when Herman Melville sailed on the *United States*, some of the members of that band from the *Macedonian* were still performing.

When all was ready, the two frigates shaped a course for America, reaching New London, Connecticut, in December 1812. Midshipman Archibald Hamilton, the son of the Secretary of the Navy, was given the honor of carrying the *Macedonian*'s battle flag from New London to Washington. Pausing just long enough to change horses, Hamilton arrived in Washington dusty, sweaty and exhausted, on the night of De-

Firing salutes with her captive upon returning to American waters via Newport and New London, the United States follows the British frigate Macedonian into New York Harbor on January 1, 1813. The captured Macedonian "comes with compliments of the season from Old Neptune," exulted one newspaper.

cember 28. A great Naval ball was in progress honoring Isaac Hull for capturing the *Guerriere,* and another officer, Captain David Porter, for capturing the British 18-gun sloop *Alert* on August 12 in mid-Atlantic. The colors of both vessels were on display at the ball.

Suddenly Hamilton appeared, pushed forward by the crowd. The band stopped playing. Hamilton's mother was in the room and at the unexpected sight of her son she almost fainted. Hamilton gave the *Macedonian*'s colors to the President's wife, and the divine Dolley Madison draped them around her shoulders. Wild cheering broke out and the punch bowls were emptied in enthusiastic toasts to Decatur. Wearing the colors of the *Macedonian,* Dolley Madison led the grand march through the ballroom.

When the news of the *Macedonian*'s loss first reached England, the British refused to believe it. The *Macedonian* was British-built and one of the finest frigates in the Royal Navy. On October 7, 1812, the London *Times* had noted that "the loss of the *Guerriere* spread a degree of gloom through the town which it was painful to observe." On December 26 *The Times* lamented: "There is a report that another English frigate, the *Macedonian,* has been captured by an American. We shall certainly be very backward in believing a second recurrence of such a national disgrace. Certainly there was a time when it would not have been believed that the American navy could have appeared upon the seas after a six month's war with England; much less that it could, within that period, have been twice victorious."

The next day the report was confirmed, and again *The Times* was forced to express British chagrin: "O miserable advocates! In the name of God, what was done with this immense superiority of force?" And on the 29th *The Times* lamented: "Oh, what a charm is hereby dissolved! What hopes will be excited in the breasts of our enemies!"

Emboldened by the early successes at sea, the American government soon changed its policy of allowing the frigates only occasional sorties into the North Atlantic. Captain William Bainbridge, having relieved Isaac Hull as commander of the *Constitution*, was ordered to lead a sweep of the South Atlantic and ultimately to conduct operations in the Indian Ocean. Accordingly, the *Constitution* and the 18-gun brig *Hornet*, commanded by Master Commandant James Lawrence, yet another of "Preble's Boys," sailed from Boston on October 26. Two days later the little frigate *Essex* cleared the Delaware capes. All three ships succeeded in escaping the British blockaders and were soon en route to a squadron rendezvous off the coast of Brazil.

Calling at Bahia, Brazil, the *Hornet* discovered a British sloop of war, the 20-gun *Bonne Citoyenne*, in that neutral port. In 1808 the plucky *Bonne Citoyenne*, herself a captured French vessel, had taken on and defeated the *Furieuse*, a French frigate of the 36-gun class, thereby earning considerable renown for herself and her crew. The *Bonne Citoyenne* was a splendid match for the *Hornet*, and Captain Lawrence immediately offered a formal challenge to the British captain. Such challenges were not unusual. While the United States and Great Britain were at war, it was still an age when chivalry counted for much, and the captains of light naval vessels in particular tended to think of themselves as duelists, even as jousting knights.

Not wishing to disturb what promised to be a superb small-ship action, Bainbridge left the *Hornet* on patrol off Bahia waiting for an answer from the *Bonne Citoyenne*, and the *Constitution* proceeded south toward Cabo Frio seeking to join up with the *Essex*. On the morning of December 29, 1812, Bainbridge sighted two sail, one standing toward him and the other making for the Brazilian coast. The vessel bearing down upon Bainbridge was H.M.S. *Java*, 38 guns, under the command of Captain Henry Lambert. The *Java*, en route to India with Lieutenant General Thomas Hislop, the new Governor of Bombay, and his entourage, had recently captured the American merchantman *William*, the other vessel Bainbridge saw. And now a British prize crew was taking the *William* into a neutral port.

The frigate Bainbridge faced was an exceptional vessel. She had started life as a pride of the French fleet, named the *Renommee*, and had been captured more than 18 months before off Madagascar. She had been extensively refitted and renamed the *Java*. She was very fast. Moreover, on this voyage, in addition to her normal crew, she had shipped an extra hundred seamen being transferred from Portsmouth to India. In short, she was a much fitter opponent for the *Constitution* than had been the *Guerriere*, though her guns were only 18-pounders, compared with the 24-pounders on the Yankee frigate.

The summer sea that day in the South Atlantic was smooth and sunlit, the winds light. Bainbridge held to a southeast course to lead his opponent away from the neutral waters in which a crippled ship might seek refuge. Lambert, with the windward advantage and the faster ship, followed in hot pursuit. By noon both ships had cleared for action and had hoisted their colors. At about 2 p.m., with both vessels on the port tack and heading in an easterly direction, the range had closed to within half a mile. Shortly afterward the *Constitution* opened fire from her port battery. The *Java* responded with a broadside. A furious cannonading began and both ships were hit repeatedly.

With her superior speed the *Java* pulled slightly ahead, and Captain Lambert tried to cross the *Constitution*'s bow so that he would be able to bring his entire broadside to bear, while the *Constitution* could only respond with her bow guns. But Bainbridge had anticipated this maneuver and quickly turned inside the *Java*, thus maintaining a position broadside to broadside (chart, page 102). Now both duelists were heading in a westerly direction and facing each other on different sides, the gun crews rushing over to the previously unused cannon. Once more Lambert put the *Java*'s helm over to try again for raking position. Again Bainbridge turned with him. The ships had resumed the original heading and were still pounding away. But by now the heavier weight of American gunnery was beginning to tell.

The *Constitution*'s 24-pounders were making a shambles of the *Java*'s hull. The British vessel's complement of midshipmen, for no apparent reason save the vagaries of combat, was suffering particularly heavy losses. Without the midshipmen's supervision, gun crews began to overlook details such as reducing powder charges as the gun barrels became hotter and maintaining a continuous supply of cartridges. The *Java*'s fire became increasingly ragged.

But now a lucky shot from the *Java* carried away the *Constitution*'s steering wheel, in the process driving a copper bolt deep into Captain Bainbridge's thigh. He had already been wounded by a musket shot in the leg. Staggering back to his feet, Bainbridge had tackles rigged so that the *Constitution*'s rudder could be controlled. The *Java* tried to tack upwind so as to gain a raking position, but her rigging had been so badly slashed that she hung up in the light air. Quickly the *Constitution* wore round and poured in two raking broadsides with ghastly effect. The *Constitution* shot away the *Java*'s bowsprit and jib boom, so that her big headsails, so important in maneuvering a frigate, dangled in the water.

Nevertheless, the *Java* retained enough headway so that the splintered end of her bowsprit fouled the *Constitution*'s rigging as the American frigate slid past. The *Java*'s Captain Lambert gave a desperate order, and British bugles sounded "Boarders Away!" The *Java*'s lieutenants drove their men forward, screaming at them and hitting them with their speaking trumpets. His cutlass in hand, Lambert ran up to lead the charge, and an American Marine in the *Constitution*'s maintop shot him through the chest.

As Lambert crumpled to the deck, the *Java*'s foremast came down with a stunning crash. The ships wrenched apart. Captain Lambert was carried below, where the *Java*'s surgeon examined him. Dr. Thomas Cook Jones later reported: "I saw him almost immediately afterward, and found that the ball had entered his left side under the clavicle, fracturing the first rib, the splinters of which had severely lacerated the lungs. I put my finger in the wound, detached and extricated several pieces of the bone. He said that he felt no annoyance from the wound in his breast, but complained of pain extending the whole length of his spine."

Lieutenant Henry Ducie Chads assumed command of the *Java*, assisted by the officers who had been passengers. The British frigate stubbornly continued to return the *Constitution*'s fire. At about 4 p.m. the *Java*'s mizzenmast toppled. The mast fell on the ship's engaged side, and the welter of flapping canvas and tarred rigging soon caught fire from the flashes of the *Java*'s own guns. The *Constitution* drew away from the burning wreck, while members of the Yankee crew set about repairing their own damaged rigging. About 5:30 p.m., when the *Constitution* returned, the British colors came down.

Bainbridge now faced a severe problem. The *Java* was carrying naval stores and a cargo of copper sheathing for ships being built at Bombay. Under ordinary circumstances this would have made a fine prize for any victorious crew. But unhappily, she was too far gone to save. The *Java* and her valuable cargo had to be destroyed. Further, the *Constitution* had captured an enormous number of prisoners, about 360 in all, 100 or so of whom were wounded. And the *Constitution* herself had been dam-

Twisting and turning, the tracks on this diagram from the British Naval Chronicle show the maneuvers of the Constitution and the Java in their fight off Brazil. The Constitution twice crossed the Java's bow—at 3:35 and 4:15 p.m.—to get in broadsides. At 5:50 the Java surrendered.

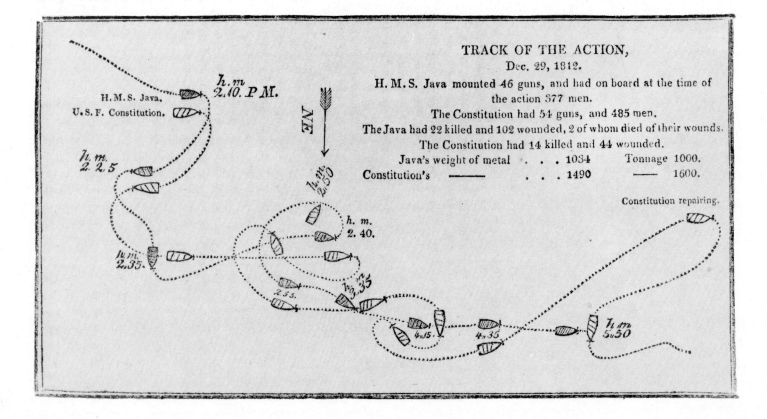

TRACK OF THE ACTION,
Dec. 29, 1812.

H. M. S. Java mounted 46 guns, and had on board at the time of the action 377 men.

The Constitution had 54 guns, and 485 men.

The Java had 22 killed and 102 wounded, 2 of whom died of their wounds.

The Constitution had 14 killed and 44 wounded.

Java's weight of metal . . . 1034		Tonnage 1000.
Constitution's ——— . . . 1490		——— 1600.

Constitution repairing.

H. M. S. Java.
U. S. F. Constitution.

h. m. 2.10. P M.

h. m. 2. 25

h. m. 2.35.

h. m. 2. 40.

h. m. 2.50

2. 55.

3. 35

4. 15.

4. 35.

h. m. 5. 50

103

Working feverishly under heavy fire from the Constitution, crewmen aboard the crippled Java clear the wreckage of masts and sails in this contemporary French watercolor. Describing his ship as "an unmanageable wreck," Acting Captain Henry Chads struck his colors, having determined that "it would be wasting lives to resist any longer."

aged. She had absorbed several hits; her sails and mizzenmast were badly in need of repair. Reluctantly, Bainbridge concluded that the cruise of the *Constitution* must end. He landed his prisoners at Bahia, where, shortly after, Captain Lambert died.

Leaving the *Hornet* to her patient blockade—the *Bonne Citoyenne*, though more heavily armed than the American, had refused so far to come out and fight—the *Constitution* set sail for Boston. Upon arriving there on February 27, Bainbridge and his crew were mobbed by ecstatic crowds. William Bainbridge, who had suffered captivity and silently borne the indignity of the *Philadelphia*'s loss, had at one stroke restored himself to the front rank of fighting captains.

News of the *Java*'s destruction reached England in the early spring of 1813. And there was more. The *Hornet* had eventually given up her fruitless blockade, but on the way home Captain James Lawrence had managed to sting the British not once but three times—by recapturing an American merchantman, taking a British prize with $20,000 in silver on board and finally, on February 24, 1813, engaging and sinking His Majesty's 18-gun brig *Peacock*.

The Royal Navy was being shamed. When the War began, any sporting

Englishman would have blissfully bet his fortune on the Navy of Nelson, with its 900 ships against America's 17. Yet the Yankees had achieved one brilliant success after another. America's only losses in 1812 were the little 14-gun brig *Nautilus*, forced to surrender to an entire British squadron, the sloop *Wasp*, eventually overwhelmed and captured by a British ship of the line, and the *Vixen*, 12 guns, taken by the British 48-gun frigate *Southampton*. By contrast, three British frigates and three other warships had been taken by the Yankees. The accounting was all on the side of the Americans.

The London *Times* summed up the situation on March 20: "The public will learn with sentiments which we shall not presume to anticipate that a third British frigate has struck to an American. Any one who would have predicted such a result of an American war this time last year would have been treated as a madman or a traitor. Yet down to this moment, not a single American frigate has struck her flag."

Britain stepped up her war effort. The Royal Navy vastly increased its force in American waters. By early 1813 Admiral Sir John Borlase Warren, in command at Halifax, alone had 15 ships of the line, each mounting 74 guns, a 50-gun ship and 15 frigates plus 20 sloops and brigs. Further, British frigate commanders were ordered to stop trying to fight singly the big Humphreys frigates with their murderous 24-pounders. And the Royal Navy hurriedly attempted to convert several ships of the line into razees for duty in American waters. After two decades of listening to taunts and jibes concerning the size of his ships, Joshua Humphreys must have been happy to hear that news.

Just as the Royal Navy had blockaded the French, so now English ships took station off every American port. The initial order for a blockade of American ports came in November 1812, after five months of war. But owing to communication problems it was not executed until some three months later. Beginning as a commercial blockade of the Delaware and the Chesapeake, it was gradually extended throughout 1813 south to the mouth of the Mississippi and north to Long Island Sound. The blockade virtually stopped America's transoceanic trade and severely crippled her coastal trade. But it was not entirely effective. Yankee privateers had been operating against British merchant shipping since the start of the War, and had already taken, according to the hand-wringing computation of marine insurers at Lloyd's, more than 500 vessels of all sizes. The blockade put a crimp in the privateers' activities, but it was unable to stop them altogether. A trio of light, fast privateers operating out of New York alone counted 65 British prizes after the blockade was imposed.

Nor could the blockade stop the Yankee Navy, which continued to slip to sea. Any snowstorm or sudden gale that might force the blockaders out for sea room was an opportunity. The tall American masts that rose over coastal harbors and had been so patiently scanned for months by the blockading British were as likely not to be there when the storm abated and the Royal Navy resumed station. Then it became a question of where in the Atlantic the American ships had gone.

And by February 1813, the Royal Navy could not even assume that the elusive Yankee frigates were in the Atlantic.

With jubilant pride, a young American seaman on the Constitution penned this victory paean after the Java's defeat. Publishing entrepreneurs sought out such eyewitness accounts for broadsides that they sold to the public as souvenirs.

Presented by the citizens of Philadelphia in May 1813 to Commodore William Bainbridge, this 18-inch silver urn commemorates the captain's "skill and gallantry in the capture of the British frigate Java." Bainbridge and his officers were decorated with medals by Congress, and they were honored at parades and banquets in half a dozen cities.

GLORIOUS NAVAL VICTORY,

OBTAINED BY COMMODORE BAINBRIDGE, OF THE UNITED STATES FRIGATE CONSTITUTION, OVER HIS BRITANNIC MAJESTY'S FRIGATE JAVA.

BY JAMES CAMPBELL, A BOATSWAIN'S MATE ON BOARD THE CONSTITUTION.

COME listen to my story the truth I will unfold,
Concerning of a frigate, she was man'd with hearts of gold,
We took a cruize from Boston, as you shall understand,
For to maintain the freedom of our own native land.

We took a new Commander, and Bainbridge was his name,
Our lot it was to have him, we could not deny the same,
He proved a Commander that was both firm and true,
You shall find in the story of the Constitution's crew.

On the 27th of October, as you shall understand,
We steered for an Island, it was called Ferdinand ;
All for to water ship my boys, and then to sail away,
Unto the Brazil coast, to beat our daring enemy.

On the 29th of December, being early in the day,
A frigate bore down on us, she was called the JAVA ;
We took her to be a seventy-four, and from them bore away,
Thinking the English Squadron to the windward of us lay.

At eleven o'clock, we made the signal of the day,
Being not directly answered, 'twas then we bore away,
At twelve we made more sail my boys, but from them we did go,
But our desire was to be along side of our most daring foe.

Our ensign and pendant we hoisted to let them understand,
They hoisted their colors, they were them of old England ;
With their union jack being hoisted, it was their British pride,
Which they were forc'd to strike to us, or sink along our side.

'Twas one when we perceived she was a single deck ship,
It being our intention their British bones to rip ;
We gave to them three cheers, and then the fray begun,
Each loyal hearted seaman then serving at his gun.

It was a little after she attempted to rake us,
But we being not inclined to let them serve us thus :
We giving them a broadside, which made them haul their wind,
To meet such a reception, they were not much inclin'd.

It was at two o'clock the bloody fray begun,
Each hardy tar and son of mars, was active at his gun,
Until their fore and mizen-mast was fairly shot away,
And with redoubled courage, we gave them three huzzas.

Her mainmast it was standing, and to windward of us lay,
And on that stick her union jack, to us they did display,
Her hull was sadly battered, and they being badly maul'd,
Unto the Constitution, down her main-jack soon she haul'd.

Our Commodore at seeing that she had her colors struck,
He wished to every officer the bravest and best of luck ;
Likewise to every seaman that was both firm and true,
Here's to brave Commodore Bainbridge & the Constitution's crew,

Two hours and three quarters, we engaged very hot,
Until one hundred and four poor Britons, lay dead upon the spot,
Which made them think the Yankees could shew them fair play,
And made them strike the union, on the close of that great day.

Come all you royal Englishmen, the truth of you I'll tell,
If you can beat the French, we you can beat as well,
For it ne'er shall be recorded, that Americans shall fly,
Great Washington he made us free, and we'll still be free or die.

Come all of our brave citizens, your tribute to us bring,
For this gallant atchievement, in this great and glorious thing,
We can beat all our enemys, like lions that is stout,
So come fill the can brave fellows, and let us drink it out.

Here's to our wives & sweethearts, for whom we fought for fame,
And when the lisping children shall sing forth their father's name,
And the pretty girls of every stamp, what more then can we do ?
So may success attend those heroes of the Constitution's crew.

BOSTON :
Printed and sold by NATHANIEL COVERLY, JNR.
Corner Theatre-Alley.

Archibald Fry's

Chapter 4

The spectacular forays of a dashing captain

aptain David Porter thoroughly mistrusted his ship. She was the light frigate *Essex*, and Porter feared that her defects, particularly of armament, would one day betray him in combat with the British. In that, Porter was prescient. For the *Essex* would, in fact, eventually bring him to grief. Yet before that day came to pass, Porter sailed his tragically flawed frigate on two of the boldest and most brilliant cruises of this, or many another, war. His objective was not to confront enemy warships, though in the end he did so, and gallantly. Rather, his purpose was to give the British a taste of their own bitter medicine by raiding their commerce and denying British shippers the very freedom of the seas they took so much for granted. In that he succeeded magnificently, scouring thousands of miles of ocean for months at a time, and taking more ships and causing more anguish in the halls of the British Admiralty than any two captains of bigger, stronger and faster Yankee frigates.

Porter's displeasure with the *Essex* stemmed not from any error in her original design. She was a splendidly built small frigate, rated at 32 guns. Almost $80,000 for her construction and fitting-out had been raised among the public-spirited citizens of Salem, Massachusetts, and when completed, the *Essex* had been donated by these citizens to the United States Navy. Her designer was William Hackett, a New England shipwright noted for building a number of successful naval vessels in the Revolutionary War. The *Essex* was meant to be his masterpiece, incorporating everything he had learned about hull design, weight and rigging. She was a finely proportioned vessel, 140 feet long, with a beam of 36½ feet and a displacement of 860 tons. She was not built of Southern live oak, as were her larger predecessors. But her constructors selected the finest of New England white oak, considered more than adequate.

During her fitting-out, the *Essex* was armed with 26 long-range 12-pounders on the main deck and 16 short-range 24-pound carronades on the spar deck, making a total of 42 guns. This combination was what Hackett had specified, and her weight and balance were such that she proved an extremely fast sailer. The Boston *Independent Chronicle* called her "as fine a ship of her size as graces the American Navy." And indeed, her early years promised a long and distinguished service life.

In 1800, under the command of Edward Preble, the *Essex* became the first United States warship to enter the Pacific, rounding the Cape of Good Hope to escort a convoy of American merchantmen home from the Dutch East Indies. As the years passed, she was sent to cruise along both the African and European shores of the Mediterranean to protect Ameri-

The light frigate Essex, scourge of British commerce on two oceans in the War of 1812, booms along with a following wind in this contemporary watercolor by Joseph Howard of Salem, Massachusetts, where the ship was built. More than 50 of the local tradesmen participated in building and fitting out the Essex, among them sailmaker John Howard, father of the artist.

can merchantmen from Moorish pirates and escort them safely through the Strait of Gibraltar into the Atlantic.

Unhappily, in 1810, when commanded by Captain John Smith, the *Essex* underwent a drastic change in armament. Though most American captains were believers in long-range cannon, which would enable them to fight a battle of maneuver, Smith was a fervent advocate of the brutal, hull-to-hull fight in which the crushing weight of short-range carronades would come into play. He therefore removed 20 of her 12-pound guns, and in their place the *Essex* was given 24 new 32-pound carronades. She retained only six of her original long-range 12-pounders, while now relying for her sting on 40 short-range carronades. The changes increased the total number of guns on board the *Essex* from 42 to 46, and boosted from 348 to 612 pounds the total weight of metal she could throw in a single broadside.

But these advantages were nullified by two highly unfortunate consequences. By disturbing the delicate balances that Hackett had built into the ship, the new guns reduced the *Essex'* sailing qualities. Worse, the rearmed frigate's lack of a large battery of long 12-pounders rendered her virtually helpless against an opponent that could successfully keep the Yankee at a distance. To succeed in any action against a comparable frigate of the Royal Navy, the *Essex* would somehow have to overcome her impaired sailing qualities to close with the enemy, and then smash and board. It was a virtual impossibility.

David Porter had complained bitterly about the *Essex'* scheme of armament when he assumed command at Gosport, Virginia, in the summer of 1811. Writing to the Secretary of the Navy, Porter asserted: "Was this ship to be disabled in her rigging in the early part of an engagement, a ship armed with long guns could take a position beyond the reach of our carronades and cut us to pieces." The Secretary's reply was small comfort to Porter: the captain could, if he chose, mount a few long 18-

Salem harbor, birthplace of the Essex, stretches tranquilly eastward to the sea in this 1797 engraving. Though launching ways existed at the boatyard (foreground) of builder Enos Briggs, the harbor was too shallow for the frigate's 18-foot draft. A new yard was established for the Essex at Winter Island, seen beyond the wharves.

TAKE NOTICE!

YE Sons of Freedom! all true lovers of the Liberty of your Country! step forth, and give your affiance in building the Frigate, to oppofe French infolence and piracy. Let every man in poffeffion of a *White Oak Tree*, be ambitious to be foremoft in hurrying down the timber to Salem, and fill the complement wanting, where the noble ftructure is to be fabricated, tomaintain your rights upon the Seas, and make the name of America refpected among the nations of the world. Your largeft and longeft trees are wanted, and the arms of them for Knees and Rifing Timber. Four trees are wanted for the Keel, which all together will meafure 146 feet in length, and hew 16 inches fquare. Pleafe to call on the Subfcriber, who wants to make contracts for large or fmall quantities, as may fuit beft, and will pay the READY CASH.

ENOS BRIGGS.

SALEM, Nov. 23, 1798.

THROUGH *the medium of the Gazette, the Subfcriber pays his acknowledgments to the good people of the county of Effex, for their fpirited exertions in bringing down the trees of the foreft for building the frigate. In the fhort fpace of four weeks, the full complement of timber has been furnifhed. Thofe who have thus contributed to their country's defence are invited to come forward and receive the reward of their patriotifm. They are informed, that, with permiffion of kind Providence, who hath hitherto favoured the undertaking,*

Next September is the time,
When we'll launch her from the ftrand,
And our cannon load and prime
With tribute, due to Talleyrand.

ENOS BRIGGS.

SALEM, JAN. 11, 1799.

Getting ready to build the Essex in 1798, Enos Briggs published a twice-weekly plea for timber (top) in the Salem Gazette, for use in the keel of the "noble structure." The response was so enthusiastic that on January 11, 1799, Briggs ran an expansive notice of appreciation (bottom).

pounders to supplement the six remaining long 12s. But he could not replace the carronades; apparently it was too expensive, since he had made one switch, now to switch back at the whim of a second captain. In any case, Porter, possibly out of anger, never did mount the authorized 18s and made do with his scant half dozen long 12s. He came from a fighting, seafaring family; he was fiercely patriotic, felt himself destined for glory and was anxious to get on with the pursuit of it.

The son of a courageous Revolutionary War captain, young David had grown up with strong ideas about both valor and the British. Like many of his contemporaries, Porter went to sea early, and received a rigorous upbringing. At the age of 18, he was commissioned a midshipman in the frigate *Constellation*, under the command of that strict disciplinarian, Thomas Truxtun. Porter was certainly not the most malleable of the youngsters aboard the ship. Though he was slight of stature, he possessed a flaming ego and an untamed spirit. In fact, chafing under his captain's rough tongue, Porter one day declared to the formidable Truxtun that he was tired of being sworn at and intended to resign from the Naval service. Whereupon Truxtun bellowed: "Why you young dog! If I can help it you shall never leave the navy! Swear at you? Damn it, Sir—every time I do that you go a round on the ladder of promotion! Go forward and let us have no more whining."

Later, Truxtun had cause to congratulate himself for resolving the matter as he did. For in the *Constellation's* running battle with the *Insurgente* in 1799, it was Porter who saved the day when he took it upon himself to lower the damaged rigging before the weight of its sails brought down the entire mast. As a reward, Truxtun assigned him to be a member of the prize crew that brought the *Insurgente* back to the United States amid the cheers of their countrymen.

Porter's life over the next decade was crammed with wild adventures. On January 1, 1800, as second lieutenant of the 20-gun schooner *Experiment* in the Caribbean, Porter defied the orders of his captain, who was about to surrender to a force of Haitian pirates, and instead rallied the crew to drive off the raiders. Home on leave in Baltimore, he stabbed and killed a drunken bully who had assaulted him, then narrowly escaped a gang of toughs bent on lynching him. A year later in the Mediterranean, Porter was with Lieutenant Andrew Sterrett on the *Enterprise* when she took the Barbary warship *Tripoli*—the first American sea victory of the Tripolitan war. And Porter was with William Bainbridge in 1803, when the *Philadelphia* ran aground and was captured off Tripoli.

During long months in a Tripolitan prison, Porter occupied his energetic mind with a variety of studies. Quartered with other American officers and midshipmen in an empty warehouse, he was spared from the backbreaking regimen imposed on the *Philadelphia's* enlisted sailors. With books supplied by the Danish consul, Porter studied naval history, mathematics and French. He even organized an informal midshipman's school where his students practiced naval tactics by pushing wooden blocks around the floors of their cells.

Released at the end of the war with Tripoli in 1805, Porter spent some time in New York, where he fell in with a wild band of drinking companions headed by Washington Irving, who nicknamed him "Sindbad" for his exploits in the Mediterranean. But after two months as a minor social lion in Manhattan, Porter was ordered by the Navy to Norfolk, where his adventures continued. On a visit to Washington, the 27-year-old Porter fell headlong in love with another visitor to the city, 15-year-old Evalina Anderson, the daughter of a prominent Pennsylvania innkeeper soon to be elected to Congress. Typically, Porter pressed his campaign so vigorously that the girl's brother ordered him out of the house. Naturally, Porter threatened to throw the brother out of the window.

But tempers cooled on both sides. Within six months Evalina Anderson and David Porter were married and on their way to New Orleans, where Porter was to serve as commander of the United States naval station for two years—and, in a twist of fate, to adopt as his son a future hero named David Glasgow Farragut (*page 124*). Brave, brilliant, impulsive and generous—this was the man who commanded the *Essex* in the fall of 1811 as war approached.

The *Essex'* new captain spent all that winter and the next spring shaping the frigate's 300-man crew to his standards on training cruises off the Virginia and New York coasts. Though the *Essex'* armament and sailing qualities may have put her at a grave disadvantage, Porter was determined to make her as deadly as possible. At all times of the day, and even in the dead of night, a sudden roll of the drums by the *Essex'* Marine band might signal the men to turn to, cutlasses and dirks in hand, for boarding and hand-to-hand combat drill. Years later, David Farragut, then a revered full admiral, observed that whenever he had been on a ship where *Essex* veterans were serving, "I found them to be the best swordsmen on board, every man with his cutlass as sharp as a razor."

Despite the added expense, Porter also saw to it that gunnery was often practiced with live ammunition, the batteries blasting away at floating wooden targets while the Marines sniped from the yards. All the while, Porter would pace the decks of the *Essex,* urging on his crew. After a particularly sharp drill, he would often issue an extra tot of rum—which naturally made the men more eager still next time around.

On June 13, 1812, the Secretary of the Navy ordered Captain Porter to get the *Essex* ready for extended sea duty as soon as possible. On June 18, war was declared against Great Britain. In two more weeks, the *Essex'* bottom had been scraped and her foremast replaced, and on July 3 Porter stood down New York Bay, setting a course for St. Augustine, Florida. Porter's orders specified that he search Florida waters for a convoy reportedly laden with specie and escorted by the 38-gun frigate *Thetis*. But he was advised that if he failed to locate the convoy, he could use his "sound judgment" in departing from the "letter of these instructions."

For almost a month, Porter searched for the money ships but failed to find them. But then on July 11, near Bermuda, the *Essex'* lookout sighted other prey: seven British ships, banded together in a flotilla, escorted by the 32-gun frigate *Minerva*. That night Porter cleverly swooped in under cover of darkness and cut out the *Samuel and Sarah*, a troop transport with 200 British soldiers bound for Quebec. Not wanting to take the soldiers on board, Porter released the ship after collecting $14,000 from

Firing her first and only broadside in a battle that lasted scarcely eight minutes, the Essex overpowers the British sloop of war Alert in the Atlantic on August 13, 1812. With "so trifling a skirmish," as Captain David Porter called it, the Alert became the U.S. Navy's first British warship prize in the two-month-old war.

the captain's strongbox. Two days later the *Essex* took the merchant brig *Lamprey*, sailing alone from Jamaica with a cargo of rum; another merchantman, the brig *Leander* with a cargo of salt and coal from Liverpool, was bagged on July 26. Both were sent to Baltimore as prizes.

The first two weeks of August yielded five additional captures in waters north of Bermuda. Each vessel was taken with nothing more than a shot across the bow. Two were sent to U.S. ports as prizes, two were burned, since Porter was by now running out of crew to man the prizes, and the fifth was loaded with British seamen and sent on its way to St. Johns, Newfoundland. Then, on the morning of August 13—a lucky 13 as it turned out—the *Essex* met the 20-gun British sloop of war *Alert*.

Porter had a plan for just such a contingency, and his crew had rehearsed it well. The *Essex'* gunports remained closed; her sails were trimmed in lubberly fashion, and a drag was streamed over the side. Believing the *Essex* to be a slow-sailing merchantman, the not very astute captain of the *Alert* quickly drew up to Porter and opened fire. The *Essex* immediately ran out her guns and returned the broadside, with crushing interest. Aghast to discover that he had been duped by the Americans, and obviously outgunned at point-blank range, Captain Thomas Laugharne struck the *Alert*'s colors in but eight minutes. The *Essex* thus won the distinction of being the first Yankee warship to capture a British warship in the War of 1812.

In keeping with the chivalrous practice of the times, Porter then allowed Laugharne to sail his ship to Newfoundland so he could disembark his crew, after which he was honor-bound to surrender the *Alert* to American authorities in New York. And that is exactly what the honorable Captain Laugharne did.

After eight weeks at sea, Porter had taken nine British ships. He had meant it to be a short cruise, and he needed reprovisioning. On September 7, he slipped through a British blockading squadron and entered Delaware Bay. No sooner had he anchored near Chester than he wrote to the Secretary of the Navy, "I have the satisfaction to reflect that I have been a great annoyance to the enemy. The injury I have done them in less than two months may be fairly estimated at $300,000. I hope, however, to have another slap at them ere long that will gall them still more."

Porter also requested that he be given another ship. Though the fight with the *Alert* had been no contest, Porter wondered what might have happened had the two ships engaged at long range instead of point-blank. He would, he wrote the Secretary of the Navy, even accept a smaller vessel, because of his "insuperable dislike to Carronades, that render the *Essex* the worst frigate in the service." But no other suitable ship was available; Porter was ordered to remain with the *Essex*, and on October 6 he was told to prepare, at once, for a long cruise.

The *Essex* was directed to rendezvous with the *Constitution* and the *Hornet* in the South Atlantic and form a commerce-raiding squadron under the command of Commodore William Bainbridge. Writing to a friend before leaving, Porter confided: "It may be many months before you hear of my arrival in the U.S., and if you hear of me at all, I hope the accounts may not be unfavorable."

Porter's instructions from Washington directed him to proceed eastward to the Cape Verde Islands, then back west across the Atlantic to the island of Fernando de Noronha, off the coast of Brazil, where Bainbridge would be waiting with the *Constitution* and the *Hornet*. From there the American squadron would be free to raid British commerce in the South Atlantic, or in the Pacific if the opportunity arose.

Departing Delaware Bay on October 28, 1812, the *Essex* reached the harbor of Praia in the Cape Verde Islands without incident, and quickly shaped a course for Fernando de Noronha. Porter was within two days' sail of the island when he made his first capture. A small ship was sighted and hailed, and when she tried to escape, Porter brought her about with a warning musket volley. She proved to be the British packet *Nocton*, carrying a $55,000 cargo of specie. Finding her "well calculated for the United States service," Porter put a prize crew on board and sent her off while he continued on his way to Fernando de Noronha.

But Bainbridge was not at the rendezvous, so Porter set sail for the next point, Cabo Frio on the coast of Brazil. On December 28, Porter came on a six-ship British convoy bound from Rio de Janeiro to England, and captured the schooner *Elizabeth*, which proved so leaky that she had to be burned. Porter raced northeast after the rest of the convoy but then lost his quarry in a storm and resumed his search for Commodore Bainbridge and his small American squadron.

However, Bainbridge was neither at Cabo Frio nor at Santa Catarina

Island, the final rendezvous spot 500 miles farther south along the coast. At last, on January 26, 1813, Porter learned from a Portuguese merchant captain that an American frigate had beaten a British frigate near Rio, and that a second American ship had been lost to the British. The captain also reported that a large British squadron of ships from England was on its way to crush the Americans.

Porter surmised from the captain's report that the victorious American frigate was the *Constitution*, and that the *Hornet* had been lost (actually she was unharmed). Speculating that Bainbridge would return to the United States after a major battle—as in fact he had—Porter made a bold decision. He would double Cape Horn, raid enemy commerce in the vast reaches of the Pacific, and live off his prizes.

By venturing into the Pacific, Porter was following in the wake of the legendary British raider commanders of the past two centuries. In 1578, Francis Drake, sailing the *Golden Hind*, rounded Cape Horn and terrorized Spanish shipping from Peru to the Philippines. Less than a decade later, in 1587, Captain Thomas Cavendish circumnavigated the globe, returning to England with a vast amount of gold taken from the annual Manila-to-Acapulco treasure ship. Porter's personal idol was Lord George Anson, who entered the Pacific in 1741, in the *Centurion*, and captured the Spanish treasure ship *Covadonga*, laden with £500,000 in gold, a treasure so immense that it required 32 oxcarts to transport it all to the security of the Tower of London upon Anson's return home. Porter wrote to a friend that he hoped to duplicate or surpass Anson's exploits, and at the expense of British commerce. Porter said he would give back to Anson's "haughty government, some of the evils to which he had subjected the pusillanimous and unprepared Spaniards."

The *Essex* had sailed from the Delaware capes with 319 officers and men, about 75 more than her usual complement. Porter planned to use these extra sailors as prize crews aboard the merchantmen he intended to capture. But they made conditions even more cramped than usual, and Porter let some of the men sling their hammocks on the roomy gun deck rather than on the berth deck. To prevent scurvy on the long, arduous voyage ahead, Porter now put in at Santa Catarina to take on as many fresh vegetables and fruits as possible. New stores of salt meat, biscuit, flour, rice, vinegar, sugar and fresh drinking water were loaded. And on January 26, 1813, Porter shaped a course south down the Brazilian coast toward Cape Horn at the tip of South America.

To his crew, Porter issued a written pronouncement. "Sailors and Marines," it began, "a large increase of the enemy's forces compels us to abandon this coast. We will, therefore, proceed to annoy them where we are least expected. What was never performed, we will attempt. The unprotected British commerce on the coast of Chile, Peru, and Mexico will give you an abundant supply of wealth; and the girls of the Sandwich Islands shall reward you for your sufferings during the passage around Cape Horn."

The *Essex* arrived off the Horn on February 13. Rather than attempt the confined inland passage through the Strait of Magellan, Porter opted for the open ocean and a voyage that would take the *Essex* clear around the outer periphery of the Tierra del Fuego archipelago. But fierce head

A COMPLETE LIST OF THE AMERICAN N

Showing the Name, Number of Guns, Commander's name, and Station of each Vessel, to July 1, 18

Names.	Guns.	Commanders.	Present Station.
Adams,	32	C. Morris,	Near Alexandria Vir.
Alert, b.	18	J. Renshaw,	New-York
Argus,	18	Lt. Allen,	On a cruise
Adeline,	—	—— ——	Chesapeake Bay
Asp.	—	Lt. Smith,	Lake Ontario
Ætna, bomb			
Analostan,	—	Smith,	Cartel Service
Boston,	32	—— ——	Washington, repairing
Constitution,	44	C. Stewart,	Boston, do.
Constellation	36	C. Gordon,	Norfolk.
Congress,	36	J. Smith,	On a cruise,
Carolina,	14	—— ——	Southern coast.
Conquest,	8	Lt. Pettigrew,	Lake Ontario.
Comet.*	14	Lt. Boyle,	Chesapeake Bay.
D. of Gloucester, b	12	—— ——	Sacket's Harbour,
Despatch,	—	Lt. Page,	Norfolk
Essex,	32	D. Porter	On a cruise
Enterprize,	14	Lt. Blakely,	Eastern coast
Elizabeth,	2	—— ——	Lake Ontario
Fair American	4	Lt. Chauncey,	Ditto
Ferret,	—	Lt. Crawley,	Southern coast
Gen. Pike,	32	A. Sinclair,	Sacket's Harbour,
Growler,	5	Lt. Mix,	Lake Ontario
Gov. Tompkins	6	Lt. Brown,	Ditto
Hornet,	18	Lt. Biddle,	New-London
Hamilton,	9	Lt. M'Pherson,	Lake Ontario
John Adams,	20	—— ——	New-York
Isaac Hull,	10	Lt. Newcomb,	Massachusetts Bay
Julia,	2	Lt. Trant,	Lake Ontario
Louisiania,	20	—— ——	————
Lady of the Lake,	3	—— ——	Lake Ontario
Macedonian, b.	38	J. Jones,	New-London
Madison,	28	I. Chauncey,	Lake Ontario
Mary, bomb,		—— ——	Ditto
New-York,	36	—— ——	Washington, repairing
Neptune,	—	Lt. Jones,	To Russia
Nonsuch,	13	Lt. Mork,	Southern coast
Oneida,	18	Lt. Woolsey	Lake Ontario
Ontario	1	Lt. Stephens,	Ditto
President,	44	Com. Rodgers,	On a c
President,	12	M'Donnough,	Lake
Petapsco,*	12	Mortimer,	Chesap
Perseverance	—	Dill,	Cartel
Pert,	3	Lt. Adams,	Lake
Raven,	8	—— ——	di
Revenge,*	16	West,	Chesap
Syren,	14	Lt. Bainbridge,	Easter
Scourge,	8	Lt. Osgood,	Lake C
Spitfire, bomb,			
Scorpion,	6	Lt. Kennedy,	Chesap
Troup,	18	—— ——	Southe
Viper,	12	Gadsden	—

STEELE'S List of the Royal Navy of Great Bri

N. B. The Ships in Italic were taken from the enemy; and the letters after each denote the power from whom taken; a. signifying American, b Batavian, d. Danis

74 Abercrombie, f. W. C. Fabie
74 Aboukir.
74 Achilles, A. P. Holles
74 Ajax, Sir R. Lawrie, bt.
74 Alfred, J. S. Horton.
74 America, J. Rowley.
74 Armada, G. Grant.
74 Asia, A. Shippard.
74 Assistance, Com. R. Mends.
64 Africa, Rr-Adm. H. Sawyer, capt. J. Bastard.
64 Ardent, G. Bell.
64 Argonaut, f. (Hos. Ship) Lt. J. James.
50 Adamant, V. Ad. W. A. Otway, capt. M. Buckle
50 Antelope, Ad. Sir J. T. Duckworth, K. B. Capt.
44 Argo, C. Quinton.
40 Acasta, A. R. Kerr
38 Africaine, f. Hon. E. Rodney
38 Alcmene, f. E. L. Graham
38 Andromache, b. G. Tobin
38 Amelia, f. Hon. F. P. Irby
38 Apollo
38 Arethusa
38 Armide, f. F. Temple
36 Aigle, Sir J. Louis, bt.
36 Astrea, C. M. Schomberg
32 Æolus, Ld. J. Townsend
32 Aquilon, W. Bowles
20 Acorn, G. M. Bligh
18 Achates, f. I. Davies
18 Ablicore, H. T. Davies
18 Amaranth, G. Pringle
18 Apelles, C. Robb
18 Arab, J. Wilson
18 Arachne, C. H. Watson
18 Ariel, D. Ross
18 Atalante, F. Hickey
16 Abundance, J. Oake
16 Acteon, f. B. C. Cator
16 Alonzo, J. Bayley
16 Avenger, U. Johnstone
14 Acute, Lt. J. A. Morrell
14 Agressor, Lt. J. Watson
14 Antelope, s. Lt. D. Boyd
12 Arrow, Lt. Scriven
10 Adonis, Lt. D. Buchan
10 Alban, Lt. W. S. Key
10 Algerine, Lt T Greensword
10 Alphan, Lt Jones
8 Ætna (Bb)
98 Barfleur, Sir E. Berry, bt.
98 Boyne, Rr-Adm. Sir H. B. Neale, bt capt. C. Jones
80 Brave, f. (PS) Lt H. Raye
74 Bahama, s. (PS) Lt J. Milne
74 Barham, J. W. Spranger
74 Bedford, J. Walker
74 Bellerophon, Rr-Adm J. Ferrier, capt. J. Halstead
74 Bellona, Rr-Adm G. J. Hope, capt. G. M'Kinley
74 Berwic, E. Brace
74 Blake, E. Codrington
74 Bombay, N. Thompson
74 Brunswic, (PS) lt J H Sparkes
74 Bulwark, Rr-adm C. P. Durham, capt. J. A. Worth
64 Bienfaifant, f. (PS) Lt W. H. Boyce
64 Bristol, E. Wyndham
50 Batavier, b. (HS) Lt. T. D. Birchall
38 Bacchante, W. Hoste
38 Belle Poule, f. G. Harris
38 Briton, Sir T. Staines kt
36 Belvidera, B. Byron
36 Brune, f.
32 Bucephalus, W. J. Lye
18 Banterer, C. Ward
18 Baracouta
18 Beagle, J. Smith
18 Blossom, I. B. Rowley
18 Bonne Citoyenne, f. G. Green
18 Briseis, I. Ross
18 Brisk, E. Boansher

16 Badger, J. L. Manley
16 Bustard, C. A. Strong
14 Basilisk, Lt G. French
14 Brevdageren, d. Lt T. P. Devon
14 Bruizer, Lt W. Price
10 Britomart, W. B. Hunt
8 Ballahou, Lt N. King
120 Caledonia, J. Coghlan
80 Christian, VII d. H. L. Ball
74 Canada, (PS) Lt W. B. Watts
74 Centaur, J. C. White
74 Chatham, Rr-adm M. H. Scot capt. R. Mansel
74 Clarence, H. Vansittart
74 Colossus, T. Alexander
74 Conquestador, Lord W Stuart
74 Cornwal, J. Broughton
74 Courageux, P. Wilkinson
74 Cressy, C. Dashwood
74 Cumberland, T. Baker
64 Caton, f. (HS) Lt. W. Brett
64 Crown, (PS) Lt W. Wickham
50 Centurion, (RS)
36 Chesapeake, a
38 Ceylon
38 Crescent, J. Quilliam
38 Clorinde, f. T. Briggs
36 Curacoa, J. Tower
32 Castor, C. Dilkes
32 Cerberus, T. Garth
32 Ceres, (RS) Lt E. Leigh
32 Circe, E. Woolcombe
32 Cleopatra, J. Pechell
32 Cornelia, W. F. Owen
32 Comus, M. Smith
22 Cossack, W. King
22 Crocodile, W. Elliot
20 Comet, G. W. Blaney
20 Cyane, T. Forrest
18 Calypso
18 Castilian, D. Braimer
18 Cephalus, E. Flyn
18 Charybdis, J. Clephane
18 Cherub, T. T. Tucker
18 Childers, J. Bedford
18 Clio, W. Farrington
18 Colibri, J. Thomson
18 Columbine, R. H. Muddle
18 Crane, J. Stuart
18 Cretan, f. C. F. Payne
18 Crocus, A. Adderly
18 Cruiser, T. R. Toker
18 Curlew, M. Head
18 Cygnet, R. Russel
18 Calliope, J. M'Kerlie
16 Charger, J. Askew
16 Corso, s. lt. G. Taylor
16 Cormorant
14 Censor, lt. M. R. Lucas
14 Centinel, lt. W. King
14 Cheerly, H. F. Pogson
14 Conquest, lt. W. Boswell
14 Constant, lt. J. Stokes
14 Cracker, lt. M. Fitton
12 Confounder, lt. J. Valobra
10 Cadmus, T. Fife
10 Chanticleer, R. Spear
10 Cheerful, lt. J. Smith
10 Cherokee, W. Ramage
10 Cordelia, T. F. Kennedy
4 Cuttle, lt. W. Paterson
74 Dannemark, d. H E R Baker
74 Defiance, R. Raggett
74 Dragon, Rr-adm. Sir F. Laforey, bt capt T. Forrest
74 Duncan, R. Lambert
64 Diadem, J. Pechell.
64 Dictator, J. Hanwell
50 Diomede, E H Fabian
44 Dolphin, A. Black
38 Doris
38 Dromedary, S. P. Pritchard
36 Dœdalus, f. M. Maxwell
36 Desiree, f. A. Farquhar
63 Dryad, E. Galwey
32 Druid, F. Stanfell
22 Daphne, P. Pipon

18 Dauntless, D. Barber
18 Demarara, W. H. Smith
18 Derwent, G. M. Sutton
18 Dotterell, W. W. Daniel
16 Diligence
16 Drake, G. Grant
14 Daring, lt. W. R. Pascoe
14 Desperate, L. W. Jenkins
14 Dexterous, lt. N. Tomlinson
14 Diligente, f. E. Ives
12 Dapper, lt. H. Harford
12 Decouverte, lt. R. Williams
12 Defender, lt. M'Cannadey
12 Depford, (tend.) lt. J. Debenham
10 Decoy, lt. J. Pearse
10 Dart, lt. Allen
10 Dominica, R. Hockings
10 Dwarf, lt. S. Gordon
8 Devastation, (Bb) T Alexander
74 Eagle, C. Rowley
74 Edinburgh, R. Rolles
74 Egmont, J. Bingham
74 Elizabeth, E. L. Gower
74 Elephant, C. J. Austen
64 Europe, (PS) lt. W. Styles
44 Experiment, (RS) lt. J. Slade
36 Euryalus, G. H. L. Dundas
28 Enterprise, (RS) lt. C Barker
18 Echo, T. Perceval
18 Eclair, J. Bellamy
18 Eclipse, H. Lynne
18 Egeria, L. Hole
18 Electra, f. W. Gregory
18 Emulous, a W. H. Mulcaster
18 Enchantress, (GS and PS) lt. J. Pasley
18 Erebus, H. J. Lyford
18 Espoir, R. Milford
18 Espiegle, J. Taylor
14 Earnest, lt. R. Templer
14 Escort, lt. G. V. Crosbie
12 Elizabeth, E. F. Dwyer
12 Evertion, lt. Murray
10 Entreprenante, f.
6 Ems, d.
80 Foudroyant, R. T. Hancock
74 Fame, W. Bathurst
74 Firme, s. (PS) Lt. H. Boyce
74 Fyen, d. (PS.) Lt. E. N. Greensword
38 Freya, d. W. J. Scott
38 Furieuse, f. W. Mounsey
36 Fortunee, G. F. Seymour
36 Franchise, f. R. Buck
36 Frederickstein, d. D F. Beaufort
32 Fox, D. Paterson
22 Fylla, d. H. Prescott
20 Favorite, R. Forbes
20 Fawn, T. Fellowes
18 Fantome, f. J. Lawrence
18 Ferret, A. Halliday
18 Forester, A. Kennedy
18 Frolic
16 Foxhound, J. Parish
14 Fancy, Lt A. Sinclair
14 Fearless, Lt C. Basden
14 Flamer, Lt T. England
14 Forward, Lt R. Bankes
14 Furious, Lt J. Mundell
12 Fairy, E. Grey
12 Fervent, Lt G. Stewart
8 Furnace, (Bb)
4 Fierce
98 Glory, (PS) Lt R. Tyle
74 Ganges, Lt F. J. Leroux
74 Genereux, Lt J. Allen
74 Glocester, R. Williams
74 Guilford, (PS.) Lt J. Crouch
50 Glatton, R. G. Peacock
50 Grampus, R. Barrie
44 Gladiator, R. Adm. W. Hargood, capt. C. Hewett
44 Gorgon, (HS.) R. Adm. F. Plokmore, capt Mainwaring
36 Galatea, W. Losack

38 Guerriere* f. capt J R Dacres
3 Glenmore, (RS.)
22 Garland, T. Huskinson
20 Ganymede, f. J. B. Purvis
18 Goree, H. D. Byng
18 Goshawk, Hon W. Napier
18 Guadalope, f. A. Stowe
16 Gannet, J. Porteous
14 Gallant, Lt. W. Crow
14 Growler, Lt. H. Anderson
10 Goldfinch, E. Waller
6 Green Linnet
4 Gleaner, T. Trickey
110 Hibernia, V Ad. Sir E. Pellew bt. 1st capt. Rr-Adm. J. Pellew, 2nd capt. C. S. Smith
74 Hannibal, Sir M. Seymore bt.
74 Hector, (PS.) Lt. A Lighterness
50 Hindostan, D. Weir
38 Horatio, Lord G. Stuart
38 Hussar, J. C. Crawford
36 Hamadryad, s. E. Chethem
36 Havannah, Hon. C. Cadogan
38 Helder, B. J. Serrell
36 Hotspur, Hon. J. Percy
32 Hyperion, W. P. Cumby
20 Hermes, P. Browne
24 Hyæna, (SS.) J. Foxton
18 Harpy, B. N. Hoar
18 Hasty, J. Dickinson
18 Hazard, J. Cooksley
18 Hecate, Hon. H. J. Peachy
18 Helena, H. Montresor
18 Herald, G. Jackson
18 Hesper, H Collier
18 Hyacinth, W. Hamilton
16 Helicon, H. Hopkins
16 Hound, J. Black
14 Haughty, Lt J Harvey
12 Hearty, Lt J Rose
10 Hope, Lt E. W. Garrett
8 Holly, Lt (SS) Treacher
4 Herring, Lieut. J. Murray
98 Impregnable, Adm. W. Young capt E. Griffiths, capt G. C. M'Kenzie
78 Impetueux, f. V. Adm. G. Martin, capt C. Inglis
74 Illustrious, V. Adm. Sir S. Hood, bt K. B. capt. W. H. Webley
74 Implacable, I. R. Watson
74 Invincible, C. Adam
74 Irresistable, (PS) R. Mansell
38 Imperieuse, s. Hon H. Duncan
38 Junon, f. J. Saunders
36 †Java, H. Lambert
36 Inconstant, E. W. C. Owen
36 Iphigenia, L. Burtis
32 Jason, hon. J. W. King
18 Jalouse, A. Lave
18 Indian, H. Jane
6 Imogen, W. Stevens
14 Insolent, f E. Brazier
12 Intelligent, lt. N. Tucker
10 Jasper, H. Jenkinson
18 Juniper, lt N. Vassall
74 Kent, T. Rogers
74 Kron, Princen, d. T. Osmer
74 Kron Pincessen, d. lt. T. Burdwood
18 Kangaroo, J. Lloyd
18 Kingfisher, E. Tritton
16 Kite, B. Crispin
74 La Hogue, hon. T. B. Capel
74 Leviathan, P. Campbell
64 Leyden, b. J. Davie
64 Lyon, Rr-Ad hon R. Stopford, capt. hon. G. Douglas

* Captured on the 19th of August 1812, by the United States' frigate Constitution, Captain Hull, and destroyed.

† Captured by the United States' frigate Constitution, Captain Bainbridge, and destroyed.

50 Leopard, W. H. Dillon
38 Lavinia, G. Digby
38 Leonidas, A. I. Griffiths
38 Loire, f. T. Brown
36 Latona, hon R. Rodney
36 Leda, G. Sayer
28 Lille Belte, d
24 Laurestinus, T. Graham
18 Lightning, B. C. Doyle
16 Leveret, Sir G. W. Willes, K.
14 Liberty, lt. G. Guise
14 Linnet, lt. J. Treacy
14 Locust, lt. R. Fair
10 Lynx,
10 Lyra, lt. R. Bloye
80 Malta f. Rr-Ad B. Hallowell capt. S. H. Inglefield
74 Magnificent J. Hayes
74 Marengo, f. lt. H. Squire
74 Marlborough, Rr-Adm. G. Cockburn, capt. B. Ross
74 Mars, H. Raper
74 Milford, Rr-Adm T. F. Freemantle, cap. J. D. Markland
74 Minden, A. Skene
74 Montaque, Rr-Adm M. Dixon, capt M. H. Dixon
74 Mulgrave, T. J. Maling
64 Monmouth, Rr-Adm T. Folsy, capt W. Nowell
50 Malabar, (SS.) F. Bradshaw
38 Macedonian,* J. S. Carden
38 Melpomene, f G. Falcon
36 Magicienne, Hon. W. Gordon
36 Maidstone, G. Burdett
36 Malacca, W. Butterfield
36 Melampus
36 Menelaus, Sir P. Parker, bt.
36 Modeste, f. Hon. Elliot
32 Medusa, hon. P. D. Bouverie
36 Mermaid, D. Dunn
32 Minerva, R. Hawkins
28 Mercury, C. Milward
20 Minstrel, J. S. Peyton
18 Metor, (Bb.) P. Fisher
18 Minorca, R. Wormeley
18 Morgiana, C. Scott
18 Moselle, H. Litchfield
18 Mosquito, J. Tomkinson
18 Mutine, N. De Courcy
16 Magnet, F. M. Maurice
16 Merope
16 Maria, lt. Blight
14 Manly, E. Collier
14 Mariner, lt. J. Russell
14 Martial, lt. C. T. Leavers
14 Morne Fortune, f. lt. J. Steele
14 Muros, J. Aberdour
10 Mullet, lt. Evans
8 Misletoe, lt. Williams
4 Mackarel, lt. T. H. Hughes
74 Namur, Rr-adm Sir T. Williams, kt capt C J Austen
74 Norge, d. J S Rainier
74 Northumberland, H Hotham
64 Nassau, d. lt. W Field
38 Niemen, f. S Pym
38 Niobe, f. W J Montague
38 Nisus, P Beaver
38 Nymphe, F P Epworth
36 Nymphen, d. J Hancock
32 Narcissus, J R Lumley
32 Nereus, P Heywood
32 Niger, (P & HS) lt. Todman
28 Nemesis, Hon J A Maude
20 North Star, T. Coe
18 Nautilus, P. Dench
18 Nimrod, F. Mitchell
16 Nancy, lt. J A Kilwick
16 Nightingale, C. Nixon
14 Netley, lt. G. Green,
14 Nonpareil, lt. J C Sherwin
98 Ocean, R Plampin

* Captured by the United States' frigate United States, Com. Decatur—The Macedonian now belongs to the American Navy.

74 Orion, Sir A C Dickson bt
36 Oiseau, f. lt. W Needham
36 Orlando, J Clavell
36 Orpheus, H Pigot
36 Owen Glendower, B Hodgson
18 Osprey
16 Oberon, J Murray
16 Orestes, W R Smith
10 Onyx, lt. C Squire
10 Olympia, lt. W Witzdeyer
10 Opossum, T. Wolridge
10 Ortenza, lt. E Blaquier
98 Prince of Wales, J E Dougles
74 Pegase, f. (PS) lt. G. Decœurdoux
74 Pembroke, J. Brisbane
74 Plantagenet, R Lloyd
74 Pompee, f. Sir J. A Wood kt
74 Poictiers, Sir J P Beresford kt
74 Princess Caroline d. H Downman
74 Princess Sophia, d. lt. Bligh
74 Puissant, f. B W Page
64 Prince Frederic, Rr-adm E Buller, bt capt J S Grove
64 Prothee, f. (PS) lt. T Bird
50 Panther, (PS) lt. J Harrison
40 Prevoyante, f. (SS)
38 Pomone, f. F W Fane
38 President, f. S Warren
36 Phœbe, J Hillyar
36 Phœnix, J. Bowen
36 Pique, f. Hon. A Maitland
36 Pyramus, J W D Dundas
28 Princess, b. (GS) J Galloway
24 Porcupine, R. Elliot
18 Papillion, J Hay
18 Partridge, J M Adye
18 *Peacock, W. Peake
18 Pelorus, J P Rowley
18 Peruvian, A F Westropp
18 Persian, C Bartram
18 Pheasant, J. Palmer
18 Philomel, G H Guion
18 Pilot, I T Nicolas
18 Plover, C Campbell
18 Podargus, W Robillard
18 Port Mahon, F W Burgoyne
18 Procris, J Norton
18 Prospero, J H Godby
18 Pylades, J Wemyes
16 Paulina, W Percival
16 Peteral
16 Phipps, d. T Wells
16 Pickle, f. lt. W Figg
16 Porpoise, T Stokes
14 Partian, J H Garetty
14 Piercer, lt. J Kneeshaw
14 Pincher, lt. S Burgess
14 Portia, H Thompson
14 Protector, lt. G Mitchener
12 Plumper, lt. J Bray
10 Patriot, lt. W Hutchinson
10 Paz, s. lt. P Dumaressy
10 Pigmy, lt. E Moore
10 Pioneer, lt. Morris
98 Queen, Lord Colville
4 Quail, lt. J Osborn
110 Royal George
110 Royal Sovereign, J Bissete
80 Royal William, (GS) Adm Sir R Bickerton, bt capt Fowler
74 Ramilies, Sir T Hardy, bt
74 Repulse, R H Moubray
74 Revenge, Sir J Gore, kt
74 Rodney, G D King
74 Royal Oak, Rr-adm. Lord A Beauclerc, capt T Shortland
64 Raisonable, E S Clay
64 Ruby Com. A F Evans
44 Regulus, J Tailour
38 Resistance, P L Rosenhagen
38 Revolutionaire, f. T E Woolcombe

* Captured by United States sloop of war Hornet, Capt. Lawrence, and destroyed.

38 Roto, d. P Somerville
36 Rhin, f. C Malcosm
36 Romulus, G W H Knight
18 Racehorse, J De Rippe
18 Racoon, W Black
18 Raleigh, G W Hooper
18 Recruit, H F Senhouse
18 Redwing, E A King
18 Reindeer
18 Rifleman, J Pearce
18 Ringdove, W Dowers
18 Rosamond, D Campbell
18 Rosario, W Henderson
18 Rose, T Mansell
18 Rover, I Finley
18 Royalist, G Downie
16 Ranger, G Acklon
16 Rapid, W Mather
16 Rattler, A Gordon
16 Raven, G G Lennock
16 Redpole, A Fraser,
16 Reynard, H Stewart
14 Redbreast, lt. Sir G Keith, bt
14 Richmond, E O Shaugnessy
14 Rinaldo, Sir W G Parker bt
12 Rebuff, lt C Jones
12 Resolute, lt J W Greene
10 Rhodian, G Moubray
10 Rolla, S Clark
112 St. Salvador del munda, s. (GS) V Adm Sir R Calder, bt capt J Nash
112 San Josef, s. Adm Ld Keith, K B & K C capt G Malcolm, capt S Jackson
90 Sussex, (HS) lt. W Cockeraft
80 San Nicolas, s. (PS) lt. J R. Mould
74 San Antonio, (PS) lt. Squire
74 San Domaso, s. (PS) lt. T Thompson
74 San Domingo, Rt Hon Sir J B Warren, bt and K B capt C Gill
74 San Ildefonso, s. (SS) lt. F Harley
74 San Juan, s. (RS) Com G V Penrose
74 San Ysidro, s. (PS) lt. G J Decœurdoux
74 Sceptre, T Harvey
74 Scipion, f. H Heathcote
74 Stirling-Castle, J Brenton
74 Suffolk, (PS) lt A Gilmour
74 Sultan, J West
74 Superb, Hon C Paget
74 Swiftsure, E S Dickson
64 Sampson, (PS) J Steventon
64 Standard, Hon C E Fleming
64 Stately, W Stewart
44 Serapis, W Lloyd
38 Salsette, H Hope
38 Shannon, P B V Broke
38 Sir Francis Drake
38 Spartan, E P Brenton
38 Statira, H Stockpole
38 Surprise, Sir T Cochrane, bt
38 Surveillante, f. E Tucker
38 Sybille, f. C Upton
38 Semiramis, Rr-Adm C Tyle, capt C Richardson
36 Stag, P Hornby
32 Solebay, V Adm R Murray, capt R Curry
32 Success, T Barclay
20 Sabrina, A R M'Kenzie
18 Sabine, E Wrottesley
18 Sambrang, b. J Drury
18 Sapphire, H Haynes
18 Sappho, H O'Gready
18 Scorpion, R Giles
18 Scout, A R Sharpe
18 Scylla, C M'Donald
18 Sea Lark, J Warrand
18 Sake
18 Sophie, N Lockyer
18 Sparrow-hawk, J Pringle
18 Spitfire, J Ellis

18 Stork, R L C
18 Surinam, b S
18 Swallow, E R
18 Sylph, W. Ev
16 Savage, W Bi
16 Shark, (RS
16 Sheldrake, J
16 Sparrow, J N
16 Spy, R Anders
16 Strombolo, (B
16 Swaggerer, lt.
16 Swift, W Mou
16 Seahorse,
14 Sea-Flower,
14 Sharpshooter,
14 Snap, G R Sa
14 Snipe, lt. C C
14 Spider, f. F G
14 Sprightly, lt. J
14 Starling, lt. C
14 Staunch, lt. H
14 Steady, lt. G
14 Strenuous, lt.
12 Sylvia, lt. R F
10 Sharpedon, T
10 Shearwater, W
10 Somers, lt. G
10 Surly, lt. R W
8 Subtle, d. lt.
74 Theseus, W P
74 Tigre, f. J H
74 Tremendous, Smith, knt
74 Triumph,
64 Trident, (GS Laugharne, cent
50 Trusty, (PS,)
58 Tenedos, H
36 Theban, S T
36 Trent, V A brough, capt
36 Tribune, G
32 Thames, C N
28 Thisbe, Rr-A ilton, bt capt
20 Talbot S Sw
20 Tartarus, J P
20 Termagant,
20 Thais, E Seo
20 Tortoise, T C
18 Thracian, J
18 Trinculo, A
18 Tweed, T E
16 Thorn, G Cr
16 Tisiphone, W
16 Tuscan, G M
14 Teaser
14 Thrasher, lt
12 Tigress, lt W
20 Thistle, J K
10 Tickler, lt S
10 Tyrian, A B
8 Thunder, (B
8 Trial, lt T S
110 Ville de Pari
100 Victory, V marez, bt
98 Union
74 Valiant, R D
74 Venerable, E
74 Vengeance, wards
74 Vengeur, T
74 Victorious, J
74 Vigo, Rr-Ad capt H M O
64 Veterian, lt
64 Vigilant, (P ville
44 Ulysses, Rr- capt W. Fo
40 Unite, f. E
38 Volontaire, Waldegrav
38 Undaunted,
36 Venus, d. K
32 Unicorn, G

PRINTED AND PUBLISHED BY JOHN LOW, NO. 17 CHATHAM-STREET, NEW-YORK.—And sold by him wholesale and

winds and a tremendous sea forced him to hazard the dangerous Le Maire Strait just east of Cape Horn between the mainland and one of the Tierra del Fuego islands. By great good fortune, the weather improved just as the *Essex* reached the passage and she made the traverse with remarkable ease. But five days later, shortly after she had rounded Cape Horn itself, the light frigate was struck by a storm of terrible intensity.

For three days, the *Essex* was forced to run south before the wind until she could head west again. On February 28, just as the wind appeared to be easing off, the frigate was struck a second time. Now the seas mounted to such extraordinary heights that the *Essex* stood in danger of being swamped. The crew, weak with fatigue and anxiety, saw only continuous lines of boiling breakers marching on them from the west. On March 3, a tremendous sea stove in the ship's boats and as she plunged sickeningly into the trough a number of her gunports were smashed from the bow to the quarter, leaving her deluged and waterlogged.

Now she swung broadside to the waves, which pounded her mercilessly. The pumps could not handle the torrents of water rushing aboard, and she began to settle. Some men stood paralyzed by fear; others fell on their knees to pray. One man cried that the ship was going down.

After being knocked down three times by the breaking seas, Porter was so groggy that he had to be helped to his cabin. A stalwart bosun's mate roared at the crew, "Damn your eyes, put your best foot forward." The men at the wheel rallied, and slowly brought the *Essex* around until she was no longer broadside to the waves. Battered and with an exhausted crew, the *Essex* struggled on—until on March 4, after five days of horror, the tempest died and she could head for Valparaiso, Chile.

The American sailors found the Chileans cordial hosts. José Miguel Carrera, who had successfully overthrown the Spanish colonial government, welcomed the visitors—in no small measure because the U.S. envoy, Joel R. Poinsett, had allied himself with the revolutionaries (page 117). While the *Essex* was being refitted and reprovisioned, Porter and his men were guests of honor at a gala round of balls and banquets. With a sailor's eye for beautiful women, Porter found the señoritas "very handsome" with "large dark eyes, remarkably brilliant and expressive." But he cared less for the local addiction to a tea called maté, which he said produced "rotten teeth and unsavory breaths."

By March 23, 1813, the *Essex* was ready for sea again, and Porter took leave of Valparaiso, heading for the offshore whaling grounds where there were sure to be British ships. Outward bound, the *Essex* overtook and boarded the Peruvian privateer *Nereyda* without a struggle. Still loyal to Spain, the Peruvians considered themselves friends of the British, and the *Nereyda* had been attacking American whaling ships. For some reason, Porter did not take her as a prize. But he did strip the vessel

Underscoring the David and Goliath nature of the War, this 1813 American broadside compares the roster of 55 U.S. Navy vessels with a British publisher's catalogue of the Royal Navy's 862 warships. One fascinating sidelight of the British list is that 174 of the vessels (proudly shown in italics) had been captured from enemies: 96 were French, 39 Danish, 18 Spanish, 18 Dutch (listed as "b," for Batavian) and three American.

of all her ammunition and throw all of her guns overboard before letting her go. A few days later, Porter recaptured the Nantucket whaler *Barclay*, which was being sailed by a prize crew from the *Nereyda*. The *Barclay*'s own crew had been imprisoned in the hold, and upon being released, the Yankee whalemen quickly agreed to have the *Barclay* accompany Porter to the Galápagos Islands.

By the middle of April, the *Essex* and her consort were off the Galápagos, with their fabulous flora and fauna. From the American whalemen, Porter learned to value the islands' giant tortoises, which weighed as much as 300 pounds and could be stored alive in the *Essex*' hold for months without appreciable loss of weight. Porter wrote that the flesh of the giant tortoise made a "wholesome, luscious and delicate food. The finest green turtle is no more to be compared to them than the coarsest beef to the finest veal." More important, the whalemen led him to the "post office" on Charles Island—a box nailed to a post, used as a message drop by both American and British whalers. A quick glance at the stack of mail disclosed to Porter the whereabouts of a number of British ships in the area.

On April 29, the *Essex* captured her first British whaler, the *Montezuma*, which surrendered after a volley of musket fire. The same day, the *Essex* took the whalers *Georgiana* and *Policy*. Both were crowded with Americans. A number of them were Nantucketers who had signed on British ships after their own whalers had been destroyed during the Revolutionary War; others were men who had at one time been impressed into the Royal Navy and then had drifted over to British merchant ships after their release. In any case, both groups retained a loyalty to the United States and cheered when the British flag came down. The three whalers were laden with cordage, canvas, paint, tar—and provisions, which, according to Porter, "removed all apprehensions of our suffering for the want of them." In addition to the naval stores, the Americans recovered 50 giant tortoises, cast overboard by the English.

The gleeful Porter was moved to issue another pronouncement. "Fortune has at length smiled on us, because we deserved her smiles," he declared. "The first time she enabled us to display *free trade and sailors' rights*, she put in our possession near half a million of the enemy's property." Porter predicted that "we will yet render the name of the *Essex* as terrible to the enemy as that of any other vessel."

He then directed that one of the captured whalers, the *Georgiana*, be fitted out as an auxiliary raider. To her six 18-pound guns were added ten 6-pounders from the *Policy*. For a crew she had 41 men from the *Essex* plus five American volunteers from her original complement. On May 9, under the command of Lieutenant John Downes, the *Georgiana* ran up the Stars and Stripes, and with three ringing cheers from the men of the *Essex*, she made off to seek her own prizes.

The *Essex*, with the *Barclay* and Porter's two other prizes, next set sail for an extended cruise around the archipelago. On May 28, the little fleet found more enemy whalers. The next morning, flying false British colors, the *Essex* approached and came alongside the *Atlantic*, a fast British whaler mounting six long 18-pounders. Believing the *Essex* to be an English warship, the *Atlantic*'s captain, Obediah Wyer, confided to Por-

Armed diplomacy by accident

The tumultuous welcome accorded the *Essex* when she called at Valparaiso, Chile, in 1813 was inspired by more than just the sight of a handsome frigate. Unknowingly, Captain David Porter had committed the U.S. Navy's first act of armed diplomacy in Latin America simply by sailing into the port.

At the time, Chile was in revolt against its Spanish overlords, and the U.S. envoy, Joel Poinsett, had sided with the rebels. Poinsett believed that soon "all South America will be separated from the Parent country. They have passed the Rubicon." So without authority he had promised the Chilean rebels U.S. support.

Though the revolutionaries had succeeded in gaining control of Chile, their hold was tenuous at best. And then, on March 14, 1813, in from the sea came the powerful *Essex*. Poinsett was astonished and the Chilean patriots overjoyed.

It was a small incident, and an accident at that. But it presaged a more significant event a decade later, when President James Monroe proclaimed his Monroe Doctrine, which bluntly demanded an end to European colonization in Latin America. As for Joel Poinsett, he continued to dabble in international politics; but he is best remembered for his introduction into the United States of the Mexican flower named for him, the poinsettia.

JOEL ROBERTS POINSETT

ter that although he was a native of America, and his wife and children lived in Nantucket, he had, after all, been born an Englishman, and he was still an Englishman at heart. Porter heard the captain out, then told the astonished man that he was seizing the *Atlantic*. Later that day, the *Essex* captured the *Greenwich*, whose captain refused to surrender until the *Essex* gave him a shot between his masts.

By now Porter's flotilla had grown to six vessels, and they all made sail for the coast of South America, where they were to rendezvous with Lieutenant Downes and the *Georgiana*. In addition to feeding his own men, Porter had to provide for more than 100 British captives and another two dozen rescued Americans. He was anxious to put them ashore and, if he could, to sell one of his prizes. On June 19, he anchored off Tumbes, Peru, where the local governor wisely treated his powerful fleet with respect, and even laid on a fete for the *Essex* men. Before long, the American fleet was more imposing still: the *Georgiana* arrived with the British whalers *Catherine*, *Rose* and *Hector* in tow.

In a little less than two months the Americans had captured eight British whalers worth more than two million dollars, including their rich cargoes of whale oil and bone. Porter reorganized his forces once again. He had the *Atlantic*, the largest and swiftest of his prizes, refitted as the *Essex Junior*, and armed her with ten 6-pound and ten 18-pound guns. The squadrons then split up. While the *Essex*, *Georgiana* and *Greenwich* returned to raid in the Galápagos, the *Essex Junior*, under Lieutenant Downes, convoyed four prizes and the *Barclay* to Valparaiso with orders to sell them and their oil.

But the Chileans had no money for either whale oil or ships. Downes was unable to sell a single one of the prizes, and had to content himself with sending the oil-laden whaler *Policy* back to the United States. The other four whalers remained moored in the harbor.

Worse, after a few weeks in Valparaiso, Downes learned from news brought overland from Buenos Aires that word of the *Essex'* depredations had reached London, and that an enraged Admiralty had sent three warships to find and destroy the *Essex*. These ships were the 36-gun frigate *Phoebe*, and the sloops of war *Cherub* and *Raccoon*, 28 and 22 guns respectively. They had called briefly at Buenos Aires, and had then sailed south to round Cape Horn and hunt down Porter in the Pacific.

Downes immediately hurried to sea in the *Essex Junior* to find Porter and warn him of the British approach.

Porter was far out in the Pacific, still sweeping the seas clean of the British whaling fleet. On July 14, off Charles Island in the Galápagos, Porter sighted three more whalers. The first vessel, the *Charlton*, meekly surrendered. The second ship, the *Seringapatam*, mounting 14 guns, exchanged a broadside with Porter's men on the prize ship *Greenwich* before lowering her colors; at this point, the third ship, the *New Zealander*, hove to.

Porter now had six ships in his little flotilla. He decided to retain the *Seringapatam* and the *New Zealander*, but sent the *Charlton* with 48 British captives around the Horn to Rio de Janeiro. He also decided to dispatch the *Georgiana* around the Horn for the United States with $100,000 worth of captured whale oil.

Nor was Captain Porter quite finished yet. On September 15, the *Essex* came upon and captured the *Sir Andrew Hammond*, while her men were in the process of cutting up a sperm whale. By now, Porter had succeeded in capturing almost every British whaler in the area.

Back home, Americans were jubilant. Wrote Porter's friend Washington Irving of the Pacific voyage: "It occasioned great uneasiness in Great Britain. The merchants who had any property afloat in this quarter trembled with apprehension for its fate; the underwriters groaned at the catalog of captures, while the pride of the nation was sorely incensed at beholding a single frigate lording it over the Pacific, in saucy defiance of their thousand ships." A Canadian newspaper grimly echoed his observation, complaining that the *Essex* had "annihilated our commerce in the South Seas." The frigate, it said, had harmed the British Empire more "than all the rest of the American Navy."

Whatever the economic and psychological effects of the cruise of the *Essex* upon the War of 1812, it was a stunning feat of naval daring. Porter had carried off an extended cruise far from American waters, had lived off the islands and the provisions of his captured ships, and had maintained the health of his crew. There was little more he could do to hurt the British. On September 30, he learned that he was being pursued when Downes in the *Essex Junior* joined his flotilla in the Galápagos. It was time to start looking for a place where he could overhaul his ships in safety before either confronting the British warships or making a run for home.

The *Essex* in particular had to be beached and her hull scoured of barnacles to render her as swift as possible. The rigging needed to be repaired and refitted. The ship was so full of rats that they were eating through the provisions and sails, and even getting into the magazines and destroying the cartridges. Moreover, the men were sorely in need of an extended rest, especially to fight the hand-to-hand combat that Porter anticipated would be necessary if the *Essex*, with her short-range carronades, encountered the British.

When Porter told his men they were heading for the Marquesas, 2,500 miles southeast of Hawaii, they were galvanized. "For the remainder of the passage they could think of nothing but the beauties of the islands," he wrote. Nor were the Americans disappointed on October 25, 1813, when the *Essex*, the *Essex Junior* and four of Porter's prizes put into Taiohae Bay on the southern coast of Nuku Hiva, largest of the Marquesas. After a year of hardship at sea, broken only by a few brief stops here and there, Porter and his men were about to embark on a seven-week South Pacific idyll to outdo their fondest dreams.

Since their discovery in 1596 by the Spanish explorer Alvara de Mendaña y Castro, the Marquesas had been visited by few white men. Before the Americans lay a paradise of white beaches and lush vegetation rising to a small mountain, where cascading waterfalls made rainbows in the sunlight.

Porter went ashore and dazzled the islanders with the fifes and drums of his Marine band, while at the same time announcing his peaceful intentions. The Nuku Hivans swam out to the ships. Laughing and chattering, they sought to exchange breadfruit for fishhooks, iron hoops and glass bottles. A handsome young woman of 18 appeared on the scene and Porter found her "to be of fair complexion and neatly attired, her skin and glossy black hair anointed with cocoa nut oil, her carriage majestic; and her whole appearance striking in the extreme."

A few days later, an aged Nuku Hivan named Gattanewa, chief of the island's Taiis tribe, called upon Porter on board the *Essex*. Gattanewa was tattooed over much of his body and quite drunk from kava, the fermented juice of a tropical root. The groggy chief scarcely blinked when Porter thought to impress him by ordering a cannon to be fired, but he brightened when the American presented a bit of scrimshaw, or carved whale's tooth, which, according to Porter, "seemed to afford him infinite pleasure."

However, the cannon may have been the reason for the chief's visit in the first place, for he soon asked Porter to assist him in his war with the Happahs, another of the 31 tribes on Nuku Hiva. Porter agreed to reflect on the matter, but he could make no decision until the repairs on his ships were completed.

With the aid of Gattanewa's villagers, the *Essex* was stripped of all her stores and careened on the beach. Charcoal fires lighted in the holds asphyxiated some 1,500 rats (although the ship quickly became reinfested with the cockroaches that thrived on Nuku Hiva). The foul bottom was scraped clean by villagers using coconut shells. The frigate's planking was treated with whale oil mixed with walnut oil obtained from the Marquesans. Her flaking copper was repaired and replaced with a supply secured from one of the captured British whalers. Finally, the frigate's main-topmast was rebuilt, and her rigging overhauled with new lines made on a ropewalk established by the boatswain.

Each day, when work ended at 4 p.m., one quarter of the ships' companies were allowed to sample the attractions of Nuku Hiva—chief among them the island's compliant women—until daybreak, while the rest remained on board and competed in wrestling, jumping, spear throwing and pitching quoits to pass the time. The only exception made in this relaxed discipline concerned the younger midshipmen, including David Farragut, who were placed under the strict control of the chaplain. The midshipmen were allowed ashore during the day, to hunt and fish with the Marquesan boys of their own ages, but were confined to the ship at night while the revelries were taking place on the island.

Reluctantly, Porter was soon drawn into the quarrels between the Marquesan tribes. In order to maintain the hospitality so essential for his crew to complete the work on the *Essex*, Porter first had to send a Marine detachment to overawe with firearms the Happahs, with whom Gattanewa was feuding. A few weeks after, he sent an expedition against a second hostile Nuku Hivan tribe, the Typees, and burned a number of their villages. With genuine sadness, Porter wrote that "the valley, which on the morning we had viewed in all its beauty, was now a long line of smoking ruins from one end to the other."

As time passed a fort was constructed, and named Fort Madison after the President. Perhaps the solid physical evidence of the American presence gave Porter an idea; perhaps he had been intending it all along. At any rate, on November 19, 1813, David Porter, acting entirely on his own authority, officially annexed Nuku Hiva to the United States. Assembling the crew of the *Essex*, the English prisoners and Gattanewa's villagers in Fort Madison, Porter read a declaration announcing that, on behalf of the United States, "I have taken possession of the island called by the natives Nooaheevah, but now called Madison's Island." He then renamed the island's lovely curving harbor "Massachusetts Bay." Explaining that the Marquesans had asked "to be admitted into the great American family, whose pure republican policy approaches so near their own," Porter affirmed, "our chief shall be their chief." The captain of the *Essex* then offered protection to the 31 Nuku Hivan tribes, including the "Tomavaheenahs," the "Attestapwyunahs," the "Tickeymahues" and the "Attakakahaneuahs" against "all their enemies, and of Great Britain."

When the news reached Washington nine months later, President Madison, preoccupied with such matters as the British invasion of Chesapeake Bay (*page 155-157*), ignored Porter's act of imperialism. As Madison's biographer later put it: "Having trouble nearer home, Chief Madison of the Attakakahaneuahs, and 30 other tribes, did not ask Congress to accept the island."

On Nuku Hiva, meanwhile, Porter's preparations for departure were complete. The ships were all seaworthy and filled with supplies for the voyage back across the Pacific. But getting the crews under way was no easy matter. When Porter canceled all shore leaves, the island girls, he recalled, "lined the beach from morning until night," and "laughingly dipped their fingers into the sea and touched their eyes so as to let the salt water trickle down their cheeks" as a signal of sorrow for the loss of their lovers.

On board the *Essex Junior*, the moping and grumbling threatened to explode into mutiny. Porter was furious. He summoned all hands to the vessel's quarter-deck, laid his cutlass on the capstan, and announced that unless the crew stopped misbehaving he would "put a match to the magazine and blow them all to eternity." The men hastily backed down.

On December 13, 1813, while the Marine band played "The Girl I Left Behind Me," the *Essex* and the *Essex Junior* made sail from Nuku Hiva, shaping a course east across the Pacific in order to stop at Mocha Island, as Porter had on the outbound voyage, for fresh meat and water.

Porter ordered the prize crew on board the *New Zealander* to proceed independently for the United States, and left the remaining four prizes under the command of Marine Lieutenant John Gamble. Porter's intent was to make Fort Madison a permanent American base of operations in the Pacific. However, within a few months of Porter's departure, the British prisoners of war and some American mutineers succeeded in recapturing the *Seringapatam* and set sail for New Zealand. Gamble attempted to reach America in the *Sir Andrew Hammond*, leaving the *Greenwich* to be burned in Nuku Hiva's Massachusetts Bay, but he and his seven crewmen were captured by a British ship off Hawaii, and did not see America again until after peace was declared in 1815. Even so, they fared better than many among Porter's force.

A sailor's views of a Polynesian paradise

When Captain David Porter, in search of a place to repair and reprovision the *Essex* after a year of raiding British shipping, reached the Marquesas Islands in the South Pacific in October 1813, he was greeted with trepidation by the first islanders he encountered. "They approached the boat with the greatest awe and agitation," wrote Porter in his journal, "and in every instance where articles were presented to them they shrank back with terror."

But the Marquesans soon overcame their shyness, and the Americans were immensely impressed by the beautiful women and by the tall, handsome men, whose bodies were covered with tattoo patterns so intricate that their skins appeared black. "On a minute examination, may be traced innumerable lines, curved, straight and irregular, drawn with the utmost correctness and symmetry," marveled Porter. The captain used his considerable artistic skill to sketch the islands and their remarkable inhabitants, as can be seen below and on the following pages.

While the Americans worked to repair the *Essex*, Porter visited several villages on the Marquesan island of Nuku Hiva, where he observed farming methods. In the rich volcanic soil, the Marquesans cultivated quantities of edible kava and taro roots, coconut palms, more than 20 varieties of bananas and many groves of tall bread-fruit trees, the most important crop.

"The bread-fruit tree is everything to the natives of these islands," wrote Porter. The islanders baked and roasted its delicious oblong fruit, made cloth from the fibers of its smaller branches, and roofed their homes with its wide leaves. With the tree trunks, wrote the captain, "they form their canoes, many parts of their houses, and even their gods. Describe to one of the Marquesans a country abounding in everything that we consider desirable, and after you are done he will ask you if it produces bread-fruit."

More than 30 different Marquesan tribes lived on Nuku Hiva. According to Porter, the islanders had no formal government: "They have only patriarchs, who possess the mild and gentle influence of a kind and indulgent father among his children."

After seven weeks in Nuku Hiva, the *Essex* was ready to sail for Chile. Although the sojourn had not been entirely peaceful—Porter had been involved in two violent skirmishes with hostile tribesmen—he left with nothing but admiration for the islanders he had befriended. Indeed, he wrote, "I am inclined to believe that a more honest, or friendly and better disposed people does not exist under the sun."

The Essex (center) lies at anchor with her prizes before the American camp at Nuku Hiva in this engraving after a sketch by Porter.

A Nuku Hivan woman appears beautifully but simply dressed in this engraving from a sketch by Porter. The robe, called a "cahu," wrote Porter in his journal, consisted of "a long and flowing piece of paper-cloth which envelopes the body to the ankles," and gave the woman "an appearance of grace and modesty not to be found among any others in a state of nature."

A 50-foot Marquesan war canoe, paddled by 18 men, passes in review for the Essex. A ceremonial craft shared by the wealthiest families, it was disassembled after each use, wrote Porter; "each piece, and indeed each paddle has its separate proprietor, and the whole is scattered throughout the valley."

Drawn by Capt. Porter.

Engraved by W. Strickland.

His tall body covered with tattoos, a
Nuku Hivan warrior holds an elaborately
carved war club and a conch horn used
to signal the start of a battle. If an enemy
warrior should chance to be knocked
over, observed Porter, "he is instantly
dispatched with spears and war
clubs, and carried off in triumph."

Clad in a feather headdress, the
strikingly tattooed Taawattaa, priest of
the Nuku Hivans, was responsible for
judging disputes, predicting the future and
healing the sick. Wrote Porter, "If
the priest tells them they shall have rain
within a certain period, they believe
him; if it does not rain agreeably to his
prediction they think no more of it."

The youth who played the man

When David Porter took command of the frigate *Essex* in August 1811, he brought on board his 10-year-old foster son, immaculately dressed, according to Porter, in a "short blue coat, with a button and a slip of lace on each side." The lad's name was David Glasgow Farragut, and it would rank with the most illustrious in the pantheon of the U.S. Navy.

Porter had been a devoted friend of the Farragut family from the time, three years before, when Porter's father had suffered a stroke and Farragut's mother had attempted to nurse him back to health. The senior Porter died and, soon after, Farragut's mother perished as well, of yellow fever. Her husband, a sailing master, was left with the care of five children. Compassionate and feeling that he owed a debt of gratitude, David Porter offered to undertake the care of young David Farragut. The youngster later recalled: "I, being inspired by his uniform, said promptly that I would go."

Appointed to the rank of midshipman at the age of nine, David was at Porter's side two years later when the *Essex* captured the British sloop of war *Alert* at the start of the War of 1812. And he soon was able to show his mettle. A number of *Alert* prisoners planned an uprising, and on the appointed night, related Farragut, one of the men of the *Alert* "came to my hammock with a pistol in his hand, gazing intently at me. I remained perfectly motionless until he passed. Then I crept noiselessly to the cabin and informed Captain Porter of what I had seen." Porter raced on deck shouting, "Fire! Fire!" rousing his crew and so confusing the prisoners that they were quickly overcome.

A year later, Farragut proved his pluck again. By now Porter had captured so many British prizes that he was running out of responsible men to command the prize crews. And when a whaler named the *Barclay* was taken, David Farragut, aged 12, was chosen to lead the crew that sailed her to the neutral port of Valparaiso. En route, the young captain put down a second, smaller mutiny—this one by the ship's navigator, Gideon Randall—by threatening to throw the rebellious seaman overboard if he persisted. Randall backed down, and "from that moment I became master of the vessel," Farragut wrote later.

With that first command, Farragut was well and truly launched on his Naval career. In 1823 he captained an armed schooner in the West Indies. During the Civil War he led the Union Navy to victory at New Orleans and Mobile. And on July 25, 1886, by an act of Congress, David Farragut, the boy who had "played the man" aboard the *Essex* and the *Barclay*, became the first full admiral of the U.S. Navy.

Young Midshipman David Farragut reports for duty to Captain David Porter aboard the frigate Essex in August of 1811.

On February 3, 1814, the *Essex* and *Essex Junior* dropped anchor at Valparaiso. It is difficult to justify Porter's decision to reenter Chilean waters after reprovisioning at Mocha Island. With the prevailing westerlies at his back he might better have dashed across the Pacific and around Cape Horn into the Atlantic with his poorly armed frigate and unwieldy converted whaler. He knew a superior British force was hunting for him along the South American Pacific coast, and that Valparaiso would be an obvious refuge. Possibly he was concerned about the four prizes with American crews that he had left in the Chilean port. More likely, the aggressive Porter, tired of raiding, was yearning for combat against a British warship. That was the gist of a letter he later wrote to the Secretary of the Navy: "I had done all the injury that could be done to the British commerce in the Pacific, and still hoped to signalize my cruise by something more splendid before leaving that sea. Believing the British would seek me at Valparaiso, I determined to cruise about that place."

For five days Porter waited in Valparaiso. Then, on February 8, 1814, two British sail appeared to the west. They were the 36-gun frigate *Phoebe* and the 28-gun sloop *Cherub*, both under Captain James Hillyar, a grizzled, 50-year-old veteran of the naval campaigns against Napoleon.

In their personalities, the two captains could not have been more different. Porter, aflame with ambition, was eager to prove himself the equal of his heroic colleagues, Hull, Decatur and Bainbridge. Hillyar, by contrast, was an earnest believer that success, not personal glory, was the ultimate goal for any officer. He was known and respected by his counterparts in the U.S. Navy. Many Americans, including Porter, had met Hillyar in the Mediterranean during the Tripolitan war. Commodore John Rodgers had once given passage to Hillyar's wife and children when they sought to leave Malta to rejoin Hillyar in Gibraltar. Now that he had tracked Porter to Valparaiso, Hillyar had a thankless assignment—to engage the *Essex* and destroy her, or at least to bottle up the American frigate and put an end to her raids on British commerce.

Straight into Valparaiso harbor Hillyar sailed—and immediately presented Porter with a chance to end the confrontation then and there. Instead of anchoring a fair distance away, the *Phoebe* bore straight down on the *Essex* until it almost seemed that Hillyar would ram into the side of the American. Hillyar never explained his action. Perhaps he felt himself safe in neutral Chilean waters, and thought to indulge in a bit of bravado. In any case, he put the *Phoebe* in dire jeopardy—with her virtually unarmed bow exposed to the full broadside of the enemy.

On board the *Essex*, Porter signaled his crew to clear the decks for action: gunners took battle stations, and the powder boys lighted the slow matches used to discharge the carronades. Boarders poised at the ship's gunwales, their dirks and cutlasses in their hands.

"The *Phoebe* was completely at my mercy," he later wrote. "I could have destroyed her in 15 minutes." Yet Porter held his fire as the *Phoebe* luffed up ever closer, the complications of Chilean neutrality obviously on his mind. Then, at the very last instant, Hillyar hailed Porter and declared that his intentions, for the moment, were peaceful. Tensely, Porter replied: "You have no business where you are. If you touch a rope yard of this ship I shall board instantly." Just then the *Phoebe*'s sails were taken aback and the British frigate fell off to the leeward, and she and the *Cherub* eventually anchored half a mile astern of the *Essex* and the *Essex Junior*. Thus began a classic wartime impasse, four ships anchored in neutral waters while their crews ached for battle.

In the harbor, insults, slogans and dares flew back and forth between the crews. The men of the *Essex* displayed a huge banner proclaiming "Free Trade and Sailors' Rights." Within a few hours the *Phoebe*'s sailors hoisted their own banner, asserting, "God and country: British sailors' best rights: traitors offend both." At night the Americans' rousing chorus of "Yankee Doodle" was countered by "The Sweet Little Cherub that Sits Up Aloft" from the Britishers. Porter commented in his journal that "the songs from the *Cherub* were better sung," but that "those of the *Essex* were more witty and to the point."

Meeting ashore, at the home of the American envoy Joel Poinsett, Porter and Hillyar attempted to work out the arrangements for the battle that both knew must come. It was an age in which chivalry still played a part, and the two captains assumed the roles of knights debating the rules for a forthcoming joust. They greeted each other with cordiality and respect. "No one would have supposed us to have been at war," wrote Porter. "Our conduct bore so much the appearance of a friendly alliance." On the question of Chilean neutrality, both captains agreed to respect the sanctity of the port of Valparaiso. Arguing that the *Essex Junior* was simply an armed merchantman, and could not be expected to stand up against the *Cherub*'s heavier guns and timbers, Porter suggested that the *Essex* and *Phoebe* fight a ship-to-ship duel. Hillyar saw no reason to forfeit his superiority and coolly declined the challenge.

On board the two frigates the sailors were exchanging their own challenges. The Americans, self-proclaimed "sons of Liberty and commerce, on board the saucy *Essex*," sent a formal offer to "their oppressed brother tars on board the ship whose motto is too tedious to mention," to meet in a frigate-to-frigate contest. A midshipman on the *Phoebe* replied with a staunch refusal that read, in anticipation of Gilbert and Sullivan: "Your vile letter which on board was brought / We scorn to answer, tho' with malice fraught / Know that we are Britons all, both stout and true / We love our king, our country, captain too / When honor calls we'll glory in his name / Acquit like men and hope you'll do the same."

A week after his arrival, Hillyar moved his two ships to a blockading station in Valparaiso roadstead, intending to bring the *Essex* to battle when she left port. If Porter had had any idea of escaping, it was now too late. But he clearly had no such idea. Instead, he now tried to entice Hillyar into a rash action. First he had two of the prizes that Downes had brought to Valparaiso eight months before towed out of the harbor and burned. Hillyar simply watched impassively. Then the *Essex* sallied out and actually challenged the *Phoebe*; shots were exchanged, but the British frigate lay off to join the *Cherub*, and Porter was forced to withdraw.

In the end it was the weather that sparked the powder keg.

On the afternoon of March 28, strong gusts of wind set the ships in Valparaiso harbor to rolling heavily. Soon the *Essex* lost one anchor, and began to drag her other. Rather than attempt to reanchor, Porter ordered the *Essex*' sails shaken out, and the American frigate raced for the sea.

The devastating cruise of the raider "Essex"

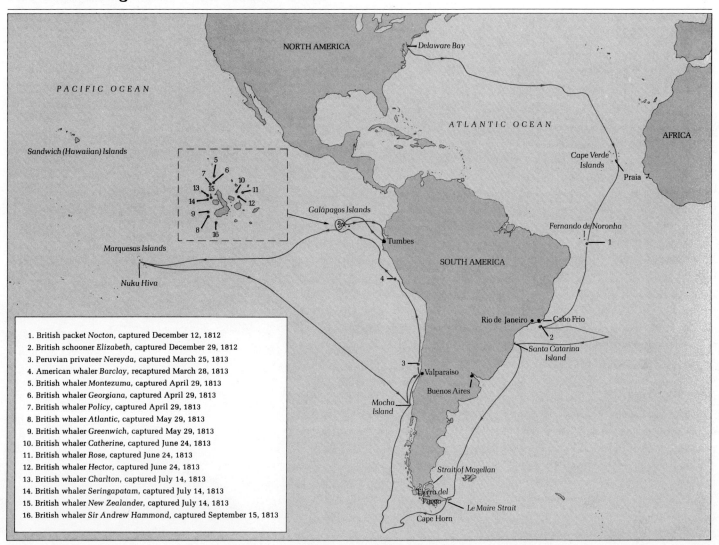

PACIFIC OCEAN

Sandwich (Hawaiian) Islands

NORTH AMERICA

Delaware Bay

ATLANTIC OCEAN

AFRICA

Cape Verde Islands

Praia

Fernando de Noronha

Galápagos Islands

Tumbes

SOUTH AMERICA

Marquesas Islands

Nuku Hiva

1

4

Rio de Janeiro   Cabo Frio

Santa Catarina Island

2

1. British packet *Nocton*, captured December 12, 1812
2. British schooner *Elizabeth*, captured December 29, 1812
3. Peruvian privateer *Nereyda*, captured March 25, 1813
4. American whaler *Barclay*, recaptured March 28, 1813
5. British whaler *Montezuma*, captured April 29, 1813
6. British whaler *Georgiana*, captured April 29, 1813
7. British whaler *Policy*, captured April 29, 1813
8. British whaler *Atlantic*, captured May 29, 1813
9. British whaler *Greenwich*, captured May 29, 1813
10. British whaler *Catherine*, captured June 24, 1813
11. British whaler *Rose*, captured June 24, 1813
12. British whaler *Hector*, captured June 24, 1813
13. British whaler *Charlton*, captured July 14, 1813
14. British whaler *Seringapatam*, captured July 14, 1813
15. British whaler *New Zealander*, captured July 14, 1813
16. British whaler *Sir Andrew Hammond*, captured September 15, 1813

3

Valparaiso

Buenos Aires

Mocha Island

Strait of Magellan

Tierra del Fuego

Le Maire Strait

Cape Horn

On her 17-month voyage into the Pacific, the Essex took 16 vessels, 12 of them while cruising in the Galápagos Islands (inset), before she was destroyed in combat. "We have completely broken up that important branch of British navigation, the whale-fishery of the coast of Chile and Peru," wrote Captain David Porter in his journal.

Within minutes, the *Phoebe* and the *Cherub*, bedecked with ensigns, motto flags and Union Jacks, bore down upon the *Essex*.

Some five miles from Valparaiso, but still well inside the three-mile limit of Chilean domain, misfortune beset the *Essex*. As the ship rounded Punta del Angeles, a wild squall struck. Porter tried to reduce sail, but the main-topsail halyards jammed. The topsails, although single-reefed, were too much to carry in that wind, and the main-topmast went by the boards, pitching four or five men overboard. Now Porter attempted to turn back to Valparaiso, but the winds were against him. There was nothing to do save run into a small bay, anchor near shore, and raise the battle flags and pendants. Grimly, Porter prepared the *Essex* for action.

The American frigate was at an enormous disadvantage. Porter was separated from his consort, out of the harbor and anchored in a crippled ship with short-range guns. Swiftly the *Phoebe* and the *Cherub* swooped down. Shortly before 4 p.m., the British ships opened fire at long range. The *Phoebe* had taken station on the *Essex*' stern and her raking fire proved tremendously destructive. Three times during the first half hour

Porter attached spring lines to his anchor cables in order to swing the *Essex* into broadside position, but each time they were shot away. The *Cherub*, after working into position on the *Essex'* starboard bow, had a less easy time of it. The Americans returned the *Cherub's* fire so accurately that the little sloop backed off to join the *Phoebe*.

To protect the *Essex'* vulnerable stern from the *Phoebe's* broadsides, Porter had three of his six long 12-pounders moved aft and fired from the stern ports. These guns were so well served that after a half hour the British ships pulled out of range, each with badly cut-up rigging.

But the *Essex* had suffered dreadful damage. The two British ships had been pounding the American frigate with 32 long 12-pounders, compared with the *Essex'* three. In the first five minutes of battle, close to a dozen of Porter's crew were killed or injured. The flying jib was the only important sail still operational; the others hung limp, their lines shot away. As for the two tiers of short-range carronades lining the *Essex'* broadsides, they had not even been fired.

At 5:30, the British returned, carefully taking position off the damaged *Essex'* starboard quarter, where the Yankee's long guns could not be brought to bear, and out of range of her stubby carronades. There was nothing left for Porter to do but cut his cable and attempt to close with the British, so that his carronades could come into range. But with the *Essex'* badly damaged rigging and the constant fire from the *Phoebe's* gunners, it was agonizingly difficult to get the vessel around. At last the *Essex'* jib was set and the American frigate drew near the British ships. The *Cherub* immediately fell off in the face of the *Essex'* heavy carronade fire, and the *Phoebe* also began to lay back.

It was now clear that the *Essex* was doomed. Porter decided to drive the vessel aground and destroy her. But contrary winds continued to push her offshore. He tried to anchor again, but the cable parted. All the while, the *Phoebe* and the *Cherub* continued to pound the Americans at long range. The carnage aboard the *Essex* by now was ghastly. One 12-pounder had been manned three times; 15 men had been slain at it, and its captain alone escaped unwounded. At one of the bow guns a young Scotsman named Bissly had a leg shot off. Turning to his American shipmates, he cried: "I left my own country and adopted the United States to fight for her. I hope I have this day proved myself worthy of the country of my adoption. I am no longer of any use to you or to her, so good-bye." With these words, Bissly dragged his mangled body to the rail and threw himself overboard.

By 5:45 p.m., the *Essex* was a hulk, drifting down upon her enemy. Hillyar's gunners continued to pour deadly fire into her. "His shot never missed our hull," recalled Porter. To end the Americans' last hopes, a terrific explosion occurred in one of the magazines and flames shot out of every main-deck hatch. Porter gave his crew permission to swim for it if they chose, and a little after 6 p.m. the *Essex'* flag was lowered.

The *Essex'* decks were so bloody that one British boarding officer fainted when he saw them. Of the frigate's crew of 255, some 58 had been killed and 65 wounded. Both Porter and his adopted son, Midshipman Farragut, had miraculously escaped injury. But death—and gallantry—had been all around them. At one point in the battle, a gun captain

Captain James Hillyar, resplendent in full-dress Royal Navy uniform in this contemporary miniature, put a devastating end to David Porter's Essex cruise. A modest, admired officer, Hillyar wrote before the battle, "I expect an awful Combat, but wish to repose my trust in God for a favorable result."

Overtaken after losing her main-topmast in a squall, the Essex (center) is caught in a murderous cross fire from the British sloop of war Cherub (right) and the frigate Phoebe, commanded by James Hillyar. "The British kept up a tremendous fire at us," wrote Captain David Porter, "which mowed down my brave companions by the dozen."

standing next to Farragut was struck in the head by an 18-pound shot, and tumbled back on the lad; the two fell down the hatchway together. Lieutenant John G. Cowell, who had lost a leg at the knee, was offered treatment ahead of rows of wounded sailors. "No doctor, none of that," Cowell told the surgeon. "Fair play's a jewel; I would not cheat any poor fellow out of his turn." But he was grievously hurt, and looking at Farragut, he cried, "I fear it is all up with me." He died soon after. The big boatswain's mate who had rallied the crew off Cape Horn had been horribly burned. Somehow he managed to dive overboard and swim ashore, where he later recovered after days spent in terrible agony.

As for the British, they had suffered a mere 15 casualties, and only five dead, most of those in the first exchanges of the battle.

With the same thoroughness with which he had fought and won his battle, Captain Hillyar now directed his full attention to burying the dead and caring for the wounded. Later, in his official report, Hillyar commended Porter. "The defence of the *Essex*, taking into account our superiority of force, and the very discouraging circumstances of her having lost her main top-mast did honor to her brave defenders, and most fully evinced the courage of Captain Porter and those under his command. Her colours were not struck until the loss in killed and wounded was so awfully great, and her shattered condition so seriously bad, as to render further resistance unavailing."

Porter was less chivalrous. He contended that the *Essex* was in Chilean territory when she was attacked, and that Hillyar had violated his earlier agreement to respect neutral waters. He bitterly recalled that he could have destroyed the *Phoebe* on their first meeting in the harbor had he not been so respectful of Chilean neutrality. Hillyar responded that he had agreed to avoid combat only in the port of Valparaiso itself. Otherwise it had been his duty to "capture the *Essex* with the least possible risk to my vessel and crew." And that was precisely what he had done.

When the survivors could travel, Hillyar put them on the *Essex Junior*, gave Porter a safe-conduct pass, and released them to return to America.

On July 5, 1814, some 21 months after leaving their homeland, Porter and 130 crewmen arrived off Sandy Hook, New Jersey, at the entrance to New York Harbor. And now, with home but 40 miles away, the *Essex Junior* was stopped by the British frigate *Saturn*. At first, Captain James Nash of the *Saturn* honored Porter's pass, but a few hours later he halted the *Essex Junior* again and detained her for an inspection of the holds.

Porter was furious. As the two ships rocked in the swell early the next morning, Porter ordered a fast whaleboat manned and lowered. Leaving a note informing Captain Nash that he had escaped, had armed himself and was ready to fight for his freedom, Porter set sail for New York. Soon afterward, the *Saturn* made sail in pursuit, but happily for Porter, a thick fog rolled in and the *Saturn* lost sight of her quarry. After sailing and rowing some 60 miles, Porter waded ashore at Babylon, Long Island. He was immediately arrested as a British spy. But when he produced his commission for the *Essex*, he was rewarded with a tumultuous greeting.

He discovered that in his own country he was a hero. It was not the loss of his ship that people remembered, but the sensational record he had made with her before she was destroyed. He had, after all, captured 22 enemy ships, probed the exotic South Pacific and eluded the British for 17 months. Americans everywhere acclaimed the cruise as a triumph of initiative, resourcefulness and courage.

On July 7 the other *Essex* men reached New York, having been released by Captain Nash, and were feted at Tammany Hall, along with their captain. "It was really pleasant," said the *American Advocate*, "to see the joy which animated the American citizens of New York where he was received with six hearty cheers. This is the way Americans receive their heroes, tho' they may have been unfortunate." In Philadelphia the veterans of Valparaiso were paraded through streets bedecked with the Stars and Stripes; at one point, some *Essex* men unhitched the horses of Porter's carriage and pulled their leader themselves. In Washington, Porter dined at the White House, where he held President Madison enthralled with tales of the voyage. The Secretary of the Navy wrote that Porter and his crew had "elevated the naval character of our country even beyond the towering eminence it had before attained."

To be sure, he and his brave but faulty frigate had been taken in the end. Yet as the President declared in an address to Congress on September 20, 1814, "this loss is hidden in the blaze of heroism with which she was defended. Captain Porter maintained a sanguinary contest against two ships, one of them superior to his own, until humanity tore down the colors which valor had nailed to the mast."

Bemoaning the defeat of the Essex, this broadside composed in Boston by an anonymous master of rhyming vituperation rails against the "In-glorious Victory" that the British achieved by pitting two warships against one.

CAPTURE OF THE ESSEX.

— & —

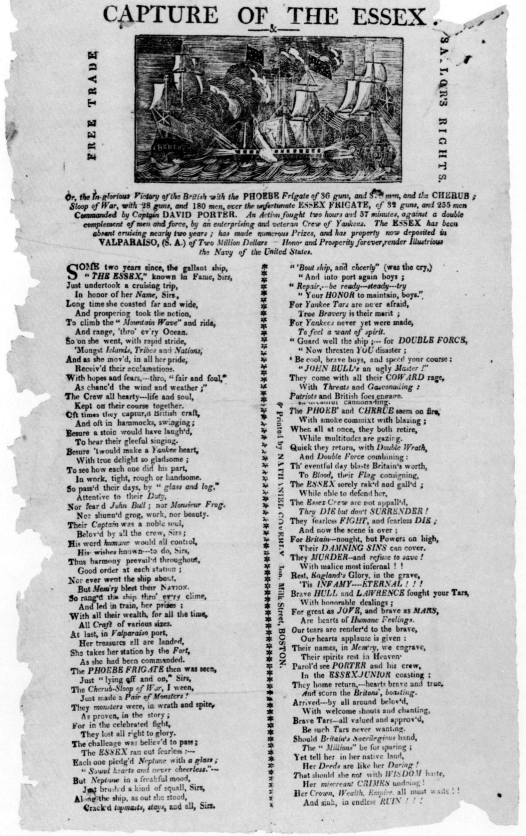

FREE TRADE

SAILOR'S RIGHTS.

Or, the In-glorious Victory of the British with the PHOEBE Frigate of 36 guns, and 3__ men, and the CHERUB; Sloop of War, with 28 guns, and 180 men, over the unfortunate ESSEX FRIGATE, of 32 guns, and 255 men Commanded by Captain DAVID PORTER. An Action fought two hours and 57 minutes, against a double complement of men and force, by an enterprising and veteran Crew of Yankees. The ESSEX has been absent cruising nearly two years; has made numerous Prizes, and has property now deposited in VALPARAISO, (S. A.) of Two Million Dollars — Honor and Prosperity forever, render Illustrious the Navy of the United States.

SOME two years since, the gallant ship,
"THE ESSEX," known in Fame, Sirs,
Just undertook a cruising trip,
In honor of her *Name*, Sirs,
Long time she coasted far and wide,
And prospering took the notion,
To climb the "*Mountain Wave*" and ride,
And range, 'thro' ev'ry Ocean.
So on she went, with rapid stride,
'Mongst *Islands, Tribes* and *Nations,*
And as she mov'd, in all her pride,
Receiv'd their acclamations.
With hopes and fears,---thro' "fair and foul,"
As chanc'd the wind and weather;"
The Crew all hearty---life and soul,
Kept on their course together.
Oft times they captur'd British craft,
And oft in hammocks, swinging;
Besure a stoic would have laugh'd,
To hear their gleeful singing.
Besure 'twould make a *Yankee* heart,
With true delight so gladsome;
To see how each one did his part,
In work, tight, rough or handsome.
So pass'd their days, by "*glass and log*,"
Attentive to their *Duty*,
Nor fear'd *John Bull*; nor *Monsieur Frog*.
Nor shunn'd grog, work, nor beauty.
Their *Captain* was a noble soul,
Belov'd by all the crew, Sirs;
His word *humane* would all control,
His wishes known---to do, Sirs,
Thus harmony prevail'd throughout,
Good order at each station;
Nor ever went the ship about,
But Mem'ry blest their NATION.
So rang'd the ship thro' ev'ry clime,
And led in train, her prizes;
With all their wealth, for all the time,
All *Craft* of various sizes.
At last, in *Valparaiso* port,
Her treasures all are landed,
She takes her station by the *Fort*,
As she had been commanded.
The *PHOEBE FRIGATE* then was seen,
Just "lying off and on," Sirs,
The *Cherub-Sloop of War*, I ween,
Just made a *Pair of Monsters!*
They *monsters* were, in wrath and spite,
As proven, in the story;
For in the celebrated fight,
They lost all right to glory.
The challenge was believ'd to pass;
The *ESSEX* ran out fearless :---
Each one pledg'd *Neptune* with a glass;
"*Sound hearts and never cheerless.*"---
But *Neptune* in a freakful mood,
Just brush'd a kind of squall, Sirs,
Along the ship, as out she stood,
Crack'd *topmasts, stays*, and all, Sirs.

"'Bout ship, and cheerly" (was the cry,)
"And into port again boys;
"Repair,--be ready--steady--try
"Your *HONOR* to maintain, boys."
For *Yankee Tars* are ne'er afraid,
True *Bravery* is their merit;
For *Yankees* never yet were made,
To feel a want of *spirit*.
"Guard well the ship;-- for *DOUBLE FORCE*,
"Now threaten *YOU* disaster;
'Be cool, brave boys, and speed your course;
"*JOHN BULL's* an ugly *Master !*"
They come with all their *COWARD* rage,
With *Threats* and *Gasconading:*
Patriots and British foes engage,
__ __ __ cannonading.
The *PHOEB'* and *CHERUB* seem on fire,
With smoke commixt with blazing;
When all at once, they both retire,
While multitudes are gazing.
Quick they return, with *Double Wrath,*
And *Double Force* combining:
Th' eventful day blasts Britain's worth,
To *Blood*, their *Flag* consigning,
The *ESSEX* sorely rak'd and gall'd;
While able to defend her,
The *Essex Crew* are not appall'd,
They DIE but don't SURRENDER !
They fearless *FIGHT*, and fearless *DIE;*
And now the scene is over;
For *Britain*--nought, but Powers on high,
Their *DAMNING SINS* can cover.
They *MURDER*--and *refuse to save !*
With malice most infernal ! !
Rest, *England's* Glory, in the grave,
'Tis *INFAMY*---*ETERNAL ! ! !*
Brave *HULL* and *LAWRENCE* fought your *Tars,*
With honorable dealings;
For great as *JOVE*, and brave as *MARS*,
Are hearts of *Humane Feelings.*
Our tears are render'd to the brave,
Our hearts applause is given:
Their names, in *Mem'ry*, we engrave,
Their spirits rest in Heaven.
Parol'd see *PORTER* and his crew,
In the *ESSEX-JUNIOR* coasting;
They home return,---hearts brave and true,
And scorn the *Britons*', boasting.
Arrived---by all around belov'd,
With welcome shouts and chanting,
Brave *Tars*--all valued and approv'd,
Be such *Tars* never wanting.
Should *Britain's Sacrilegious* hand,
The "*Millions*" be for sparing;
Yet tell her in her native land,
Her *Deeds* are like her *Daring !*
That should she not with *WISDOM* haste,
Her *miscreant CRIMES* undoing !
Her *Crown, Wealth, Empire*, all must waste ! !
And sink, in endless *RUIN ! ! !*

Printed by NATHANIEL COVERLY, Inn, Milk Street, BOSTON.

Chapter 5

"Don't give up the ship!"

arly in 1813 the politically powerful Marquis of Lansdowne arose in Parliament with a complaint that sounded like a sigh of the Empire: "Some time ago it was imagined that in the event of a war with America the first operation would be the destruction of her navy. What the fact has turned out to be, I am almost ashamed to mention. If anyone were asked what had been the services of our navy in this war, he would unfortunately find some difficulty in giving an answer."

Lord Lansdowne's lament accurately reflected British popular opinion about the Royal Navy's inability to subdue the Americans. Not only had three major British frigates been lost, but the *Essex* had already made her first successful foray *(page 111)* and now was thrusting into the Pacific. Meanwhile Stephen Decatur threatened daily to break out of New York with both the *United States* and the British-born *Macedonian*, now under Yankee colors. Moreover, American privateers continued to come and go, moving steadily toward the total of 991 British vessels that would be captured before the War was done.

Although the Royal Navy remained the world's largest maritime force, British power and policy were based on an absolute, unquestioned mastery of the seas, and the individual successes scored by the Yankee upstarts might encourage other underdog nations to nip and snap at the lion. Only a dramatic naval victory could quell the fears of lords and commoners, lift the gloom in Royal Navy wardrooms and silence the grumblings in British fo'c's'les.

Such a British victory was, in fact, close at hand. Yet by a supreme irony, the Americans would emerge from their defeat with perhaps the greater profit, for the dying words of a gallant young New Jersey frigate captain struck down in the encounter would infuse the fledgling U.S. Navy with an even more vigorous determination to fight and win.

At noon on June 1, 1813, the American frigate *Chesapeake*, freshly painted and flying a broad banner emblazoned with the phrase that had become America's watchword, Free Trade and Sailors' Rights, cleared Boston Harbor and set course directly toward the single British frigate that stood between her and the open sea. On her sunlit quarter-deck stood Captain James Lawrence, dressed in full uniform—cocked hat, gold epaulets, blue coat, white trousers and top boots.

At 31 Lawrence was in the very prime of an enviable life. He had established a brilliant record in the Navy, serving as a lieutenant under both Isaac Hull and Stephen Decatur aboard the schooner *Enterprise* in Tripoli (he was second-in-command of the *Intrepid* the night Decatur took the little ketch into Tripoli harbor and burned the *Philadelphia*). Modest and unassuming, Lawrence was supremely popular with his peers. It was possible to admire the heroic Decatur despite his overwhelming ambition, to empathize with the capable Bainbridge because of his misfortunes, to respect the bellicose Porter with his bluff quarter-deck mannerisms, and to take delight in the hearty Isaac Hull. But to know James Lawrence was to adore him. On one occasion in the Mediterranean, the beggar-poor midshipmen, intent on honoring Commodore John Rodgers with a party, concluded that their meager allowances

In this allegorical painting celebrating the War of 1812, a flag-bearing American seaman, freed of his shackles, crushes a crown beneath his foot as the goddess Liberty offers him a hero's laurel. The 26 stars in the flag correspond to the number of states in the Union between 1837 and 1845, the period, experts think, during which the picture was painted.

JOHNNY BULL in a Fret

Oh these Wasps & Hornets! the dreadful little Insects, how they sting! Oh wee is me! why did I disturb their Nest!!

A bloodied and enraged John Bull, Britain's portly equivalent of Uncle Sam, swipes ineffectually at a swarm of stinging insects in this American cartoon gloating over the discomfort that U.S. ships—including the sloops of war Wasp and Hornet—were causing the longtime ruler of the seas. In another cartoon using the same symbols, John Bull groaned that he "little thought such diminutive insects could give me such a sting."

would not permit invitations to the commodore's lieutenants. But when they realized that to omit all the lieutenants would mean the absence of Mr. Lawrence, every purse was emptied on the table. Amid wild cheering, it was found that the small coins just added up to a sum that would permit the inclusion of Lawrence, the only lieutenant so honored.

Even his enemies revered him. After his *Hornet* took the *Peacock* off the South American coast in February 1813, surviving British officers presented Lawrence with a certificate in which they recorded their gratitude for the manner in which he had attended to their needs. His Majesty's officers noted that they had ceased to consider themselves prisoners after Lawrence and his crew had opened their sea chests to give every captive decent clothes to replace those ruined in battle. One British sailor, requiring an amputation, would not submit to the surgeon's saw until Lawrence sat beside him, held his hand and promised to adopt his son should the sailor not survive.

Following his victory over the *Peacock*, Lawrence had been promoted to captain and reassigned to command of the *Constitution*, but then to his dismay his orders were changed: he would get the *Chesapeake* instead. He considered the *Chesapeake* an unlucky vessel, partly because she had served as flagship to Commodore Richard Valentine Morris during that feckless officer's disastrous Mediterranean tour of duty in 1802, partly because of her humiliation in the *Leopard* affair in 1807. Lawrence sent four letters protesting his assignment to the Secretary of the Navy, but failed to elicit so much as an answer. When he boarded the *Chesapeake* on May 20, 1813, all he had to go on was an order that directed him to take his ship to sea as soon as feasible.

The key word was feasible. Although the *Chesapeake* herself was physically ready for sea, the crew was not. She had recently shipped a large draft of new officers and sailors. They had had few gunnery drills and no sail exercises while under way, and they had not yet developed a sense of pride and unity.

Worse yet for Lawrence, patrolling off Boston was His Britannic Majesty's ship *Shannon*, one of the best frigates in the Royal Navy and a vessel with a score to settle: the *Shannon* was the ship that had lost the kedging contest with the *Constitution* 13 months before, after which the *Constitution* had gone on to defeat the *Guerriere* and the *Java*. Captain Sir Philip Bowes Vere Broke of the *Shannon* was bent on retribution. He and his men—known in the Royal Navy as "the Shannons"—had been together since 1806 and were honed to a razoredge. When a parsimonious Admiralty failed to provide Broke with enough powder for extra gunnery exercises, the captain had dipped into his own pocket for funds. To inspire his Shannons during endless drills, Broke would offer a pound of his best tobacco to the first gunner to hit the target.

Knowing the *Shannon* was at the peak of her capabilities while his *Chesapeake* was at her nadir, Lawrence nevertheless decided by June 1 that he must comply with his orders and attempt to run the blockade. And he chose to try to dispose of the *Shannon* rather than elude her.

Broke was expecting him. Earlier the *Shannon* had stopped a Yankee merchantman and Broke had sent a challenge to the Americans to come out and fight. In fact Lawrence never received the dare, but Broke did not know this, and he waited in full confidence that his gauntlet would be picked up. To his vast delight on that Tuesday morning, he saw the tall masts of his adversary in Boston Harbor beginning to fill with canvas. The word passed quickly among the Shannons: "She's coming out!"

At about 1:30 p.m., as the *Chesapeake* passed the Boston Lighthouse, Lawrence mustered the crew and made a short speech in which he urged his men to "*Peacock*" the enemy—a reference to his victory over the British vessel just four months before. It was perhaps only then that he fully realized the unpromising state of his crew's morale. Instead of shouting the huzzahs that usually greeted a captain's hortatory oration, the men began to grumble and complain that they had not yet received prize money from past cruises. Lawrence hurriedly ordered the ship's purser to issue prize money chits, and then sent the crew to the guns.

Aboard the *Shannon*, meanwhile, Captain Broke assembled his crew. The tanned sailors were shoeless and stripped to the waist; they wore bandannas around their heads to keep sweat from their eyes and to protect their ears from the roar of the guns. Drawn up in the gangways were Royal Marines, wearing scarlet jackets, blue trousers, white cross-belts and black headdresses with crimson plumes. Broke first reminded his men of America's galling successes at sea, and then spoke of their own hard training and longtime comradeship. "You will let them know today that there are Englishmen in the *Shannon* who still know how to fight," he concluded. "Don't cheer. Go quietly to your quarters. You have the blood of hundreds of your countrymen to avenge."

By 4 p.m. the ships were seven miles apart, and began to close for action, each one maneuvering to try to obtain an advantageous position. At a little before 6 p.m., with both ships heading in a westerly direction within 50 yards of each other, the *Shannon* opened fire. The *Shannon's* guns were loaded with round shot and canisters of musket balls. When this fusillade struck the *Chesapeake*, a cloud of torn hammocks, splinters, fragments of her bulwarks, and cut rigging seemed to rise over her. In this first broadside Captain Lawrence was hit in the knee, and his sailing master, William White, was killed. But the *Chesapeake* replied instantly, letting go her own broadside with good effect.

Aboard the *Shannon* splinters flew, a British cannon was dismounted, and one smoking 32-pound cannon ball, after piercing the hull, almost rolled into a powder scuttle. It was kicked away at the last moment by the bare foot of an Englishman. Then, as the fast-sailing *Chesapeake* forged ahead and momentarily stole the wind from the British frigate's sails, James Lawrence made a direful decision.

If the *Chesapeake* had continued to pass the *Shannon* to windward, then had fallen off around her bow for a rake, the outcome of the battle might have been different. But Lawrence, refusing to surrender his windward advantage, attempted to luff up briefly into the wind to slow his speed and then resume his course and continue the broadside-to-broadside battle. It was a complicated maneuver—and one that almost instantly brought disaster. A British shot killed the man at the *Chesapeake*'s wheel just as the helm was put over. Moments later the jib sheets were shot away and the fore-topsail yard plunged into the slings. Always responsive to her rudder, the handy *Chesapeake* came around too far and hung up in the wind, caught in irons, as sailors say.

With her weakly armed stern now directly exposed to the *Shannon*'s broadsides, the *Chesapeake* began to drift back on the British frigate, taking fearful punishment as shot hurtled along her entire length. A cask of musket cartridges, left by the green crew on the *Chesapeake*'s quarter-deck when the ship was cleared for action, was hit by a shot and exploded, killing and maiming nearby men.

In the smoke and confusion the *Chesapeake* wallowed down on the *Shannon*, until her port quarter hooked itself on the *Shannon*'s starboard anchor. A boatswain aboard the *Shannon* lashed a rope around the *Chesapeake*'s rail just before the swipe of an American cutlass took off his left arm. Captain Broke waved his sword, called for boarders to follow him, then scrambled over the hammock nettings and leaped onto the deck of the *Chesapeake*.

Captain Lawrence too had seen the need for boarders, and ordered his

Sword in hand, Captain Philip Bowes Vere Broke of the British frigate Shannon leads a boarding party onto the American frigate Chesapeake off Boston on June 1, 1813, following a fight that lasted only 15 minutes. It was one of the swiftest frigate victories in history, and was sweet revenge for the British after a long string of American successes.

bugler to sound the call. But the bugler was new at his job, and craven to boot. At first he could not be found; when finally located, he was so paralyzed by fear that he was unable to sound a note. At that moment James Lawrence collapsed on deck, struck by a musket ball in the groin. As he was carried below to the surgeon, he shouted to his men, "Keep the guns going. Fight her till she strikes or sinks." And then he called out his last order, the words that would ring throughout the U.S. Navy and the nation for decades after: "Don't give up the ship!"

On hearing Lawrence's words, the ship's chaplain, Sam Livermore, grabbed a pistol, shot one British sailor and was going after others with a broadsword when Captain Broke personally cut him down. The British boarders swarmed forward, driving the disorganized defenders to the fo'c's'le. There the cornered Americans put up a desperate fight.

Captain Broke was hit in the head by a musket butt; then a cutlass slash laid open his skull, exposing his brain for some three inches. But the British had won the deck and, as the two ships broke apart, some men from the *Shannon* hoisted British colors on the *Chesapeake*. In the confusion the British ensign was mistakenly bent on the hoist not above but beneath the Stars and Stripes—and the men left on the *Shannon*, taking this as an indication that the Americans had prevailed, immediately reopened fire, killing some of their own countrymen on the *Chesapeake*. When the hoist was lowered and the ensign went up again, this time above the American flag, the *Shannon* ceased firing.

The struggle was over. Of the *Shannon*'s crew, 34 men were dead or dying and 43 wounded. The American toll was 56 men killed and 85 wounded. The battle had lasted just 15 minutes.

With both captains near death, a lieutenant named Provo Wallis took command of the *Shannon*, and the two ships set sail for Halifax. James Lawrence was beyond help. The musket ball had penetrated his abdomen and peritonitis soon set in. He lived four more days in agony, repeating his exhortation again and again: "Don't give up the ship!"

When the badly damaged vessels reached Halifax, the size of the casualty lists touched off an outpouring of grief. The *Chesapeake* still bore much of the grisly litter of battle. "Internally the scene was one never to be forgotten by a landsman," said a man who visited the American ship. "Pieces of skin with pendant hair were adhering to the sides of the ship, and in one place I noticed portions of fingers protruding as if thrust through the outer wall of the frigate."

After his death Lawrence had been wrapped in an American flag and placed on the quarter-deck of the *Chesapeake*. Now, in Halifax, six Royal Navy captains served as his pallbearers while a band and 300 members of the British 64th Regiment of Foot rendered honors. The procession of mourners to the cemetery was long, with officers and men from both the *Chesapeake* and the *Shannon* joining in poignant tribute to a gallant captain. Wrote one of the American officers at the funeral: "I can truly say that all appeared to lament his death, and I heard several say that they considered the blood which had been shed on the *Chesapeake*'s deck as being as dear to them as that of their own countrymen." Six weeks later, under a flag of truce, Lawrence's body was removed to New York and reburied in Trinity churchyard.

Surrounded by grieving crewmen, the gallant Captain James Lawrence lies fatally wounded on the deck of his Chesapeake during her losing battle with the Shannon. Above Lawrence's head in this emotional contemporary engraving flutters a ribbon bearing his immortal last words: "Don't give up the ship."

Captain Broke, one of the bravest and most skilled of the Royal Navy's frigate commanders, never again served at sea. His brain was irreparably injured. In England he was received in triumph and knighted in 1815, but lived as an invalid for the next 27 years. In 1841 he died during a brain operation.

At word of the capture of the *Chesapeake*, London went wild with delight. Guns at the famous old Tower boomed salutes to Broke and his Shannons. Stirring tales were told and retold—of the fierce old bosun who had lashed the ships together and lost his arm and of some British middies who had raced up the rigging to clear out with their cutlasses one of the *Chesapeake*'s fighting tops. As time passed there was a story that it was a grenade thrown by Broke himself, rather than a cannon ball, that set off the keg of musket cartridges on the *Chesapeake*'s deck.

The swelling pride was occasionally punctured by a critical judgment. While the afterdinner port was passed one night at the Duke of Wellington's table, British Admiral Sir Isaac Coffin had enough of posturing and foolish talk. It was a lucky thing, he observed, that Broke "fell in with the unprepared *Chesapeake*, and not with Hull and the *Constitution*. If he had, no Tower guns would have been heard celebrating the *Shannon*'s victory."

In America the mood was grim. The British were now clearly on the offensive. Admiral Sir George Cockburn had entered Chesapeake Bay with two ships of the line, three frigates and two sloops. He remained there through the spring and into the summer of 1813, dominating a broad expanse of water that was vital to American shipping. The frigate *Constellation* was bottled up near Norfolk, Virginia, and boatloads of British troops made forays up the innumerable creeks and rivers that feed into Chesapeake Bay. American supplies were captured. Small American ships were burned. But it was an operation that at times defeated its own purpose; the arrival of British Redcoats and Marines commanded by arrogant officers often stiffened local resistance.

Thus a British attempt to capture the *Constellation* was frustrated by raw American militiamen. On June 22, 1813, a British force of some 1,500 men under the command of Colonel Sir Thomas Sidney Beckworth attacked Craney Island, guarding the approach to the Elizabeth River, in which the *Constellation* was moored. The militia stopped Beckworth in his tracks, taking 40 prisoners and killing or wounding a large number of the enemy. Perhaps in pique, Beckworth then attacked a nonmilitary target, the village of Hampton on the James River, where a night of looting, rape and murder gave abundant evidence of the coarsening conduct of the War.

The U.S. Navy had no more given up the fight than had Americans ashore. Commodore Rodgers with the *President* had escaped from Boston in a fog on May 1, and he remained at sea throughout the summer of 1813, collecting prizes in the North Atlantic and the North Sea. The little *Argus* roamed the Irish Sea, taking 20 vessels before she was captured by H.M.S. *Pelican*. The American *Enterprise* captured the *Boxer*, 14 guns. And on September 10, 1813, Master Commandant Oliver Hazard Perry took a small fleet of brigs, schooners and sloops into action against a British squadron on Lake Erie and secured for his country naval control of the Great Lakes (pages 146-151).

The American corvette *Adams*, cut down to a sloop of war, prowled the sea for the first seven months of 1814, taking 10 enemy merchantmen before being chased up Maine's Penobscot River, abandoned, and finally burned by the British. The last day of the previous year, the *Constitution* had slipped out of Boston and in three months at sea captured another four prizes. On April 29 a new sloop of war named the *Peacock* took H.M.S. *Epervier*, 22 guns, and by November had captured 14 merchantmen as well. In late June the *Wasp*, namesake of the sloop lost in 1812, captured H.M.S. *Reindeer*, 19 guns. And on September 1 the *Wasp* sank H.M.S. *Avon*, 18 guns, before mysteriously disappearing herself.

With a British flag flying above the Stars and Stripes, the captured Chesapeake follows the Shannon into Halifax Harbor in Canada a few days after their battle. Crowds on shore sent up a welcoming cheer, but the Shannon's crew remained silent so as not to disturb Captain Broke, who lay below severely wounded.

For the British, even apparent triumphs turned sour in this maddening little war. Late in the summer of 1814 Admiral Sir Alexander Cochrane with 44 vessels glided into Chesapeake Bay to join Cockburn's fleet. The admirals landed troops, who burned Washington and then attacked Baltimore, home port of many of the most active—and, to the British, most odious—American privateers. But again, untrained American militia held the enemy at bay (pages 155-157).

In England this latest news was greeted with dismay. Many in Parliament saw the burning of Washington as wanton arson, without strategic advantage. The rebuff at Baltimore added to their chagrin. Moreover, England, an industrial nation that depended on international trade for survival, stood in danger of losing out in the world's marketplaces because of the War. The country needed safety for its merchant ships and a resumption of commerce with America; in short, Britain needed peace.

The British began to reappraise their war effort against Jonathan Yankee, who had proved himself so unexpectedly stubborn. The two nations had already begun peace negotiations in the Belgian city of Ghent, but now the British looked on the talks as more than a diplomatic minuet. In secret Cabinet circles a new British policy evolved: English arms would seek to win as many victories as possible—but only in order to wrest concessions at the negotiating table and force a speedy peace.

The U.S. government was ignorant of this change of heart in London.

Among gifts showered upon Captain Philip Bowes Vere Broke for his capture of the Chesapeake were the ornate silver plate at left, 44 inches in diameter, from the people of his native county of Suffolk, and this gold-decorated sword and scabbard presented to him by the City of London. Broke was also knighted.

All the Americans knew was that the British seemed to be focusing their efforts against U.S. coastal cities. At the head of an almost destitute nation, the anxious President James Madison reverted to the cautious policy he had been talked out of at the start of the War. In the fall of 1814 the big frigates were ordered to take station at major cities to act as coastal defense vessels. And there they remained until the new year, when it became apparent that the British probably were not going to mount more direct attacks on large coastal cities. A degree of calm returned to Washington. Now Stephen Decatur was given permission to attempt an escape from New York in the *President*, which was faster than his old command, the *United States*, and thus better able to evade the blockading British ships.

On the night of January 14, 1815, with a snowstorm blowing and a heavy sea running, the frigate *President* stood out to sea from New York. Her captain hoped the storm had driven the British blockade ships south, and that the swift *President* could thrash her way out undetected. The plan seemed to be working—until 8 p.m., when the *President's* pilot, blinded by the storm and unable to fix his position, ran the *President* hard aground on a sandbar off New Jersey's Sandy Hook peninsula.

It took two hours of sail maneuvering and the help of the tide before the *President* was worked free and back into deep water. In the process the frigate displaced a portion of her false keel and damaged her rudder, with grave harm to her sailing qualities. A return to port would have been more than judicious—it was imperative. But because the gusty winds were against him, Stephen Decatur had no choice but to take his lamed frigate farther out to sea.

Still hoping to elude the Royal Navy blockade, the *President* ran east through the cold, blowy night—until the morning's first light revealed three, then four sail, looming dead ahead and only two miles distant. Decatur, having sailed the *President* directly into Captain John Hayes's blockading squadron, could do no more than turn and make a run for it in his crippled ship.

Heaving the *President's* cables, boats and extra spars overboard, and even jettisoning her fresh water and other provisions, Decatur desperately struggled to escape. At about 11 a.m. the British experimented with ranging fire, which fell short. But by 5 p.m., with the rest of the squadron following as best they could, Captain Henry Hope had worked the *Endymion*, a 38-gun frigate, to within point-blank range of the *President's* starboard quarter. Soon the *Endymion* was hitting the *President* repeatedly, while the American frigate, because of her position, could bring hardly a gun to bear.

Decatur attempted to turn broadside to the enemy and board. But Captain Hope maneuvered the *Endymion* away, determined to hold the *President* at bay until the rest of the British squadron came up. At dusk Decatur decided that the only way to escape defeat was to vanish into the night. He swung off, heading south, and the *Endymion* did also. Now the ships were broadside to broadside and slugging away in the gloom.

After two hours the *Endymion's* sails were in tatters; the braces leading to her spars were shot away and her masts were tottering. With most of her guns knocked out of action, she ceased firing and wallowed helplessly in the ocean troughs. Eleven of her men were dead and another 14 wounded.

But in the brutal mauling match, the *President* too had paid dearly, and had suffered many more casualties. Three of Decatur's five lieutenants were now dead, including Archibald Hamilton, the youth who had raced the *Macedonian's* colors to Washington; he was cut in half by a heavy shot. Decatur himself had been struck in the chest and head by splinters of wood. Though the wounds were not severe enough to put him out of action, they caused him great pain and much loss of blood.

In all, about one fifth of the *President's* 450-man crew were casualties. And though they had beaten the *Endymion* Stephen Decatur still had to outrun the remaining British ships. Into the night sailed the *President*— into darkness and defeat.

Just before midnight the 38-gun British frigate *Pomone* closed within musket shot on the port bow of the *President*. The 38-gun frigate *Tenedos* took position two cables' length astern of the American, and the *Majestic*, a 56-gun razee, also came up astern. Decatur was a realist, and further resistance could result only in the needless sacrifice of his men and of his battle-scarred frigate.

The American flag came down, and Decatur was rowed over to the *Majestic*. There he offered his sword to Captain John Hayes, who "felt proud in returning the sword of an officer who had defended his ship so nobly." The *President* was taken as a prize to Bermuda. Decatur was put on board the *Endymion* with Captain Hope for the trip. It was a stormy voyage, and Decatur had the satisfaction of seeing most of the *Endymion's* shot-damaged masts come down in the gale.

In Bermuda the British received Decatur with great courtesy. He had written immediately after the battle to his wife; the letter was delivered under a flag of truce so swiftly that Susan Decatur was one of the first persons to learn of the battle. Decatur was paroled and placed aboard the frigate H.M.S. *Narcissus*, and on February 22 he reached New London— where he received some astonishing news.

The War was over. The Treaty of Ghent had been signed on December 24, 1814, and had been ratified by the British on December 28. The text of the treaty had been on its way across the Atlantic when Decatur fought his battle. It had reached Washington on February 13 and had been formally ratified by the United States on February 17, while he was en route to New London.

Decatur must have had doubts about the reception he would receive in New London as the commander of the only 44-gun American frigate to be lost during the War, but he was accorded a hero's welcome. Ropes were attached to his carriage and he was drawn by the town's citizens to his lodgings. He was a guest of honor at a great ball and fireworks display given to celebrate the return of peace. And when he arrived in New York on February 28, he learned that the ships' carpenters at the Brooklyn Navy Yard had pledged 1,600 unpaid days of work toward building him a new frigate.

Still fretful lest he be officially criticized for the loss of the *President*, Decatur wrote to Washington and requested a court of inquiry to rule on his conduct. He was exonerated on April 17, when the board reported

Office of the Philadelphia Gazette, Feb. 12th

Laus Deo!

Glorious News ! ! !

PEACE.

An express passed this city this morning for the Southward. He brought a letter dated last night, at New-York, which we delivered to Mr. Havens, who, politely shewed us its contents, which are as follow:

"A British Sloop of War,* with Mr. Carrol, and a Treaty of PEACE has just arrived—signed on the 24th December.

When the Express left New-York, at eleven o'Clock, last night, the city was brilliantly illuminated.

☞ No Mail from New-Orleans.

* *Favorite, J. Maxwell of 20 guns.*

"Praise to God" reads the Latin headline of this Philadelphia Gazette broadside heralding the signing of a peace treaty between the United States and Great Britain on Christmas Eve, 1814. Though the treaty was ratified in Washington on February 16, 1815, the combat at sea continued for another four months because of the difficulty of getting messages to cruising warships.

that he had "evinced great judgment and skill, and heroic courage. His conduct and the account of his officers and crew are highly honorable to them and to the American navy, and deserve the warmest gratitude of their country."

Nevertheless, the loss of the *President* was a blow to American pride, and the War of 1812 seemed to have ended on a melancholy note. Then came the incredible news of perhaps the most dazzling of all American naval victories—in a battle fought by the *Constitution* under Charles Stewart, another of Preble's Boys, after the War was officially over.

A childhood companion of Stephen Decatur in Philadelphia, Stewart first went to sea in his early teens as a cabin boy on a merchantman bound for distant shores. The sea spell took hold; he continued in the merchant trade until 1798, when at 20 he was commissioned a lieutenant in the new Navy.

The young officer was less than an instant success in the Yankee Navy. Commodore Truxtun later complained that Lieutenant Stewart had "made a point of keeping out of the way of the commander of the squadron he was sent out to join, as much as possible." But Truxtun could hardly complain about Stewart's obedience. Once, in the Caribbean, Truxtun ordered his squadron to sea while Lieutenant Stewart was in the midst of repairing the mainmast of his little schooner, the *Experiment*. Stewart put to sea anyway, towing the mast behind him.

In the Tripolitan war, Stewart had commanded the brig *Siren* and provided cover for the *Intrepid* on the night Decatur and Lawrence burned the *Philadelphia*. At war's end Stewart obtained an extended furlough from the service and made several profitable voyages as a merchant captain. But by 1811 he was back in the Navy, hoping for a major command. He received the 38-gun *Constellation* in late 1812, prepared her for sea and forthwith got under way.

His timing could scarcely have been worse. Just as the *Constellation* was beating out the narrow channel at Hampton Roads on a wintry day in February 1813, Stewart encountered Admiral Cockburn standing into the Chesapeake Bay with a fleet bent on conducting the first punitive raids in the region. Stewart could do nothing in the face of such overwhelming force. He took the *Constellation* up the Elizabeth River, and there she remained blockaded for the rest of the War. But not Stewart. He made such a nuisance of himself demanding another frigate that he was finally given command of the *Constitution*, and on December 17, 1814, slipped her through the British blockade at Boston into the open ocean.

Stewart headed south, cruising off Bermuda, where he took the merchantman *Lord Nelson* on December 24. Then, when the hunting grew thin, he set course for the Madeira islands. But there was little game to be found. At noon on February 19—two days after the War, unbeknownst to those on the *Constitution*, had formally ended—several officers gathered on the starboard gangway and began bemoaning their lack of success. Overhearing them, Captain Stewart, with a prescience seemingly summoned from his Celtic heritage, remarked: "I assure you, gentlemen, that before the sun again rises and sets you will be engaged in battle with the enemy, and it will not be with a single ship." ⊕

Action on the lakes:
Twin debacles for Britain

The great American frigate victories of the War of 1812 were mostly single-ship actions. But there were two occasions on which the United States Navy sent out fleets to engage the British. The warships in these encounters were smaller than frigates, and both battles took place on fresh water: one on Lake Erie, the other on Lake Champlain. The results, however, were as disastrous as any frigate defeat to the image of an invincible Royal Navy.

In the summer of 1813 the British controlled Lake Erie, a vital trade route between the East and American territories to the west. The task of winning the lake fell to 27-year-old Master Commandant Oliver Hazard Perry, who set forth from Ohio's Put-in-Bay on September 10 with nine vessels mounting a total of 54 guns. Inscribed on Perry's battle flag (pages 2-3) were the last words of Captain James Lawrence, who had been slain on board the frigate *Chesapeake* three months before: "Don't give up the ship."

Perry found the British about 10 miles north of Put-in-Bay. The enemy had six vessels mounting 63 guns, and for most of the fight the Royal Navy had the best of it. Perry's flagship *Lawrence* was reduced to a wreck; the American commander was forced to transfer to the brig *Niagara*. But then superior American gunnery slowly turned the tide. After more than three hours of furious combat, Perry could signal to shore: "We have met the enemy and they are ours."

Almost exactly one year later, the drama was repeated to the east on Lake Champlain. This time the British were on the offensive, launching attacks down from the north by land and by lake in hopes of isolating New England.

While British and American troops struggled for the town of Plattsburg, New York, the Royal Navy tried to break through a Yankee fleet guarding Plattsburg Bay. The British had 16 vessels, led by the 37-gun *Confiance*. The American fleet, under Commodore Thomas Macdonough in the 26-gun *Saratoga*, also numbered 16 ships; they were anchored across the narrow bay in such a way that the British would have to plunge head on into American broadsides.

The battle lasted almost two and a half hours. At the climax the *Saratoga* forced the bigger *Confiance* to strike her colors. Three other British ships also surrendered, and the remaining 12 fled. A great cheer arose from the American fleet—at which point the British on land lost heart and surrendered, thus ending the threat to New England.

Leaving his disabled flagship Lawrence *(left), her ensign still waving, Commodore Oliver Hazard Perry carries his battle flag as he is rowed to the brig* Niagara *(right) during the height of the action on Lake Erie in 1813. All told, 83 of the* Lawrence's *103 men were killed or wounded during the fierce battle.*

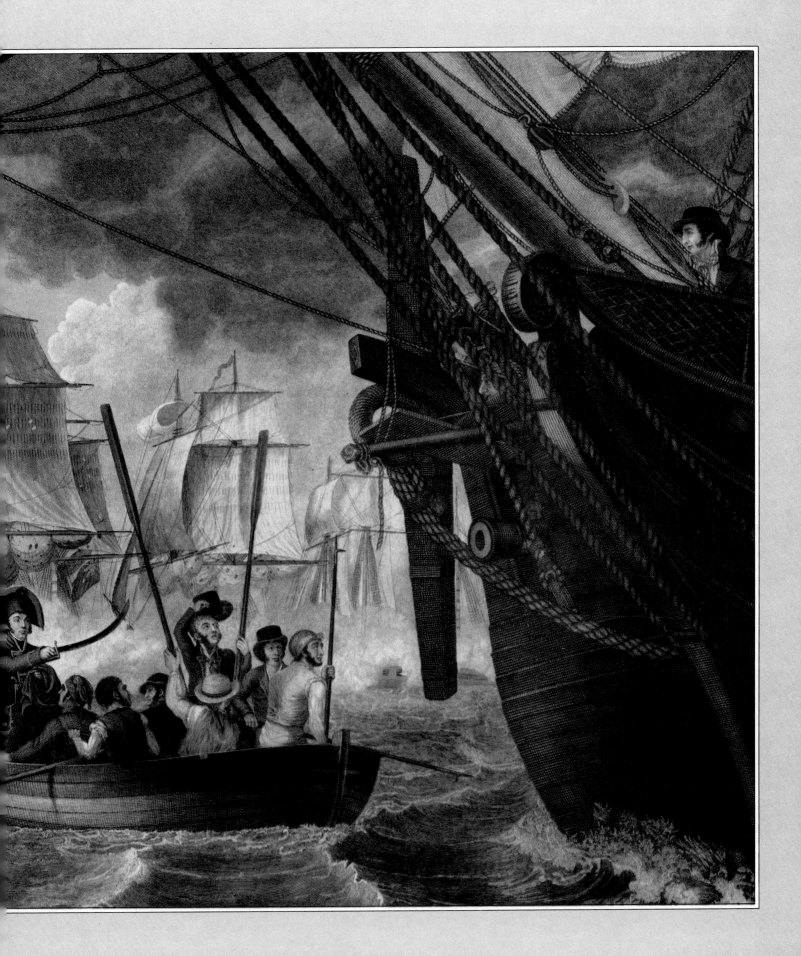

Broadsides thundering point-blank to port and starboard, the 20-gun American brig Niagara (center) charges into the center of the British line at a decisive moment in the struggle for control of Lake Erie. Following the Niagara's lead, other vessels in the American squadron engaged the enemy at close quarters until, eight minutes after the Niagara's daring maneuver, the British flagship Detroit hauled down her colors, as did three of her sister ships, signaling defeat for the Royal Navy.

Sandwiched between the British Confiance and the Linnet, the American flagship Saratoga cuts loose with cannon on all sides in this artist's rendering of the Battle of Lake Champlain on September 11, 1814. On shore, American civilians cheer the action, while in the distance smoke billows from land battles in the village of Plattsburg. To the left of the main naval action, British gunboats hastily escape under fire, while to the right, American gunboats bombard the beleaguered British fleet.

ebruary 20 began with a thick fog that left water droplets glistening on the frigate's rigging. A little after noon the fog parted, and a ship could be made out sailing along under easy canvas. The *Constitution* quickly turned in pursuit, crowding on sail until she drew close enough for her crew to see that the stranger was a frigate.

Now, with studding sails set for greater speed, the *Constitution* pressed onward and soon sighted a second ship, dead ahead on the horizon. Since both alien ships were on the starboard tack and holding to the same course, Captain Stewart surmised that his quarry was a pair of frigates cruising in company. By late afternoon he had greatly narrowed the gap between the *Constitution* and the aftermost ship, which Stewart hoped to tackle singly before her consort could join the fight. But just as he was nearing firing range, the *Constitution* suddenly heeled to a sharp gust—and lost her main-royal mast. Suddenly the *Constitution* found herself in a situation reminiscent of the dilemma of the *Essex:* an American frigate partially dismasted and facing two enemies.

Yankee topmen swarmed up to fit a spare spar to the main-topgallant mast and resplice the rigging. Within an hour the *Constitution* was in pursuit once again, but in that interval the two British ships had managed to join forces, and Captain Stewart had missed the chance to fight them one at a time.

In the traditional preliminary to action, a double ration of grog was brought up for the *Constitution*'s crew. Nothing speaks more eloquently of the crew's fettle than the fact that before the men could get their hands on the stuff the older hands tossed the grog tub into the scuppers. According to a midshipman, the veterans said they "didn't want any Dutch courage on board."

By 6 p.m. all three ships had reduced to fighting sail, and in bright moonlight the British and American flags were hoisted. Five minutes later the *Constitution* opened fire on the sternmost ship, both British vessels replied, and the battle was on.

The aftermost ship was H.M.S. *Cyane*, a frigate of 32 guns, Captain Gordon Falcon commanding. Keeping her company was H.M.S. *Levant*, not a frigate after all, but a sloop of war of 18 guns under Captain the Honorable George Douglass. During the chase neither British commander had wished to avoid battle. But they had kept their distance until dark in the belief that it would improve their chances of working as a team against the big American frigate.

Now, with all ships firing as fast as their guns could be reloaded, smoke quickly filled the small triangle between them. Scarcely damaged, the *Constitution* ceased firing after 15 minutes. She was drawing ahead of the *Cyane*, pulling up on the *Levant*. Captain Stewart ordered his guns double-shotted, and the *Constitution* delivered a crushing broadside into the smaller ship. But as the *Constitution* was preparing to finish the kill, Captain Stewart saw the *Cyane*, behind him, begin to luff up into the wind to gain raking position.

Charles Stewart, with the smartly trained men of the *Constitution*, now executed a superb feat of seamanship. The *Constitution* came up into the wind, the main- and mizzen-topsails were backed and the head-

In the last and most dramatic victory of her brilliant career, the Constitution (center) sends a full port broadside into the British frigate Cyane (right) while the British sloop of war Levant futilely attempts to lend assistance to her companion's ineffective counterfire. The Constitution defeated both foes, and was ready for combat three hours later.

sails cast loose. She glided to a halt, then gathered sternway just off the starboard bow of the *Cyane* and backed down into position to deliver a tremendous diagonal rake the length of the enemy. Under the force of this ferocious fire, the *Cyane* quickly fell off, her headsails in tatters. The two ships were very close, the Marines in both tops rattling away as fast as their muskets could fire. Clearly the *Cyane*, her guns being dismounted and her men falling on bloody decking, could not long continue to take this sort of punishment from a bigger, stronger opponent so splendidly handled. As the *Cyane*'s guns fell silent, the *Constitution* again turned her attention toward the *Levant* in what was becoming a deadly change-partners dance at sea.

As the crew of the *Constitution* sheeted home, the big frigate surged forward and emerged from the smoke of battle to catch the *Levant* making a turn and presenting her stern. The *Constitution* poured in two tremendous broadsides, probing the entire length of the *Levant*. The smaller ship staggered under the shocks and wobbled away out of control. Now it was back to the *Cyane*.

The *Constitution* wore round just in time for Stewart to make out the bigger British ship limping up behind him. But the *Constitution*, her crew as adept on the yards as they were at the guns, turned swiftly on the enemy frigate, winding up astern and blasting British masts with another broadside. Forty minutes after her first gun had been fired, the *Cyane*'s halyard blocks creaked and her flag came down.

Incredibly, the battle was not yet done. By 8 p.m. the *Levant*, having made emergency repairs, came rushing back to the scene—a brave little bulldog, loyal and true. One broadside from the *Constitution* almost leveled the badly damaged sloop, and shortly after that her colors too came fluttering down.

Aboard the *Cyane* and *Levant* there were 35 killed and 42 wounded out of 313 men. The *Constitution* had suffered but four killed and 10 wounded of her 456-man crew. After the battle the British captains, Falcon and Douglass, taken aboard the *Constitution* and sitting in Stewart's cabin, began blaming each other for the crushing defeat. "Gentlemen," Stewart said, "there is no use in getting warm about it; it would have been the same whatever you might have done. If you doubt that, I will put you all on board and you can try it over."

Captain Charles Stewart had fought the last big frigate action of the War of 1812 with great bravery and consummate skill. Although each of the British ships was smaller than the *Constitution*, their combined weight of broadside exceeded that of the American. Whatever the respective strengths of armament, the seamanship with which the *Constitution* had been handled against two enemy vessels amounted to a virtuoso performance. Commodore Preble, had he been alive, would have slapped his knee in admiration of one of his boys.

On March 10 the *Constitution* brought her two prizes into the port of Praia in the Cape Verde Islands. But at noon the next day the sails of several ships, set on a course to enter the roadstead, were seen looming above the low, heavy sea fog. The force, consisting of three frigates, was commanded by British Captain Sir George Collier. It had been the blockade group through which Stewart and the *Constitution* had slipped when leaving Boston. For 85 days and across thousands of wave-tossed miles, Collier had been hunting the *Constitution* after learning of her escape—and now, at last, he had tracked her down.

Within seven minutes after sighting Collier, the crew of the *Constitution* had cut her cables, loosed her topsails and got the Yankee frigate under way. Signals instructed the American prize crews on the *Cyane* and *Levant* to follow. As the American flotilla emerged from harbor the British cracked on all canvas, boiling along at 10 knots on a course intended to cut Stewart off from his prizes.

Observing this, Stewart signaled the *Cyane* and *Levant* to part company. The *Cyane* immediately tacked to the northwest, expecting at least one of Collier's ships to pursue. But, to the amazement of the Americans, Collier allowed their captured frigate to sail unscathed over the horizon without a single pursuer. Sir George instead veered his entire force after the tiny *Levant*, by far the least valuable of his three possible quarries. The *Levant* led her pursuers on a merry chase and eventually succeeded in anchoring back in Praia. Disregarding the neutrality of that port, Admiral Collier thereupon ordered his ships to open fire on the *Levant*, which surrendered quickly enough—after English shot had flown over her and plowed into several houses in town.

A campaign of punishment on Chesapeake Bay

"The ruin, the desolation, the heartless misery that we left them to brood over will forever make the citizens of the United States hate us with that hatred which no words can allay or time eradicate." So wrote Frederick Chamier, a midshipman and member of the British invasion force sent to Chesapeake Bay in the summer of 1814.

The British intention was to capture the cities of Washington and Baltimore, and thus bring the Americans quickly to terms in the war they had been so audaciously waging against their mother country. The plan failed, but before the British retreated they managed to wreak a devastation that the Americans would long remember. The campaign had its genesis in a blockade of the Chesapeake that the British had maintained since February 1813. The admiral in charge was Sir George Cockburn, a choleric man with a vast contempt for Americans.

Rather than send his vessels back to Bermuda for fresh provisions, Cockburn sent raiding parties ashore for supplies. "Should resistance be offered or menaces held out," he ordered, the landing parties were to "consider the town as a fortified post and the male inhabitants as soldiers; the one to be destroyed and the other, with their cattle and stock, to be captured."

Before long the Chesapeake area was dotted with burned villages and ransacked farms. The climax came on May 3, when Cockburn put ashore 19 bargeloads of men at Havre de Grace in Maryland. After shelling the town and overruning a small redoubt, the British plundered and burned 40 of the community's 60 buildings.

The weak resistance of the Americans at Havre de Grace helped convince the British that they were free to "chastise the savages," as the London *Times* put it. More forces were sent to the Chesapeake and plans drawn to sweep up the Bay and deal a stunning blow at the heart of the upstart nation.

British landing parties under Admiral George Cockburn (foreground, right of center) loot and burn Havre de Grace, Maryland, in May 1813.

156

A valiant turnabout: the tale of two cities

On August 19, 1814, Admiral Alexander Cochrane, now in command of the British fleet, landed a force of 4,500 men at Benedict, Maryland, on the Patuxent River and commenced a cross-country drive on Washington, only 35 miles away. The troops were experienced regulars, veterans of Wellington's campaigns against the French, and they easily brushed aside 7,000 American militiamen who met them on August 24 outside of Washington.

By late afternoon of the same day, the British forces were in the 15-year-old American capital. On all sides of them, buildings and roadways lay un-

finished amid pools of stagnant water. Many of the 9,000 inhabitants had fled into the countryside at first news of the British invasion. Shortly after entering the city, the Redcoats were ordered to burn all the public buildings, and soon the Capitol, the Treasury, the War Office, the Arsenal and the White House were in flames.

The torching of Washington was a great symbolic triumph for the British. But their next target, the port of Baltimore, was strategically much more important. Besides being an old and prosperous city of about 40,000 inhabitants —the third largest city in America—

While Washington erupts in smoke and flames, President James Madison— or "Maddy," as he is dubbed in this British cartoon of 1814—flees the nation's capital amid the catcalls and jeers of his countrymen. Two English sailors, Jack Tarr and his messmate, observe the proceedings and compare Madison's fate to that of Napoleon Bonaparte, Britain's recently defeated archenemy.

Baltimore was a major shipbuilding center. And from its harbor sailed hundreds of the privateers that preyed on British merchant shipping.

Cochrane moved his fleet north to a position at Baltimore's front door, the mouth of the Patapsco River. But here the defenses were far more formidable than those on the road to Washington. The American in command was Major General Samuel Smith, a 62-year-old veteran of the Revolutionary War who had been at work since August fortifying the city and Fort McHenry, guarding the harbor. Now, as fresh militia streamed in from nearby states, he had no fewer than 50,000 men under him.

On September 12, Cochrane put his troops on shore—and met disaster. His army commander was shot off his horse by American snipers and died on the spot. The British soldiers met stiff resistance from the American advance guard, and Fort McHenry held out through an entire day and night of bombardment by the British fleet.

With his men rapidly losing heart and soaked to the skin by torrential rain, Cochrane, on the 14th, ordered the troops to return to the ships. Within a month the fleet sailed for the West Indies, never to return.

Hove to in Baltimore harbor on September 13, 1814, a massive British fleet begins its historic bombardment of Fort McHenry, lobbing great bombs, each weighing 190 pounds, into the American redoubt. The siege continued for 25 hours and the fort was rocked by 400 direct hits. But the American flag continued to fly in proud defiance, prompting Francis Scott Key (top right), a patriot and poet, to pen his famed ode, "The Defense of Fort McHenry." The poem was later given another title and put to music as "The Star-Spangled Banner."

Nevertheless, the little American Navy, which had begun the frigate actions of the War of 1812 with Isaac Hull's victory over the *Guerriere*, had ended them with Charles Stewart's defeat of H.M.S. *Cyane* and *Levant*. Against the most formidable navy then sailing the seas, the Yankees had more than held their own. In 26 major ship actions of all kinds, the Americans had been victorious 14 times, defeating, destroying or capturing 16 Royal Navy frigates, sloops and other warships while losing 12 vessels of their own. However, that was not the full measure of the accomplishment. Of those 26 major engagements, 14 had been single-ship actions, and when one American encountered one British vessel on equal terms, the American had achieved victory no fewer than a dozen times.

The London *Times* summed up the Royal Navy's lamentable tally: "Scarcely is there an American ship of war which has not to boast a victory over the British flag; scarcely one British ship in 30 or 40 that has beaten an American. With the bravest seamen and the most powerful navy in the world, we retire from the contest with the balance of defeat so heavily against us."

The Treaty of Ghent, ending the War, was remarkable for its lack of formal substance. It restored to both Britain and the United States some minor territories captured during the fighting, provided for a commission to determine a northwestern boundary between Canada and the United States, and generally reestablished conditions as they had existed before the War. The treaty made no official mention of either British impressment of American seamen or the right of neutral trade. But by unwritten agreement it was understood that impressment would be ended immediately (it was) and that Americans could trade as they chose (thereafter they did).

The United States had secured for itself freedom of the seas and henceforth would be recognized as a maritime power, to be respected the world over. The crucible of 1812 shaped America's destiny just as surely as a few innovative shipbuilders and a handful of stout-hearted captains had shaped a navy.

There remained one small matter to be resolved. During the War of 1812, the Dey of Algiers had formally allied himself with the British. Yet if he had hoped for easy pickings from the Americans, he was grossly disappointed. During the conflict the Dey had captured only the *Edwin*, a small brig out of Salem, Massachusetts. And now, with the War over and the United States Navy gaining in strength, President Madison decided to suppress the Barbary corsairs once and for all.

William Bainbridge and Stephen Decatur were ordered to take squadrons to the Mediterranean and bring the Dey of Algiers to terms. When Bainbridge was delayed in getting his squadron to sea, Decatur sailed from New York in his flagship, the spanking new 44-gun *Guerriere*, named after the first British frigate to be defeated by the Americans in the War of 1812. Accompanying him were nine other warships. In short order Decatur captured the Algerian frigate *Mashuda*, 46 guns, swept up the 22-gun brig *Estedio* and forced his own terms not only on Algiers but on Tunis and Tripoli as well. Those states agreed to demand no more

The finest hour of a Yankee privateer

To the Royal Navy, Yankee privateers were the vermin of the seas. The letters of marque they carried authorizing them to plunder enemy ships made them little better than pirates in British eyes. Their privately armed sloops and brigs, rarely as large as the smallest frigate, preyed on unarmed merchantmen and generally fled at the sight of a British warship. But at least one privateer—Samuel Chester Reid of New York City—proved himself a match for the Royal Navy. In fact Reid may have unwittingly played an indirect role in the galling British defeat at the Battle of New Orleans on January 8, 1815.

Reid's part of the story began a little over three months before that battle, when he sailed his seven-gun brig *General Armstrong* into the harbor at Fayal in the Azores to take on drinking water.

Shortly after he arrived, he spied a squadron of three British ships making for the island. Commanded by Captain Robert Lloyd, the vessels were the 18-gun brig *Carnation*, the 38-gun frigate *Rota* and the 74-gun ship of the line *Plantagenet*. They were en route to Jamaica with 2,000 men to join Admiral Alexander Cochrane for an attack on New Orleans.

Samuel Reid, hero of Fayal, is portrayed impeccably garbed amid the smoke of battle in this 1815 painting.

Though Portugal was neutral in the War, and Reid was presumably safe within its territorial waters, he suspected that the British would attack him, neutral port or no. He therefore set his 90-man crew to work rowing the *Armstrong* toward shore into waters too shallow for the biggest British warships to follow. Sure enough, that night the British attacked in four launches carrying about 160 men. Reid gave them a murderous broadside of grapeshot. More than a dozen attackers were killed and wounded before the launches retreated back into the gloom.

Enraged by the stinging repulse, Captain Lloyd vowed to crush the privateer. He now sent 12 boats filled with men and armed with swivel-mounted carronades against the Americans. "As soon as they came within proper distance," Reid later recalled, "we opened our fire which was warmly returned from the enemy's carronades and small arms. In a moment they succeeded in gaining our bow and starboard quarter and the word was Board!"

As the British hacked at the netting Reid had thrown up to block them, the Americans fired their muskets into the faces of their assailants and cut at them with pikes and cutlasses. The British gained the deck and were pressing aft when Reid rallied his men and drove the enemy back over the side.

Whether the British casualties were as Reid recorded them, 120 killed and 130 wounded, or as they were later reported by the British, 34 killed and 86 wounded, they were bad enough to make Lloyd lose all composure. He ordered the *Carnation* to attack the *Armstrong*. Reid endured the siege as long as he could. Then, realizing his lost position, he scuttled his ship and took refuge with his men in a nearby monastery.

Although the little brig went down a flaming wreck, Reid's gallant defense caused the British to remain at Fayal for nearly a fortnight making repairs. Cochrane, in turn, was compelled to postpone his departure for New Orleans, giving Andrew Jackson time to force-march 2,000 Tennessee militiamen to the city and crush the invaders.

Reid's effect on the outcome at New Orleans is a matter of conjecture. But in 1890, when Reid's son offered his father's saber as a gift to the United States, the Senate responded by voting to strike a gold medal in the privateer's honor. Declared Senator Daniel W. Voorhees, "No such battle would have been fought, no such victory won, but for the stubborn and invincible courage of Captain Reid and his crew at Fayal."

tribute of any kind, to promptly release without ransom all the prisoners they currently held and henceforth to exchange prisoners in wartime rather than make them slaves.

Returning to the United States, Decatur—by now dubbed the "hero of the Mediterranean"—settled in Washington with his wife, Susan. He bought land near Lafayette Square, across from the White House, and commissioned Benjamin Latrobe, designer of the Capitol, to build him a mansion. In January 1816 Decatur reported for duty as a Commissioner of the Navy, a position analogous to a Lord of the British Admiralty. It was an easy and prestigious life, and the impetuous Decatur chafed at it. Approaching his 41st year, he still sought action, still felt compelled to defend the most rigid code of personal honor. In 1820 that compulsion cost him his life.

It is hard to understand why Decatur chose to meet James Barron on a field of honor. After the disastrous affair between the *Chesapeake* and the *Leopard*, Barron had passed his five-year exile from Naval service working in the merchant marine. Finally, in February 1819, he asked that his Navy commission be reinstated. Barron had long held Decatur accountable for the court-martial verdict against him. Now, when the Secretary of the Navy delayed in granting his application, he blamed Decatur, as Navy Commissioner, for that too. Newly aggrieved, Barron entered into angry correspondence with Decatur, who replied—needlessly and perhaps cruelly—that if the choice were his, Barron would never reenter Naval service.

When Barron continued his barrage of protest, Decatur, in exasperation, attempted to break off the exchanges. He wrote Barron that he would pay "no further attention to any communication you may make other than a direct call to the field." Barron responded that Decatur was "at liberty to view this as a call" and Decatur forthwith accepted the challenge. The confrontation was set to take place on a well-known dueling field called the Valley of Chance near Bladensburg, Maryland, on March 22, 1820.

On that day Decatur, who had confided to friends that his intention was only to wound his opponent, rose early and slipped out of the house. He joined Bainbridge, who had agreed to act as umpire, and another friend for breakfast before the trio proceeded to Bladensburg. At the appointed time Barron arrived at the field with his seconds. Eight paces were marked off. Decatur won the toss and elected to take the lower ground to the north.

While the pistols were being loaded by Commodore Bainbridge, both principals voided their urine so as not to risk medical complications if they were wounded. As they took their positions, Commodore Barron said: "I hope, sir, that when we meet in another world, we shall be better friends than we have been in this." Decatur replied: "I have never been your enemy, sir!"

The duelists were to fire after Bainbridge said "one" but not after the word "three" in a sequence that ran "present—one—two—three." After cautioning the two men to make ready, Bainbridge started to recite the sequence, speaking quickly so as to lessen the chance of good aim and a mortal wound.

الهلاطر ادجيد مع المريكان وكان عدد البنقب المريكانين اربعة فراقط وقربط واربعة السكونات وبقى الحرب الحوخسته ساعات فرمان ١٢٣٠ سنة

At the word "two," two reports sounded as one and a puff of smoke curled up from each pistol. Barron pitched, groaning, to the ground—he had been hit in the hip, exactly where Decatur had said he would aim. Decatur straightened, dropped his pistol, clapped his right hand to his side and then fell senseless. He had been shot in the abdomen, the ball severing major blood vessels. Both combatants were carried from the field, Barron saying, "God bless you, Decatur." Decatur's response was a weak "Farewell, farewell, Barron."

Decatur was brought back to his house by 10:30 a.m. and was placed on a sofa in the parlor. At his insistence, his wife and nieces were led upstairs. He was in extreme agony, remarking that he did not know "any man could suffer such pain." When he realized his wound was mortal, he observed that he did not so much regret his death as the manner of it; had it found him on the quarter-deck, it would have been most welcome. Between 9 and 10 o'clock that night Stephen Decatur died.

Surrounded by U.S. warships, led by Captain Stephen Decatur's frigate Guerriere (at left, flying a pennant), the Algerian frigate Mashuda (center) fights on though doomed, off the Spanish coast on June 17, 1815. The inscription below this contemporary Arabic watercolor describes the battle as lasting "nearly five entire hours" and gives the year as 1230—the Muhammadan date.

And what befell the others among Preble's Boys? Neither William Bainbridge nor David Porter adjusted comfortably to the stagnant routine of the peacetime Navy. In 1831 Bainbridge became involved in an acrimonious dispute with the Secretary of the Navy over a matter of personal expenses; he was consequently suspended from the service for a year, until the matter was finally resolved in his favor. But the squabble left him bitter, and ill health sapped his strength. He died two years afterward, at the age of 59, deliriously calling for his pistols and cutlass so as to "board the enemy."

David Porter was embroiled in an even more serious conflict with his superiors in 1824, when he took it upon himself to land 200 men on the Spanish-owned island of Puerto Rico to redress an insult to one of his officers. The Spaniards apologized and no one was hurt. But such truculence ran counter to American diplomatic policy in the Caribbean at the time. Porter was court-martialed for disobeying orders and resigned forthwith from the Navy. Yet time eventually mellowed the proud and disputatious captain of the *Essex*. After further adventures, including a stint in the Mexican Navy, he entered the U.S. Foreign Service and ended his days as American resident minister at Constantinople, where he died of heart disease in 1843 at the age of 63.

Isaac Hull and Charles Stewart, on the other hand, showed themselves well suited to high position in the Navy of later years. Hull commanded various Navy yards, and cruised far and wide as commodore in command of the Pacific and Mediterranean fleets. While in Rome in the 1830s, he renewed his acquaintance with British Captain James Richard Dacres, his erstwhile foe of the *Guerriere* battle. The two could be seen walking together, arm in arm, the tall, thin Dacres and the short, stout Hull, engaged in deep conversation, no doubt fighting the engagement all over again.

In 1843, just before Hull died of a stomach ailment, the meticulous old captain called an undertaker to his home in Philadelphia so that he could order his final arrangements. His last words were ones that he had never uttered before in his life: "I strike my flag."

Charles Stewart outlived them all. For a spell he was in command of the Mediterranean fleet and had charge of the 74-gun *Franklin* in 1821 when she was dispatched to protect United States interests in the Peruvian War of Independence against Spain. Like Porter, he was court-martialed—on the basis of a canard alleging, among other things, that he ran contraband into Peru. But he was cleared of the charges and, unlike Bainbridge, refused to let the experience sour him. He continued to serve and eventually rose to rear admiral, the only one of Preble's Boys to achieve that exalted rank. He was 83 and still on the Navy's rolls in 1861 when the Confederates shelled Fort Sumter. He immediately applied for active sea duty. With expressions of regret, Lincoln's government turned down his offer. Stewart retired for good the next year, and lived to see the Union victorious before he died of cancer in 1869 at the age of 92.

So they passed into history, the small band of gallant Americans whom Commodore Preble had once labeled "a pack of boys." Later, after some months of witnessing their exploits in the Mediterranean,

A sad and senseless postscript in a British prison

One of the most sorrowful chapters in the War of 1812 occurred weeks after peace was made. By March 1815 some 6,000 Americans were confined in grim Dartmoor Prison in southwest Devon. Some of them had been there for years. When news of the ratification of the Treaty of Ghent reached the prison, the Americans went wild with joy. "We made old Dartmoor shake under us with our shouts," recalled one prisoner. "There could be no doubt of our being soon set at liberty."

But several weeks passed and the men remained incarcerated. The United States government, all but bankrupt, was having trouble raising funds to bring them home. Tensions rose un-

til, on the afternoon of April 6, a group of Americans playing a game of catch lost a ball over the inner wall dividing the prison yard from the soldiers' barracks. When the guards refused to return the ball, several infuriated Yanks, trying to retrieve it, started knocking a hole in the wall with loose bars of iron taken from a prison window.

The commandant of the prison, fearing a massive escape attempt, ordered guards to fire into the yard. "There were men firing on us for more than ten minutes, and the pattering of balls against the buildings seemed like a hail storm," recalled one man. When the shooting stopped, seven Americans were dead and 54 wounded.

Both nations regarded the incident as a sad and senseless postscript to a war that everyone was glad to see come to an end. The British Admiralty agreed to pay part of the expense of repatriating the prisoners, and by June they were beginning to arrive home. "On first setting foot on my native soil, tears gushed from my eyes," one American later wrote. "I should have kneeled down and kissed the earth of the UNITED STATES."

Shocked and terror-stricken, American prisoners scatter in all directions as a rank of guards (just below the center of the picture) fires a smoking volley during the 1815 Dartmoor Prison massacre.

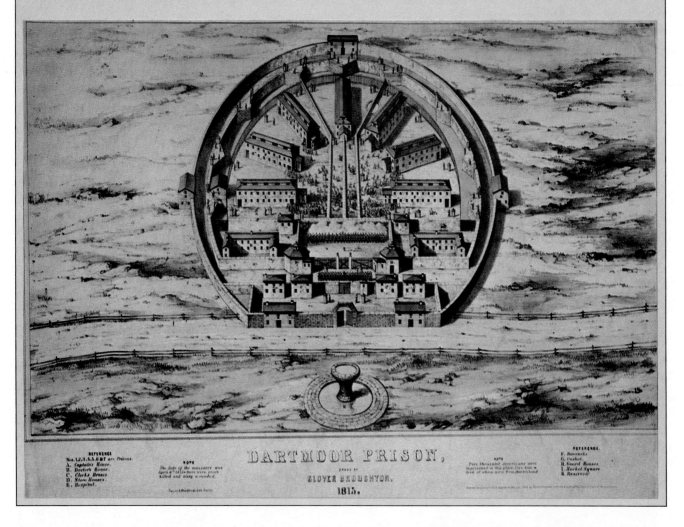

DARTMOOR PRISON,

DRAWN BY

GLOVER BROUGHTON.

1815.

the old commodore had been reminded of the way he had first characterized his young officers. Preble permitted himself a small, wry smile. If he had in fact called them boys, he acknowledged, then they were "very good boys."

And what of the men who designed the frigates that took the boys to war? Life did not work out well for Joshua Humphreys. His son Clement was lost at sea on a merchantman in 1803. His wife, Mary, died unexpectedly in 1805 at the age of 47. He gave up shipbuilding and retired to his house in Haverford, Pennsylvania, where he lived until 1838, virtually forgotten in his own time. Josiah Fox, as well, seems to have spent his energies as a shipbuilder with the completion of the first frigate. In 1811 he moved inland and purchased a large tract of land near what is now Colerain, Ohio, and there he lived comfortably as a gentleman-farmer until his death in 1847.

Of the grand fighting frigates, the *Constellation* and the *Constitution* lived on long beyond their service career, and after they had passed through numerous incarnations, both found a new life as museum ships. The *Constellation*, once nicknamed the "Baltimore Race Horse," was returned to the city where she had been born. The *Constitution*, as well, was eventually sent home to honored rest at the U.S. Navy yard in Boston *(pages 164-169).*

The two captured frigates—the *President* and the *Chesapeake*—were taken to England, where they were displayed as prizes of war for a time, and no doubt served as models for His Majesty's shipwrights. The *President* was broken up by the Royal Navy in 1818, and her timber and fittings scattered to the winds. Two years later the *Chesapeake* also was scrapped, but she continued to live, after a fashion. By remarkable coincidence, the ship that was built at Gosport, Virginia, was broken up at a yard in Gosport, England—after which her almost indestructible live oak was used in its entirety to rebuild a flour mill in Wickham, eight miles from Portsmouth. And there her timbers even today stand and serve in the still-working Chesapeake Mill.

Of the other two frigates, the *Congress* was broken up by the U.S. Navy in 1836, and the *United States* was burned and sunk in 1861 at the Norfolk Navy Yard to prevent her from being captured by Confederate forces. Yet even in her last moments of agony the *United States* played a modest role in history. For as the flames flickered along her rigging, they spread to nearby vessels, including the steam frigate *Merrimack*, which also burned and sank.

History rarely marks the close of one era and the advent of another with such pinpoint precision as it did in this instance. On May 30, 1861, the burned-out hulk of the *Merrimack* was raised from the mud by engineers of the Confederacy. Rather than rebuild the steam frigate's wooden walls, they plated her over with great sheets of rolled iron two inches in thickness, and soon afterward she sailed out to do battle with the Union ironclad, *Monitor*.

The iron warship had burst upon the world. And with its coming, the majesty, beauty, grace and gallantry of the great wooden frigates had passed forever.

Saving a gallant ship from the "harpies of the shore"

In the autumn of 1830 it seemed at last that the rot of age and the parsimony of the U.S. Congress were about to accomplish what nary a foe had been able to achieve—the death of "Old Ironsides," as the U.S.S. *Constitution* was fondly called. She had last fired a shot in anger in February 1815. She performed peacetime duties until July 1828, when she was withdrawn from service. By 1830 the greatest frigate of them all had been pronounced unseaworthy and awaited an uncertain fate at her berth in Boston Harbor.

But then a young Harvard graduate came to the *Constitution*'s rescue. He was Oliver Wendell Holmes, who later would be widely famed as an essayist and the father of one of America's most distinguished jurists. Deeply angry over the great ship's impending fate, Holmes wrote a stirring poem that began, "Ay, tear her tattered ensign down!" and scornfully chided the "harpies of the shore" who would sell Old Ironsides for scrap lumber. He wrote:

Oh better that her shattered hulk
Should sink beneath the wave;
Her thunders shook the mighty deep,
And there should be her grave.

Picked up by newspapers and printed widely in broadsides, the poem struck a chord of patriotism in Americans everywhere. Such a roar of indignant protest filled the halls of Congress that funds were soon appropriated to restore the *Constitution* for further service. And although her fighting days were over, she went on to serve for a century and more as an American Naval vessel.

Over the years she was flagship for the Mediterranean, Pacific and African Squadrons, circumnavigated the globe, and saw duty as a training ship and as a receiving ship for transient sailors. In 1849 she was host to Pope Pius IX in Italy, the first time a reigning pontiff had set foot on United States territory—for such were her decks considered. And in the 1930s she was visited by more than four and a half million people during a 22,000-mile cruise to 74 East, West and Gulf Coast ports.

Her last duty was in her birthplace, Boston, where she rests today as a museum ship and a tribute to the old frigate builders' art, bearing as well the distinction of being the oldest commissioned ship in the U.S. Navy.

With a ceremonial salvo and her crew lining the rigging, the flag-bedecked Constitution celebrates George Washington's birthday while on a visit to the British base of Malta on February 22, 1837. Royal Navy warships in the harbor responded in kind, in recognition of the fact that the old animosities between England and her former colonies had finally died.

One of the earliest photographs of the Constitution shows her set for relaunching after undergoing extensive repairs at the Portsmouth, New Hampshire, Navy Yard in 1858. This particular restoration followed a tour of duty in African waters during which she captured her last prize—an American slaver flouting an 1807 law banning slave importation.

In her most plebeian incarnation, the Constitution serves as a floating barracks for Navy recruits at Portsmouth Navy Yard. This duty lasted about 15 years, until 1897, when she was towed to Boston for her 100th-anniversary celebration.

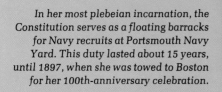

With the Constitution as a backdrop, Girl Scout leaders hand the Boston Navy Yard commandant, Rear Admiral Philip Andrews, $200 to help finance yet another restoration. The work, performed between 1927 and 1931, cost nearly one million dollars, of which more than two thirds was raised by public subscription and the sale of souvenirs crafted from old wood and metal removed from the frigate during her restoration.

Looking as trim as the day she was built, the Constitution passes through the Panama Canal during her 1931-1934 good-will cruise around the U.S. coastline. The frigate, which had last moved under canvas in the 19th Century, was towed from port to port by the U.S.S. Grebe, a World War I minesweeper, seen here following her through the canal.

In contrast to the stark modern skyline
looming over Boston Harbor, the ornately
rigged Constitution is gently towed
along by tugboats during her annual
"turnaround cruise." The purpose
of the two-hour exercise, which takes
her just a few miles from her berth,
is to reverse her position at the dock, thus
ensuring that she will weather evenly.

Bibliography

Allen, Gardner W., *Our Navy and the Barbary Corsairs*. Houghton Mifflin, 1905.

Anthony, Irvin, *Decatur*. Scribner's, 1931.

Archibald, E. H. H., *The Wooden Fighting Ship*. Arco, 1968.

Carson, the Honorable Hampton L., *The Humphreys Family of Haverford and Philadelphia*. Wickersham Press, 1922.

Chapelle, Howard I., *The History of the American Sailing Navy: The Ships and Their Development*. Bonanza Books, 1949.

Chidsey, Donald Barr, *The Wars in Barbary*. Crown, 1971.

Clark, William Bell, *Gallant John Barry 1745-1803*. Macmillan, 1938.

Coggins, Jack, *Ships and Seamen of the American Revolution*. Promontory Press, 1969.

Coles, Harry L., *The War of 1812*. The University of Chicago Press, 1965.

Cooper, J. Fenimore, *The History of the Navy of the United States of America*. A. and W. Galignani, 1839.

Dearborn, H. A. S., *The Life of William Bainbridge, Esq. of the United States Navy*. Princeton University Press, 1931.

Dearden, Seton, *A Nest of Corsairs*. John Murrary, 1976.

Donovan, Frank, *The Tall Frigates*. Dodd, Mead, 1962.

Engle, Eloise, and Arnold S. Lott, *America's Maritime Heritage*. Naval Institute Press, 1975.

Eskew, Garnett, "Our Navy's Ships and Their Builders, 1775-1961." Unpublished manuscript, U.S. Naval Academy.

Evans, Henry C., Jr., *Chile and Its Relations With the United States*. Duke University Press, 1927.

Fairburn, William Armstrong, *Merchant Sail*, 6 vols. Fairburn Marine Educational Foundation, 1945-1955.

Faris, John Thomason, *The Romance of Forgotten Men*. Harper & Brothers, 1928.

Farragut, Loyall, *The Life of David Glasgow Farragut*. D. Appleton, 1879.

Ferguson, Eugene S., *Truxtun of the Constellation*. The Johns Hopkins Press, 1956.

Foley, John P., *The Jeffersonian Cyclopedia*. Funk and Wagnalls, 1900.

Gleaves, Albert, *James Lawrence: Captain, United States Navy: Commander of the "Chesapeake."* G. P. Putnam's Sons, 1904.

Grant, Bruce, *Isaac Hull: Captain of Old Ironsides: The Life and Fighting Times of Isaac Hull and the U.S. Frigate Constitution*. Pellegrini and Cudahy, 1947.

Gurn, Joseph, *Commodore John Barry, Father of the American Navy*. P. J. Kenedy & Sons, 1933.

Harris, John, *"Old Ironsides": Her Birth, Heroes and Victories*. Globe Newspaper Company, 1977.

Headley, the Reverend P. C., *Life and Naval Career of Vice-Admiral David Glasgow Farragut*. William H. Appleton, 1865.

Henderson, James, *The Frigates: An Account of the Lesser Warships of the Wars from 1793 to 1815*. Adlard Coles, 1970.

Hollis, Ira N., *The Frigate Constitution: The Central Figure of the Navy Under Sail*. Houghton Mifflin, 1931.

Horgan, Captain Thomas P., *Old Ironsides: The Story of USS Constitution*. Burdette, 1963.

Horsman, Reginald, *The War of 1812*. Knopf, 1969.

Lewis, Charles Lee:
Famous American Naval Officers. L. C. Page, 1924.
The Romantic Decatur. University of Pennsylvania Press, 1937.

Long, David F., *Nothing Too Daring*. U.S. Naval Institute, 1970.

Lord, Walter, *The Dawn's Early Light*. W. W. Norton, 1972.

Lossing, Benson J., *The Pictorial Field-Book of the War of 1812*. Harper & Brothers, 1896.

Lowrie, Walter, and Walter S. Franklin, eds., *American State Papers*, Vol. 1, *Documents, Legislative and Executive of the Congress of the United States*. Gales and Seaton, 1834.

McKee, Christopher, *Edward Preble*. U.S. Naval Institute, 1972.

Maclay, Edgar Stanton, *A History of the United States Navy: From 1775 to 1894*, Vols. I and II. D. Appleton, 1897.

MacNeil, Neil, *Forge of Democracy*. David McKay, 1963.

Magoun, F. Alexander, *The Frigate Constitution and Other Historic Ships*. Bonanza Books, 1928.

Malone, Dumas, *Jefferson the President*. Little, Brown, 1974.

Martin, Tyrone G., *A Most Fortunate Ship*. Globe Pequot Press, 1979.

Miller, Nathan, *The U.S. Navy: An Illustrated History*. American Heritage, 1977.

Molloy, Leo T., *Commodore Isaac Hull, U.S.N.: His Life and Times*. The Hull Book Fund, 1965.

Muller, Charles G., *The Darkest Day: 1814 The Washington-Baltimore Campaign*. J. B. Lippincott, 1963.

Muller, John, *A Treatise of Artillery*. Museum Restoration Service, Ottawa, Canada, 1965.

Nicolay, Helen, *Decatur of the Old Navy*. D. Appleton-Century, 1942.

Office of Naval Records:

Naval Documents Related to the Quasi-War Between the United States and France. U.S. Government Printing Office, 1937.
Naval Documents Related to the United States Wars With the Barbary Powers, Vol. III. U.S. Government Printing Office, 1941.

Padfield, Peter, *Guns at Sea*. St. Martin's Press, 1974.

Paullin, Charles Oscar, *Commodore John Rodgers: Captain, Commodore, and Senior Officer of the American Navy: 1773-1838*. Arthur H. Clark, 1910.

Peabody Museum of Salem:
"Don't Give Up the Ship": A Catalogue of the Eugene H. Pool Collection of Captain James Lawrence. Peabody Museum of Salem, 1942.
"Josiah Fox Papers." Unpublished manuscript.

Porter, David, *Journal of a Cruise Made to the Pacific Ocean*. Gregg Press, 1970.

Porter, David D., *Memoir of Commodore David Porter of the United States Navy*. J. Munsell, 1875.

Potter, Elmer Belmont:
The Naval Academy Illustrated History of the United States Navy. Galahad Books, 1971.
Ed., *The United States and World Sea Power*. Prentice-Hall, 1955.

Pratt, Fletcher:
The Navy: A History. The Story of a Service in Action. Garden City, 1941.
Preble's Boys: Commodore Preble and the Birth of American Sea Power. William Sloane Associates, 1950.

Pullen, Hugh Francis, *The Shannon and the Chesapeake*. McClelland and Stewart, 1970.

Rippy, Fred J., *Joel R. Poinsett, Versatile American*. Duke University Press, 1935.

Roosevelt, Theodore, *The Works of Theodore Roosevelt: The Naval War of 1812*, Part 2. P. F. Collier, 1882.

Roscoe, Theodore, and Fred Freeman, *Picture History of the U.S. Navy*. Bonanza Books, 1956.

Smelser, Marshall, *The Congress Founds the Navy, 1787-1798*. University of Notre Dame Press, 1959.

Smith, Edgar Newbold, *American Naval Broadsides*. Philadelphia Maritime Museum and Clarkson N. Potter, 1974.

Smith, Philip Chadwick Foster:
The Artful Roux: Marine Painters of Marseille. Peabody Museum of Salem, 1978.
The Frigate Essex Papers: Building the Salem Frigate, 1798-1799. Peabody Museum of Salem, 1974.

Spears, John R., *The History of Our Navy*.

Scribner's, 1897.

Stevens, William O., *The Story of Our Navy*. Harper & Brothers, 1919.

Story, Dana A., *The Building of a Wooden Ship*. Barre, 1971.

The Story of the U.S. Frigate Constitution (Old Ironsides). John Hancock Mutual Life Insurance Company of Boston, 1931.

Tucker, Glenn, *Dawn Like Thunder: The Barbary Wars and the Birth of the U.S. Navy*. Bobbs-Merrill, 1963.

Turnbull, Archibald Douglas, *Commodore David Porter: 1780-1843*. Century Co., 1929.

Turner, Harriot Stoddert, *Memoirs of Benjamin Stoddert, First Secretary of the Navy*, Vol. XX. Records of the Columbia Historical Society, 1917.

United States Frigate "Constitution": A Brief Account of Her History, Together with Data for Model Builders. The Bureau of Construction and Repair, Navy Department, Washington, D.C., 1932.

Wilkinson-Latham, Robert, *British Artillery on Land and Sea 1790-1820*. David & Charles, 1973.

Acknowledgments

The index for this book was prepared by Gale Partoyan. The editors give special thanks to the following: Professor Salvatore Bono, University of Perugia, consultant *(pages 34-39)*, Roy H. Andersen, artist *(pages 68-75)*, John Batchelor, artist *(pages 20-21, 85-87)*, Commander Tyrone G. Martin, USN (Ret.), consultant *(pages 68-75, 85-87)*, William A. Baker, consultant *(pages 20-21, 85-87)*, William L. Hezlep, artist *(page 127)*, and Peter McGinn, artist *(end-paper maps)*.

The editors also wish to thank: In the United Kingdom: London—R. Williams, Department of Prints and Drawings, British Museum; Pieter van der Merwe, Historical Section, E. H. H. Archibald, R. M. Quarm, J. E. Tucker, Picture Department, Mrs. J. Moore, Department of Photographs, Patricia Blackett and T. H. Wilson, Weapons and Antiquities Department, National Maritime Museum; David Brown, The Naval Historical Library; Deal—Mr. J. Lee St. Lawrence; Llanvair Grange—Sir Harry and Lady Llewellyn; Nacton—J. H. Hurlock; Portsmouth—Colin White, The Royal Naval Museum; Wickham—Bruce Tappenden, The Mill House. In France: Paris—Hervé Cras, Director for Historical Studies, and Denise Chaussegroux, Researcher, Musée de la Marine; Avignon—Georges de Loÿe, Curator, Musée Calvet. In the United States: Washington, D.C.—Decatur House; Dr. Timothy Nenninger, Navy and Old Army Branch, National Archives; Captain Harry C. Allendorfer Jr., USN (Ret.), Director of Maritime Preservation, National Trust for Historic Preservation; James M. Perry; Truxtun-Decatur Naval Museum; Robert A. Carlisle, Photojournalism and Public Inquiries Branch, U.S. Navy; Rear Admiral J. D. H. Kane Jr., USN (Ret.), Director of Naval History, Commander T. A. Damon, Director, U.S. Navy Memorial Museum, William S. Dudley, Assistant Head, Research Branch, Charles R. Haberlein Jr. and Agnes F. Hoover, Photographic Section, John C. Reilly Jr., Ships History, U.S. Naval Historical Center, Brigadier General E. H. Simmons, USMC (Ret.), Director of Marine Corps History and Museums, John Vajda, U.S. Navy Library, Washington Navy Yard; La Jolla, California—Mrs. Paul Wormser; Avon, Connecticut—Alexandra Rollins Garfield, Curator, Dietrich Fine Arts Collections; Darien, Connecticut—Richard Valentzas; Boynton Beach, Florida—Joel Barlow; Coconut Grove, Florida—Mrs. John T. Wainwright; Portland, Maine—Maine Historical Society; Annapolis, Maryland—Captain Jack Darby, Commanding Officer, U.S. Naval Academy; Dr. W. W. Jeffries, Director, James Cheevers, Curator, Mrs. Alexandra Welch, Curator, The Robinson Collection, Mrs. Winifrede Peters, U.S. Naval Academy Museum; Baltimore, Maryland—Hugh Bennett Jr.; Berkeley Cooley, Lynn Cox, Romaine Somerville, Maryland Historical Society; Marion Butterwick and Mrs. Hugh M. Martin, Star-Spangled Banner Flag House; Boston, Massachusetts—Commander Robert Gillen, Commanding Officer, U.S.S. *Constitution*, Petty Officer Paul Ciriello, Peter Sterling, Director, Robert Badmington, Curator, USS Constitution Museum Foundation; Massachusetts Historical Society; Brighton, Massachusetts— Milton Feinberg; Cambridge, Massachusetts—Hart Nautical Museum, Massachusetts Institute of Technology; Falmouth, Massachusetts—John Harris; Hingham, Massachusetts—Alicia Williams; Manchester, Massachusetts—Evan Randolph, descendant of Commodore Truxtun; Salem, Massachusetts—Ernest S. Dodge, Director, Markham W. Sexton, Photographer, Kathy Flynn, Peabody Museum of Salem; Durham, New Hampshire—Dr. David F. Long; Brooklyn Heights, New York—Warren Sturgis; New York, New York—Roger Mohovich, Curator of Broadsides, and Wendy Shadwell, Print Room, The New-York Historical Society; Harry Shaw Newman, The Old Print Shop; Davenport West Jr.; Charles Windsor; Paoli, Pennsylvania—Edgar Newbold Smith; Philadelphia, Pennsylvania—Richard Dietrich, Dietrich Fine Arts Collections; James E. Mooney, Director, Nancy Robertshaw, Assistant to the Director, Linda Stanley, Peter Parker, Historical Society of Pennsylvania; John M. Groff, Assistant Curator, Philadelphia Maritime Museum; Providence, Rhode Island—Richard B. Harrington, Curator, The Anne S. K. Brown Military Collection; Newport News, Virginia—Larry Gilmore and Beth Meisner, The Mariners Museum of Newport News, Virginia.

Quotations and information from *Nothing Too Daring* by David F. Long, © 1970, United States Naval Institute, Annapolis, Maryland, are reprinted by permission of the publishers. A particularly valuable source of quotations was *The Tall Frigates* by Frank Donovan, Dodd, Mead and Co., 1962.

Picture Credits

Index

Numerals in italics indicate an illustration of the subject mentioned.

A

Adams (U.S. corvette), 77, 141
Adams, John, 9, 22, 26
Admiral Duff (British frigate), 44
Aeolus (British frigate), 81
Africa (British ship), 81
Alert (British sloop), 99, *111-112*, 124
Algiers, 7, 9, 10, 11; history of, 34, *36-37*; vs. U.S., 21, 41, 158-159, *160. See also* Barbary corsairs
Allen, Lieutenant William H., 64
American Advocate, 130
American Revolution. *See* Revolutionary War
Anderson, Evalina, 110
Andrews, Rear Admiral Philip, 167
Anson, Lord George, 113
Argus (U.S. brig), 46, 51, 80; and War of 1812, 77, 78, 94, 141
Atlantic (British whaler), 116-117, *map 127*
Avon (British ship), 141
Azores, Battle of Fayal, 158-159

B

Bainbridge, Midshipman Joseph, 50
Bainbridge, Captain William, 47, *49*, 51, 53-54, 59, 61, 62, 65, 109, 133, 158, 161; and Decatur's duel, 159-160; Porter and, 112-113, 125; quoted, 52, 59-60; urn presented to, *104*; and War of 1812, 77-78, 92, 100-102
Baltimore, Md., British attack on (1814), 142, 155, 156
"Baltimore Race Horse," 163
Barbados (British West Indies), 13
Barbarossa (Red Beard) brothers, 34, *35*
Barbary corsairs, 7-11, 27, 33; history of, 34, *35-39*; U.S. final defeat of, 158-159. *See also* Tripolitan war
Barclay (U.S. whaler), 116, 117, 124, *map 127*
Barreaut, Captain (French), quoted, 32
Barron, Commodore James: and *Chesapeake* affair, 64, 65; vs. Decatur, 159-160; quoted, 159, 160
Barron, Commodore Samuel, 61, 62
Barry, Commodore John, *10*, 27; signal book of, *31*
Beckworth, Colonel Sir Thomas Sidney, 141
Belvidera (British frigate), 79-80, 81, 83
Benedict, Md., 156
Bermuda, 110, 144, 145
Betsey (U.S. merchant ship), 84
Bible Reading on Board (painting), Earle, *97*
Birch, Thomas, painting by, *cover*
Bissly (Scotsman), quoted, 128
Blake, General-at-Sea Robert, 9

Bonhomme Richard (U.S. ship), 42, 92
Bonne Citoyenne (British sloop), 100, 102
Boston (U.S. frigate), 25
Boston, Mass.: *Independent Chronicle, 107*; U.S. Navy yard at, 163, *167, 168-169*
Boxer (British ship), 141
Brazil: Porter and, 112-113; and War of 1812, 100, *diagram 102*
Briggs, Enos: boatyard of, *108*; timber ad of, *109*
British Naval Chronicle, diagram 102
British Royal Navy, 13, 14, 27, 50, 53; and Barbary corsairs, 8-9, 10, 42, 45-46; blockade of U.S. by, 77-78, 100, 104, 112, 135, 143, 145, 154, 155; and captured U.S. frigates, 163; crews of, 27; guns of, 26; Jamaica convoy, 83, 94; officers' lives aboard ship, 96-97; and Revolutionary War, 44-45; U.S. Navy compared with, 77, *114-115*; and West Indies, 27-30. *See also* Impressment policy; War of 1812
Broke, Captain Philip Bowes Vere, 81, 82, 83; gifts to, *142*; vs. Lawrence, 135-139, *137, 140-141*; quoted, 136
Buenos Aires, Argentina, 117, *map 127*
Burr, Aaron, 43
Bush, Lieutenant William S., quoted, 88
Byron, Captain Richard, 79

C

Cabo Frio, 100, *map 127*
Cadiz, 45
Calhoun, John Caldwell, 67
Canary Islands, 2, 76-77, 94
Cannon, *19. See also* Guns
Cape Cod, 27
Cape Hatteras, 17
Cape Horn, 113, 115, 117, 125, *map 127*, 128
Cape of Good Hope, 107
Cape St. Vincent, 7
Cape Verde Islands, 112, *map 127*, 154
Carden, Captain John Surman, 93-98
Caribbean Sea. *See* West Indies
Carnation (British brig), 158-159
Carrera, José Miguel, 115
Cathcart, William Leander, 41
Catherine (British whaler), 117, *map 127*
Cavendish, Captain Thomas, 113
Centurion (Anson's ship, British), 113
Cervantes, Miguel, *Don Quixote*, 39
Chads, Lieutenant Henry Ducie, 102; quoted, 103
Chamier, Midshipman Frederick, quoted, 155
Charles, King (Spain), 34
Charlton (British whaler), 117, *map 127*
Cheeseman, Forman, 16
Cherub (British sloop), 117, 125-128, *129*
Chesapeake (U.S. frigate), 2, 32-33; vs. Barbary corsairs, 43; British defeat of

(1813), 133, 135-*139, 137, 140-141, 163*; and *Leopard* affair (1807), 63-65, 135, 159; and War of 1812, 48, 77
Chesapeake Bay, British invasion of, 120, 141-142, 145, *155*
Chesapeake Mill, 163
Cheves, Langdon, 67
Chile, and War of 1812, 113, 115, 117, 125-128, *map 127*, 130
Civil War, 161; Farragut and, 124; iron warships in, 163
Claghorne, Colonel George, 16, 24
Clay, Henry, 67
Cochrane, Admiral Sir Alexander, 142, 156; and New Orleans, 158, 159
Cockburn, Admiral Sir George, 141, 142, 145, *155*; quoted, 155
Coffin, Admiral Sir Isaac, quoted, 139
Collier, Captain Sir George, 154
Confiance (British ship), 146, *150-151*
Congress (U.S. frigate), 33; vs. Barbary corsairs, 61; fate of, 163; and War of 1812, 77, 78
Constellation (U.S. frigate), 22, 24, 25, 26, 27, 30-32, *33*, 42, 43, 109; vs. Barbary corsairs, 61; as museum ship, 163; and War of 1812, 77, 141, 145
Constitution ("Old Ironsides," U.S. frigate), 22, 24-26, 27-29, *28*, 48, *85*; vs. Barbary corsairs, 45-46, 52, 54, *58-59*, 59-61, 62; design of, *86-87*; *Essex* and, 112, 113; fate of, 163, *164-169*; vs. *Guerriere*, 49, 80-89, *82, 85, 88*, 90-93, 94, 96, 98, 99, 101, 135, 139, 141, 158, 161; guns of, 19, 20; vs. *Java*, 85, 100-*102, 103*, 135; Lawrence and, 135; Nicholson's appeal for sailors for, *27*; paintings of, *90-93*; Stewart and, 145, 152-154, *153*, 158; victory broadside by, *105*
Cornè, Michele Felice, paintings by, *90-93*
Covadonga (Spanish treasure ship), 113
Cowell, Lieutenant John G., quoted, 129
Creamer, Jack, quoted, 95, 98
Crews, 26-27; life of, aboard frigates, *68-75*; Nicholson's appeal for, *27*
Curaçao (Dutch West Indies), 32
Cyane (British frigate), 152-154, *153*, 158

D

Dacres, Captain James Richard, 83-90, *89*, 98, 161; quoted, 84, 89, 90
Dale, Captain Richard, 32-33; vs. Barbary corsairs, 42-43, 46
Dan, Father Pierre, *Histoire de Barbarie et de Ses Corsaires, 38*, 39
Dartmoor Prison massacre (1815), *162*
Decatur, Lieutenant James, 57-58
Decatur, Captain Stephen, 2, 24, 46, 47, 50, 51, 125, 133; vs. Barbary corsairs, 55-61, *56-57*, 135, 158-159, 160; vs. Barron, 159-160; and *Chesapeake* affair, 63-65; dirk of, *50*; quoted, 47, 50, 77, 98, 159,

160; sword of, *55*; and War of 1812, 76-77, 78, 93-99, 133, 143-145
Decatur, Susan, 144, 159, 160
Declaration of Independence, 43
Deguyo, John, 65
Delaware River, *6-7*, 18; Bay, 27, *map 127*
Detroit (British ship), *148-149*
Detroit, surrender of, 92
Don Quixote, Cervantes, 39
Donegal (British ship), 46
"Don't give up the ship!" Lawrence, 3, 138, *139*, 146
Doughty, William, 16, 27, 33
Douglass, Captain the Honorable George, 152, 154
Downes, Lieutenant John, 116, 117, 118, 126
Drake, Sir Francis, 15, 27-28, 113
Dutch East Indies, 107

E
Earle, Augustus, paintings by, *97*
Eaton, William, 43
Edwin (U.S. brig), 158
Elizabeth (British schooner), 112, *map 127*
Elizabeth River, 141, 145
Endymion (British frigate), 143-144
Enterprise (U.S. schooner), 41, 42, 46, 49, 51, 77, 109, 133, 141
Epervier (British ship), 141
Essex (U.S. frigate), 49, 63, 77, 100, *106-107*, 107-113; vs. *Alert*, 111, 124; vs. Barbary corsairs, 41, 50, 61; British defeat of, *129*, *131*, 152; in Pacific, 107, 113-130, *121*, *map 127*, 133
Essex Junior (U.S. warship), 117, 118, 120, 125, 126, 130
Estedio (Algerian brig), 158
Experiment (U.S. schooner), 109, 145

F
Falcon, Captain Gordon, 152, 154
Farragut, Admiral David Glasgow: and Porter, 110, 119, *124*, 128-129; quoted, 110, 124
Fayal (Azores), Battle of, *158-159*
Fernando de Noronha (island off Brazil), 112, *map 127*
Fort McHenry (Baltimore harbor), *157*
Foss, John, quoted, 7
Fox, Josiah, 14-16, *15*, 19, 27, 32, 163; drafting curves of, *15*
Franklin (U.S. ship), 161
Frazier, Daniel, *56-57*, 58
French Navy, 9, 11, 14, 78; guns of, 26. *See also* Napoleonic Wars; Quasi-War
Frigates, defined, 13-14
Furieuse (French frigate), 100

G
Galápagos Islands, 116, 117, 118, *map 127*
Gamble, Marine Lieutenant John, 120
Gattanewa (Nuku Hivan chief), 119, 120
General Armstrong (U.S. brig), 158-159
Genêt, Citizen, 22

Georgiana (British whaler), 116, 117, *map 127*
Ghent, Treaty of, 142, 144, 158, 162
Gibraltar, 43, 62, 125; Strait of, 8, 10, 45, 108
Golden Hind (Drake's ship), 113
Gordon, Captain Charles, 65
Gray, William, 83
Great Britain. *See* British Royal Navy; War of 1812
Grebe (U.S. minesweeper), *167*
Greenwich (British whaler), 117, 120, *map 127*
Grundy, Felix, 67
Guadeloupe (French West Indies), 32
Guerriere (British frigate), 65, *90-93*; vs. *Constitution*, 49, 81, 83-92, *90-93*, 94, 96, 98, 99, 135, 158, 161
Guerriere (U.S. ship), 158-159, *160*
Guns, *19*, 26, 29-30, 32-33; carriage for, *20-21*; and War of 1812, 78

H
Hackett, Colonel James, 16
Hackett, William, 107, 108
Haitian pirates, 109
Halifax (British ship), 65
Halifax Harbor, Canada, *140-141*
Hamburg sailors, *39*
Hamilton, Midshipman Archibald, 98-99; death of, 144
Hamilton, Paul, 77, 78
Hartt Shipyard (Boston), 16, 85
Hassan, Pasha (Dey of Algiers), 21; quoted, 7. *See also* Algiers
Havre de Grace, Md., *155*
Hayes, Captain John, 143; quoted, 144
Hector (British whaler), 117, *map 127*
Heerman, Surgeon's Mate Lewis, 57
"Hew to the line, let the chips fall where they may," 18
Hibernia (British ship), *64*
Hillyar, Captain James, 125-130, *128*; quoted, 128, 130
Hislop, Lieutenant General Thomas, 100
Histoire de Barbarie et de Ses Corsaires, Dan, *38*, *39*
Holmes, Oliver Wendell, "Old Ironsides," 164
Hope, Captain Henry, 143, 144
Hornet (U.S. brig): cartoon of, *134*; *Essex* and, 112, 113; vs. *Peacock*, 134-135; and War of 1812, 77, 78, 100, 102
Howard, John, 107
Howard, Joseph, painting by, *106-107*
Hull, Captain Isaac, 28-29, 47, *49*, 51, 125, 133, 161; paintings commissioned by, *90-93*; quoted, 80, 84, 88, 90, 91, 161; and War of 1812, 80-92, 94, 98, 99, 100, 139, 158
Hull, General William, 92
Humphreys, Clement, 163
Humphreys, Joshua, 11, *12-13*, 14, 15-18, 19, 22-24, 27, 29, 33, 46, 104, 163;

quoted, 14, 16
Humphreys, Mary, 163

I
Ibn-Nosseyr, Musa, 8
Impressment policy (British Royal Navy), 11, 27, 62-67, *65*, 116; and end of War of 1812, 158
Insurgente (French frigate), 30-32, *33*, 42, 43, 51, 109
Intrepid (U.S. prize ketch), 54, 55, *60*, 61, 131
Iron warships, 163
Irving, Washington, 110; quoted, 118
Israel, Lieutenant Joseph, 61

J
Jackson, Andrew, 159
Jamaica, 158; convoy, 83, 94
James, Reuben, 58
James River, 141
Java (British frigate), 85, 100-102, *diagram 102*, *103*, 135
Jay, John, Jay's Treaty (1794), 22
Jefferson, Thomas, 10, 43; vs. Barbary corsairs, 41, 42, 44; and *Chesapeake* affair, 65; medal to Preble from, *61*; quoted, 9, 41. *See also* Tripolitan war
Jersey (British prison ship), 44, *45*
John Adams (U.S. corvette), 41-42, 77
Jones, John Paul, 42
Jones, Dr. Thomas Cook, quoted, 102
Julius II, Pope, 34

K
Karamanli, Yusef (Pasha of Tripoli), 41, 54, 62. *See also* Tripoli; Tripolitan war
Knox, General Henry, 11, 14, 15, 16

L
Lake Champlain, Battle of (1814), 48, 146, *150-151*
Lake Erie, Battle of (1813), 2, 141, *146-149*
Lambert, Captain Henry, 100-102
Lamprey (British merchant brig), 111
Lansdowne, Marquis of, quoted, 133
Latrobe, Benjamin, 159
Laugharne, Captain Thomas, 111-112
Lawrence (U.S. ship), *146-147*
Lawrence, Captain James, 47, 48, 51, 133-135; and *Chesapeake* (1813), 133, 135-139; last words of, *3*, 138, *139*, 146; and Tripolitan war, 135; and War of 1812, 100, 102
Le Maire Strait, 115, *map 127*
Leander (British merchant brig), 111
Leiser, Jacob, 9
Leopard (British frigate), vs. *Chesapeake*, 64, 65, 135, 159
Levant (British sloop), 152-154, *153*, 158
Lincoln, Abraham, 161
Linnet (British ship), *150-151*
Little Belt (British sloop), 65-66, 78, 83
Livermore, Sam, 138

Lloyd, Captain Robert, 158-159
Lord Nelson (British merchant ship), 145

M
Macdonough, Commodore Thomas, 47, 48, 146
Macedonian (British frigate), *cover, 76-77,* 93-99; Decatur and, 133, 144
Madison, Dolley, 99
Madison, James, vs. Barbary corsairs, 158-159; cartoon of, 156; and *Chesapeake* affair, 64; quoted, 130; and South Pacific, 119, 120, 130; and War of 1812, 77, 78, 143
Magellan, Strait of, 113, 115
Maidstone (British frigate), 46
Majestic (British razee), 144
Malta, 42, 43, 50, 53, 61, 125; *Constitution* at (1837), *164-165*
Marquesas Islands, 118-120, *121-123, map* 127
Martin, Daniel, 63, 65
Mashuda (Algerian frigate), 158, *160*
Mediterranean Sea. *See* Barbary corsairs
Melville, Herman, 98
Mendaña y Castro, Alvara de, 118
Merrimack (Confederate frigate), 163
Mexico: Navy, 161; and War of 1812, 113
Midshipmen's Berth (painting), Earle, *97*
Minerva (British frigate), 110
Mocha Island, 120, 125, *map* 127
Monitor (Union ironclad), 163
Monroe Doctrine, 117
Montezuma (British whaler), 116, *map* 127
Morgan, John, 16, 17-18; quoted, 17-18
Morocco, 7, 9, 48. *See also* Barbary corsairs
Morris, Lieutenant Charles, 81, 84
Morris, Gouverneur, 43
Morris, Lewis, 43
Morris, Lewis Robert, 43
Morris, Commodore Richard Valentine, 43-44, 45, 46, 135
Morris, Robert, 14

N
Naples, Italy, 61
Napoleon I (French Emperor), 8, 32
Napoleonic Wars, 77, 125, 156
Narcissus (British frigate), 144
Nash, Captain James, 130
Nautilus (U.S. schooner), 46, 51, 61; and War of 1812, 77, 81, 104
Nelson, Admiral Horatio, 78, 79, 104; "Band of Brothers of," 47; quoted, 13-14, 62
Nereyda (Peruvian privateer), 115-116, *map* 127
New London, Conn., 144
New Orleans, Battle of (1815), 158, 159
New York (U.S. frigate), 41-42, 50
New Zealander (British whaler), 117, 120, *map* 127
Niagara (U.S. brig), *146-147, 148-149*
Nicholson, Lieutenant John B., 95-96
Nicholson, Captain Samuel, 27, 28; appeal

for sailors by, *27*
Nocton (British packet), 112, *map* 127
Nuku Hiva (Marquesas Islands), 118-120, *map* 127; Porter's sketches of, *121-123*

O
"Old Ironsides" (poem), Holmes, 164
Orne, Captain W. B., 84; quoted, 89
Ottoman Empire, and Barbary corsairs, 34

P
Pacific Ocean, Porter in, 107, 113-130
Panama Canal, *167*
Parker, Captain (English master), 28
Patapsco River, 156
Patuxent River, 156
Peacock (British brig), 102, 134-135
Peacock (U.S. sloop), 141
Peale, Rembrandt, painting by, *40*
Pelican (British ship), 141
Penobscot River, 141
Penrose, William, 11, 13
Penrose, Mrs. William, 13
Perry, Commodore Oliver Hazard, 2, 141, *146-147;* quoted, 146
Peru, struggle of, with Spain, 161; and War of 1812, 113, 115-116, 117, *map* 127
Philadelphia (U.S. frigate), *12-13;* vs. Barbary corsairs, 41, 46, 49, 51, *52,* 53-55, *54,* 60, 62, 65, 102, 109, 133, 135; guns of, 19
Philadelphia Gazette, 144
Phoebe (British frigate), 117, 125-128, *129,* 130
Pincke (N.Y. ship), 9
Pius IX, Pope, 164
Plantagenet (British ship), 158-159
Plattsburg, N.Y., 146, *150-151*
Poinsett, Joel Roberts, 115, *117,* 126; quoted, 117, 121, 122, 123
Policy (British whaler), 116, 117, *map* 127
Polly (U.S. merchant brig), 7, 10
Pomone (British frigate), 144
Porter, Captain David, 31-32, 47, *49,* 51, 99, 107-113, 133, 161; and Farragut, *124;* in Pacific, 107, 113-130; quoted, 111, 112, 113, 115, 116, 118, 119, 120, 125, 126, 127, 128, 129; sketches by, *121-123*
Porter, Peter B., 67
Portsmouth, N.H., Navy Yard, *166*
Portugal: treaty of, with Algiers, 10; and War of 1812, 159
Preble, Commodore Edward, *40,* 44-45, 84, 107; vs. Barbary corsairs, 49, 53-62; "Internal Rules and Regulations" of, 52-53; medal to, *61;* "Preble's Boys," 46, *47-49,* 50-53, 145, 154, 161-163; on prison ship, *45;* quoted, 41, 45, 46, 54, 55, 58, 61, 161, 163
Preble, Brigadier General Jedediah, 44
President (U.S. frigate), *33, 80;* vs. Barbary corsairs, 41, 42-43, 61; and War of 1812, 65, *66,* 77, 78, 79, 83, 141, 143-145, 163
Press gangs. *See* Impressment policy
Privateers, 44, 104; and War of 1812, 133,

142, 156, *158-159*
Prize money, 27, 29
Protector (U.S. frigate), 44
Puerto Plata, Hispaniola, 29
Puerto Rico, Porter and, 161
Punta del Angeles,127

Q
Quasi-War (France vs. U.S.), 8, 22, 27-32, *28-29, 33,* 41, 42, 47, 48, 51, 109; Barry's signal book from, *31*

R
Raccoon (British sloop), 117
Randall, Gideon, 124
Randolph (U.S. frigate), 13
Randolph, John, quoted, 67
Ratford, Jenkin, 63, 65
Razees, 14
Read, Lieutenant George, 89
Reid, Samuel Chester, *158-159;* quoted, 159
Reindeer (British ship), 141
Renommee (French frigate), 100
Retaliation (U.S. schooner), 51
Revere, Paul, 25
Revolutionary War, 9, 13, 15, 41, 42, 44, 92, 107, 116, 156; British prison ship, 45
Rodgers, Commodore John, 65-66, 125, 133-134; quoted, 80; and War of 1812, 78-79, 80, 83, 94, 141
Rose (British whaler), 117, *map* 127
Rota (British frigate), 158-159
Rous, Admiral Rais Mahomet, 42
Roux, Antoine, Sr., painting by, *25*

S
Saint Kitts, 30, 32
Salem Gazette, 109
Salem, Mass., harbor, *108*
Sally (U.S. sloop), 29
Samuel and Sarah (British troop transport), 110
Sandwich (French ship), *28-29*
Sandwich Islands, 113, *map* 127
Santa Catarina Island, 112-113, *map* 127
Santa Margaretta (British frigate), 28
Sargasso Sea, 94
Saratoga (U.S. ship), 146, *150-151*
Saturn (British frigate), 130
Selim I, Sultan (Ottoman Empire), 34
Serapis (British ship), 42, 92
Seringapatam (British whaler), 117, 120, *map* 127
Shannon (British ship), 81-82; vs. *Chesapeake,* 135-139, *137, 140-141*
Sir Andrew Hammond (British whaler), 118, 120, *map* 127
Siren (U.S. brig), 46, 51, 55, 77, 135
Slavery, Barbary corsairs and, *36-39*
Smith, Captain John, 52, 78, *108*
Smith, Robert, 45; quoted, 47
Smith, Major General Samuel, 156
Somers, Master Commandant Richard (Dicky), 51, 61

Southampton (British frigate), 104

Spain: vs. Barbary corsairs, 9, 34; Chile vs., 117; Drake vs., 113; Peru vs., 161; Porter and, 161; and Quasi-War, 29

Spitfire (U.S. brig), 65

Stanser, Dr. Robert, 63

Sterrett, Lieutenant Andrew, 109; quoted, 42

Statesman, The (London), 77

Stewart, Captain Charles, 47, *48*, 51, 55, 61, 161; and *Constitution*, 145, 152-154, 158; quoted, 145, 152, 154; and War of 1812, 77-78

Stodder, David, 16

Stoddert, Benjamin, *22*, 45; quoted, 22, 29

Strachen, John, 63, 65

Strachen, Sir Richard, 46

Syracuse, Sicily, 51, 61

T

Taawattaa (Nuku Hivan priest), *123*

Talbot, Commodore Silas, 29; quoted, 29

Tenedos (British frigate), 144

Thames (British frigate), 44

Thetis (U.S. frigate), 110

Tierra del Fuego archipelago, 113, 115, *map 127*

Timbers, *16-17*; Briggs' ad for, *109*

Times, The (London), 92, *99-100*, 104, 155, 158

Trinitarian Fathers, *38*

Tripoli, 7, 159. *See also* Barbary corsairs; Tripolitan war

Tripoli (Tripolitan warship), 42, 109

Tripolitan war, 41-46, 47, 52, 53-62, 109, 125, 133, 135, 145

Trippe, Sailing Master John, 57

Truxtun, Captain Thomas, 27, 30-32, 43; quoted, 19, 32, 109, 145

Tunis, 7, 8-9, 34, 43, 159. *See also* Barbary corsairs

U

United States (U.S. frigate), *cover, 6-7, 10,* 22, 24, 26, 27, 46, 50; Decatur and, 133, 143; guns of, 19; and War of 1812, *76-77,* 78, 85, 93-98, *99,* 163

U.S. Constitution, 10

U.S. Foreign Service, 161

U.S. Naval Act of 1794, 21

U.S. Navy, birth of, 7-11; British Royal Navy compared with, 77, *114-115;* and end of frigates, 163; life aboard frigates, *68-75. See also* Quasi-War; Tripolitan war; War of 1812

U.S. Navy Department, 43; creation of, 22

V

Vengeance (French frigate), 32

Viper (U.S. ship), 77

Vixen (U.S. schooner): vs. Barbary corsairs, 46, 51-52; and War of 1812, 77, 104

Volontaire (French frigate), 51

Voorhees, Daniel W., quoted, 159

W

Wadsworth, Midshipman Henry, 61

Wallis, Lieutenant Provo, 138

"War hawks" (U.S. Congress), 67

War of 1812, 8, 47, 48, 77-104, 107-113, 133-158; allegorical painting of, *132;* British blockade during, 77-78, 100, 112, 135, 143, 145, 154, 155; causes of, 11, 27, 62-67, *65,* 116, 158; in Pacific, 107, 113-130; Treaty of Ghent ending, 142, *144,* 158, *162;* U.S. declaration of, *78*

Ware, William, 63, 65

Warren, Admiral Sir John Borlase, 104

Washington, D.C.: British burning of (1814), 142, 155, *156;* Navy Yard, 81

Washington, George, *10,* 11, 22; quoted, 9, 10

Wasp (first) (U.S. sloop), cartoon of, *134;* and War of 1812, 77, 104

Wasp (second) (U.S. sloop), 141

Wellington, Duke of, 139, 156; quoted, 92-93

West Indies, 13, 94. *See also* Quasi-War

Whalers (British), Porter vs., 116-119, *map 127*

Wharton, John, 13, 16

Wharton and Humphreys shipbuilding firm (Philadelphia), 11, 18, 24. *See also* Humphreys, Joshua

William (U.S. merchant ship), 100

Winter Island (Salem, Mass.), *108*

Winthrop (U.S. frigate), 45

Wyer, Captain Obediah, 116-117

Printed in U.S.A.

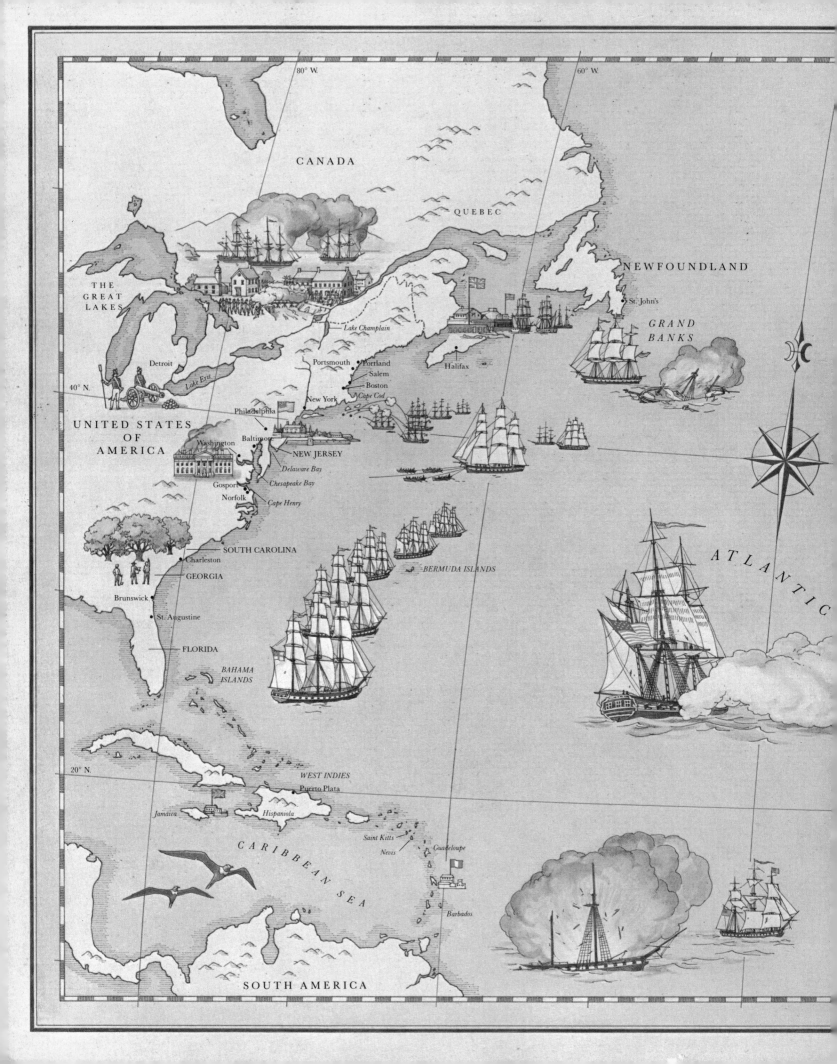